Italian Slow and Savory

Italian Slow and Savory

A Cookbook by Joyce Goldstein

Photographs by Paolo Nobile

CHRONICLE BOOKS

SAN FRANCISCO

Library of Congress Cataloging-in-Publication
Data available.

ISBN 0-8118-4238-X

Manufactured in Singapore.

Designed by Vanessa Dina
Typesetting by Kristen Wurz
Food styling by Marco Melissari
Prop styling by Federica Bianco di San Secondo

Distributed in Canada by Raincoast Books
9050 Shaughnessy Street
Vancouver, British Columbia V6P 6E5

10 9 8 7 6 5 4 3 2 1

Chronicle Books LLC
85 Second Street
San Francisco, California 94105

www.chroniclebooks.com

PHOTO CREDITS:

Ristorante Zenobi; 132, Contrada Riomoro; 64010 Colonnella
(TE); Tel. +39 0861 70581; www.ristorantezenobi.com : p. 46,
making pasta

Gioie di Fattorie; Villa Fiore; 64010 Torano Nuovo (TE);
Tel. +39 0861 82269; Fax. +39 0861 807126 : p. 46, *condiments:
Dried tomatoes paté*

Antica Macelleria Cecchini; 11, Via XX Luglio; 50022 Panzano
in Chianti (Fi); Tel. +39 055 852020; Fax. +39 055 852700;
email: macelleriacecchini@tin.it : p. 213, *Butcher's shop*

Gastronomia Di Angelo; 18, Via Molviano; 64010 Sant'Onofrio
Campli (TE); Tel +39 0861 553845 : p. 164, *Porchetta*

Consorzio L'Escaroun; Comunità Montana della Valle Stura;
Agnello Sambucano Presidia; Attention: Ms Romana Fiandino;
19, Piazza Renzo Spada; 12014 Demonte (CN); Tel. +39 0171
955555; Fax. +39 0171 950949: p. 8, *Two Lambs eating*

Razza Piemontese Presidia; Mr Sergio Capaldo; Mob. +39 335
6770566; sergio.capaldo@libero.it : p. 165 *Calf (Razza
Piemontese)*, p. 15, *Cattle grazing, calves*

Marino Felice & C.; 25, Via Caduti per la Patria; 12054
Cossano Belbo (CN); Tel. +39 0141 88129 : p. 46, *Mr. Marino
Felice working at the mill*

Gioie di Fattorie; Mr. Fiore; Villa Fiore; 64010 Torano Nuovo
(TE); Tel. +39 0861 82269; Fax. +39 0861 807126 : p. 76, *farro
perlato, farina di farro, farricello, polenta di farro*

Food Old Time srl; Mr Raffaele Grilli; 2/4, Via Francesco
Crispi; 64023 Moscaino S.A. (TE); Tel. +39 085 8069110;
Fax +39 085 8069686; www.foodoldtime.com;
info@foodoldtime.com : pp. 22 & 24, *pane di prata
(organic bread from abruzzo)*

Laboratorio Caseario Ioanna Domenico; Mr Ioanna
Domenico; Contrada Molino a Vento; 71032 Biccari (FG);
Tel. +39 0881 593246 : p. 15, *pecorino from foggia*, pp. 6 & 68,
pecorino from foggia, ricotta dura, caciocavallo podolico from gargano

Azienda La Marzuola; Loc. Marzuola; 27045 Calvignano (PV);
Tel/Fax +39 0383 871123 : p. 15, *grape harvest*

Azienda Agricola Umberto Rizzo; Loc. Olivaro; 74020
Maruggio (TA) and Azienda Agricola Saracino Giovanni;
Loc. Fontanelle; 74020 Maruggio (TA) : p. 2, *olive trees*, p. 135,
olive trees

Gorlagricola - Tenuta Castello; Via Vittorio Vento 81; 27020
Alagna Lomellina (PV); Tel. +39 0382 818110 : p. 76, *rice
cultivation*, p. 78, *rice field*

Associazione dei Trifulau; Mr. Agostino Aprile; 2, VC.
Montello; 12046 Montà (CN); Tel. +39 0173 976307 :
p. 76, *Mr. Stefano Grosso, truffle hunter*

Acknowledgments

Joyce Goldstein would like to say *GRAZIE* to: my favorite editor, Bill LeBlond, who not only reads and edits well but cooks well, too. Copy Editor Goddess Sharon Silva for yet another fabulous job; your wish is my command. Designer Vanessa Dina for an elegant and sumptuous looking book. Photographer Paolo Nobile for his evocative visions of *la bell'Italia*. Stylists Marco Melissari and Federica Bianco di San Secondo, for showing that classic old-time dishes can be positively dazzling in a contemporary setting. Amy Treadwell for keeping us all on schedule and for her attention to the details. Maureen and Eric Lasher who continue to support my work with enthusiasm. Gary Woo and Paul Buscemi for their impeccable taste buds, culinary skills, and for helping me with zealous recipe testing and tasting. Cooking is always fun with them in the kitchen. Jeffrey Meisel for his wine expertise and passion for Italy. The Slow Food Organization for continued inspiration and the amazing Salone del gusto. Dun Gifford and Sara Baer-Sinnott of Oldways for trips to Puglia, Rome, and elsewhere. Greg Drescher for all those fabulous Mediterranean conferences at Greystone. Larry and Laura Martin for arranging for the trip to the Abruzzo, continued friendship, and supplying me with fresh hot peppers. Liana Gualtieri for inviting me and my daughter, Rachel, on the Abruzzo trip. We still talk about digging for truffles in the snow. Livia Colantonio and Paolo Nodari for their Umbrian hospitality. Rolando Beramendi for inviting me to teach in Tuscany. Fred Plotkin for the amazing trip to Friuli and for his excellent dining recommendations. Lynne Kaufman for having me lead food and wine trips to Italy for the University of California Travel with Scholars Program. Robert Wilk and Tamara Andruszkiewicz for their Venetian hospitality. Ron Schwarz and Michael Barcun for the hospitality of their Venice apartment kitchen where we could actually cook the food from the Rialto Market instead of just looking at it, and for all those joyful reunion dinners. Alexandra Greeley, food editor at *Vegetarian Times,* for asking me to write about *farro.* Bob Long for his fabulous wines and enthusiastic Italian dinners. Frankie Whitman for sending samples of Niman Ranch *lardo,* pancetta, and guanciale. Paul Ferrari for importing fine Italian foodstuffs so I could test recipes with accuracy. Giacomo Santoleri for lentils, *farro,* olive oil, and hospitality. Ari Weinzweig at Zingermans for his fine palate and great products. Mark Furstenberg for stimulating discussions about food and politics. Michael Romano and Danny Meyer for shared memories of Italian food and hospitality and their loving execution of both at Union Square Café. Ernesto Illy for friendship and all that coffee to keep me going. And my wonderful family, thanks for eating every bite.

CONTENTS

"Siete in Italia!"

INTRODUCTION

"Pazienza, Signora!"

Some years ago, I went to Italy to live for a time. When I arrived, I was the typical young, ambitious American. I had grown up in New York, so I was speedy, driven, and circumspect. I walked swiftly through the streets, head down, eyes unswerving, focused on my intended destination. I had always prided myself on my efficiency, on my ability to get many errands done in the shortest possible time. In a single morning, I imagined myself going to the market, the post office, the bank, the drugstore, and the dry cleaners, with energy to spare. Why "waste time" with frivolous pursuits when I could be filling every minute productively.

And then I came up against the Romans and their *la dolce far niente* lifestyle.

I would take the bus to the post office early, only to find that to mail a simple letter I needed to go to three different windows: one to buy a stamp, a second one where the stamp was put on the letter and a clerk recorded the letter in a ledger, and a third one where the letter actually went into the mail. In addition, the concept of a line at each window was foreign to the average Italian, who instead preferred to hang back, only to plunge forward suddenly when he or she saw a lull in the action or decided to take advantage of another customer's hesitation at the window. Not surprisingly, my visit to the post office would consume the entire morning.

On my way to the market, I would stop at the dry cleaners to drop off a sweater and would be told to pick it up on a specific day the following week. When I would show up on the appointed day, the clerk would look at me incredulously because no one had even started cleaning my sweater. He would then say, "Come back Friday, *signora,*" and only then would the work that had been contracted for a week earlier commence.

The apartment my former husband and I were renting had no refrigerator, so marketing was a daily necessity. As this was the pre-*supermercato* era, it also required an epic journey, with every foodstuff available in a separate shop. I made the rounds, traveling from the butcher to the vegetable market to the fish stand to the dairy store to the *salumeria* to the pasta shop to the bakery to the wine shop. In other words, the entire morning could be spent in gathering what I needed for a simple dinner for two.

At first, I was frustrated at every turn, and muttered under my breath about the inefficient, disorganized Italians. What a way to run a country! I must have appeared both vexed and perplexed, because wherever I went, someone, with the shrug of a shoulder and a knowing smile, would say to me, *"Pazienza, signora"* ("Be patient, madam"). It was a humbling experience. *"Siete in Italia, signora."* ("You're in Italy, madam.") Everyone said essentially the same thing: "Eventually everything will get done, in due time, in *our* time. So, slow down and enjoy your life."

It took me a few months to accept the way things worked and to assume the rhythm of daily Roman life. Italians seemed to get things done without working hard at it. I saw people savoring every moment of the day, enjoying their surroundings, watching the action in the piazza, listening to neighborhood gossip at the coffee bar, pausing to admire a cute baby, fiercely debating politics, or whispering about the scandalous actions of a famous movie star. I learned to chat over the artichokes, instead of grabbing two and running home. I talked about how to prepare a certain cut of meat with the butcher. I admired my neighbor's plants on the balcony and heard about a good bakery nearby. I discussed fashion at the beauty shop and was told where to get the best sweaters on sale. Gradually, my days became easier, and richer. I started to fit in. I came to understand the wisdom of slowing life down.

I was finally seduced by Italy, and the Italians, and became a willing participant in *la dolce far niente*.

Now, some thirty years later, and after many crazy, exhausting, adrenalin-fueled decades of running restaurants, I have begun reminiscing about my time in Italy. The contrast in lifestyles is dramatic. I realized that once again it was time to slow down and enjoy my life in a more fulfilling, more leisurely way. This change of pace reinspired my approach to cooking as well. Now, as a mature person and seasoned cook, I have a greater appreciation of *pazienza* and the pleasures of slow cooking and an increased awareness of the importance of culinary traditions.

Nowadays, too much emphasis is placed on what's new in food and restaurants. It is not necessary to create a new style of cuisine or invent a new dish every week. On the other hand, when someone chooses to cook traditional food, it is not evidence of a lack of imagination. For some cooks, tradition means faithfully reproducing old favorites with local ingredients and a personal palate. For others, it means discovering old recipes and cooking them with a contemporary hand. Tradition grounds us in a good way; it is a touchstone. It can inspire us to create something personal in our own kitchen, linking innovation with tradition. The late baker Lionel Poilâne once observed, "Using old ways is a glorious way to make new things. The man with the best future is the one with the longest memory." In other words, if our food is not connected in some way to the culinary past, it probably won't have much of a future.

Why Slow Cooking

In this era of fast, easy cooking, we eat often and quickly, but not always well, and seldom memorably. It is not uncommon for people to forget what they ate last evening, much less last week. For too many of us, mealtime has become one more chore to complete, and the pleasure of relaxed dining is now more typically a rare event than the norm.

In food, and in life, many of the best things are worth our time and effort. Yes, it is easy to like fast foods and fast cooking; they give instant gratification and a certain level of predictable satisfaction. It is like dating a good-looking person who lacks character. It may be fun for an evening, but it is not going to be a long-lasting love affair. Cooking is like that, too. When I am in a rush, my repertoire of fast and easy dishes serves me well. I can whip up a quick pasta or sauté a *scaloppina* in record time. But the foods I love to cook—the tastes and aromas that I remember most vividly—are the slowly simmered soups, stews, vegetables, and pasta sauces.

Fast food temporarily fills us up, but it will never replace the deep satisfaction and sense of well-being that come from taking time to relax and savor the food and the company. Many of us are nostalgic for old-fashioned family dinners when everyone did not have an obligation or appointment afterward, or those evenings with friends when we sat for hours, eating slowly, enjoying food and conversation. We remember those meals, those unforgettable tastes, those aromas that, even today, can summon up a face, a date, an occasion. Those meals enriched our lives.

It's no surprise that the Slow Food movement started in Italy. When a McDonald's was opened in Rome's famed Piazza di Spagna, many Italians were outraged by what they saw as a blatant affront to their lifestyle. Members of the Slow Food organization, and most Italians, believe that meals prepared in the traditional way, using the best local and artisanal ingredients, with time as a major seasoning, are not only healthful but also infinitely more pleasurable and sustaining. Opposed to antisocial, eat-and-run fast food, Slow Food's mission is to promote the "revival of the kitchen and the table as centers of pleasure, culture, sociability, and community." Its members are "dedicated to the invigoration and proliferation of regional, seasonal culinary traditions."

The Italians have a great deal to teach us about relaxation at the table. No matter how many things they might have to do during the day, when it's mealtime, everything comes to a halt. They go to the table in anticipation of enjoying their favorite dishes, and they relax. They want their beloved *spezzatino di vitello,* their rib-sticking *polenta pasticciata,* their richly layered *lasagne al forno*. They want food that reminds them of home and hearth. Indeed, we all need this kind of cooking and those powerful taste memories to connect us with our traditions. When these are gone, we are at a loss.

While we may not be able to experience leisurely dining every day, we can make an attempt to slow down our pace by cooking slow and savory stews, soups, grains, and vegetables a few nights a week. *Italian Slow and Savory* celebrates low-maintenance cooking: Assemble the dish, put the pot on the stove or in the oven, and forget about it for an hour or two. You may need to check on it occasionally, but otherwise you can get on with life—maybe even sit down and have a glass of wine, read the paper, or talk with your family—while it cooks.

Tradition and Change

For generations, Italian cooks resisted change and novelty, a reluctance illustrated by a single example: the tomato arrived in Italy in the 1500s, but it took three hundred years before Italian cooks allowed it in the kitchen. Until the 1970s and 1980s, unsung heroes worked at the country's stoves, cooking their regional dishes with good-quality raw ingredients in homes and restaurants. When Italians went out to eat, they wanted familiar regional recipes, the kind of food that mamma made. But today things are changing in the food world. Despite the Slow Food movement, with its respect for tradition and sustainability, mass marketing and public relations now drive much of the food industry.

Years ago, when I lived in Rome, a "foreign" restaurant was one that served food from Tuscany or Emilia-Romagna. Nowadays, restaurants serving cuisines from many regions of Italy and from around the world are a regular part of the culinary landscape. For example, in Venice, an Italian friend asked if I wanted to eat at a restaurant that serves Venetian food with Asian accents. Food magazines are filled with articles on the French-inspired *nuova cucina* or the fashionable *cucina creativa,* or new hip wine bars, and the latest avant-garde Italian restaurants. Such places have chefs who are known by name and who cook the food of many other regions and other countries. They understand the power of food magazines to stimulate business, so plate presentations have become more stylized. This trend toward the internationalization of the Italian menu may be a good thing for tourists and for locals seeking greater culinary variety, but I wonder what it bodes for the home cook and for the country's many traditional trattorias and restaurants. Is classic regional cuisine too rustic, too predictable, too familiar to survive in an era obsessed with culinary trends and celebrity chefdom? In the competitive restaurant market-place, will Italian chefs feel pressured to serve dishes drowning in truffle oil or in ginger and lemongrass to attract customers? Will down-home

dishes such as *coda alla vaccinara* and *pollo alla cacciatora* fade away to be replaced by foie gras and tuna tartare with vanilla and sesame?

In 1990, to counteract the rush toward abandonment of traditional recipes, Slow Food began publishing a regularly updated guide to *osterie* in Italy in which it describes small, local eating places that serve regional recipes. The idea is to promote lively, informal establishments where making food is still a craft, "where you can enjoy the dishes and wines of the territory you are in."

Over the years, Italy has been a culinary and cultural touchstone and inspiration for many of my friends and fellow restaurateurs. We like to talk about our early, formative dining experiences in Italy and how they changed the way we cook and eat. Italy formed the standards by which we measure our own personal style of cooking and our sense of hospitality. We used to be able to count on the fact that when we went back, year after year, our favorite places would still be there, and the food would still be as we remembered it. For us, those culinary traditions are as much a part of Italian culture as the Roman Forum, the ruins of Pompeii, or the Piazza San Marco. We don't want our beloved classics to be replaced by complex dishes that reflect the cult of the chef, that lack a sense of place and taste of the region. We don't want change just for the sake of change.

This book is an opportunity to share some of my favorite slow-cooked Italian dishes—dishes that have stood the test of time—so that you can join me in keeping them alive in home kitchens. It is fine to personalize them, of course. I am not discouraging either creativity or variety. Just remember to shop with care and cook with respect and grace.

Slow cooking makes good use of economical ingredients. Less-expensive cuts of meat become tender with time and promise a big payoff in rich flavor. The dishes are not difficult to prepare, yet they are long on the stove top or in the oven, which calls on the *pazienza* of the cook. But once they are made, whether over the weekend or on an afternoon or evening when you are not rushed, you will have fast, easy, and delicious dinners for later on in the week.

Most slow cooking produces comfort food, something we all need in today's stressful world. When my family is coming to dinner and I ask them what they'd like to eat, nine times out of ten it's a slow-cooked stew, pasta sauce, or baked dish that they request. That is why you'll enjoy *Italian Slow and Savory,* with its time-tested, classic regional recipes. This is food with deep, satisfying flavors guaranteed to evoke long-lasting memories.

How Slow Is Slow?

Cooking time is relative, so no specific amount of time qualifies a dish to be labeled slow. We expect stews to cook in an hour and a half to three hours, so they are definitely slow. Bean soups take at least an hour, maybe longer. That's slow, too. However, you can cook green beans in about five minutes, so when I find a recipe that calls for cooking them in thirty minutes, that's also slow. Most fish present a similar situation. They usually cook in six to ten minutes, so if I discover a fish recipe that takes thirty to sixty minutes, I mark it slow. In other words, recipes made with ingredients that might ordinarily be prepared quickly, but are slowed down in order to coax another flavor or texture from them, typically qualify for inclusion.

Preparation time is not a criterion. Some recipes take a great deal of time to assemble, but cook quickly. They are not included here. Some recipes go together quickly, but then cook slowly. Others need extensive preparation time and also cook slowly. Both are candidates for slow and savory. The pasta sauce that takes time to simmer to reach perfection is included, even though cooking the pasta itself is fast. So, again, slow is a relative concept.

Kitchen Equipment

You do not need exotic equipment to cook slow and savory dishes. Dutch ovens or stew pots made of heavy cast iron or enamel-coated cast iron and outfitted with tight-fitting lids and two loop handles are ideal for making countless dishes. In England, these same pots are called casseroles, while in France they are primarily known as *marmites,* and they can be used both in the oven and on the stove top. Lodge manufactures them in plain cast iron, while Le Creuset and Staub make them in enameled cast iron in many attractive colors. If you stew or braise for varying numbers of diners, you will need pots in different sizes. Be patient when cleaning this cookware. If anything sticks or scorches, do not scour the pot with steel wool. Fill it with hot water and let it soak for a few hours; most of the debris will lift off easily.

Terra-cotta baking dishes with lids, terra-cotta gratin dishes, glass baking dishes, and heavy sauté pans and sauce-pans with lids are useful, too. In Italy, these various vessels have diverse names, such as *tiella, tortiera, tegame, caldaio, caldariello, caldarotto, pigneti,* and *casseruola*. You will also need a stockpot or two, a large heavy skillet, a colander, a sieve, a collection of sharp knives, and a food mill, food processor, or blender.

Two other pieces of kitchen equipment support slow and savory cooking: the microwave oven and the slow cooker or electric crockpot. I used to be a snob about the microwave oven, but I have become a convert. When it comes to reheating left-overs, it is the most efficient tool you can use. All slow-cooked dishes can be reheated quickly in a microwave, without loss of flavor and texture and with no pots or pans to clean.

I used to be a snob about slow cookers, too. As a passionate cook, I thought they were for lazy noncooks who threw things in and let the machine do the work. But now I think, what is wrong with that? In the old days, before every home had a stove with an oven, Italians would carry their assembled dishes to the oven of the local bakery or would slip them into a wood-burning brick oven in the backyard, where they cooked slowly in the residual heat after the bread had finished baking. Today, slow and savory foods are cooked on top of the stove or in the oven. If you have a slow cooker, you will be delighted to know that, while it is not a brick oven, nor a classic piece of equipment in the Italian kitchen, it will work beautifully for some of dishes in the following pages, especially stews, any *ragù,* and soups.

After testing many of these recipes on the stove top and in the slow cooker, I have found that the major difference between the two methods is the amount of liquid needed. You do not have to adjust the liquid measurement for soups, but if you use a slow cooker for any of the stews or for a *ragù,* cut back on the liquid by about half. Also, to convert the timing, estimate three to four hours on low for every hour on the stove top, or two to two and a half hours on high for every hour. Finally, in slow cooking, steam collects on the underside of the lid and drips back down into the food, watering down the pan juices. To intensify the flavor of these juices once the dish is cooked, pour them into a saucepan and reduce them on the stove top.

Notes on Ingredients

The Italians, with their innate sense of style, have created a cuisine that combines full flavor with simple technique. But as most professional cooks know, simplicity is difficult to do well. It requires both the best ingredients and culinary finesse. You must know how to let the primary ingredients shine, rather than drown them with too many other flavors.

One of the best ways to showcase ingredients is to taste as you cook, and to make seasoning adjustments along the way. Although I do not instruct to do so in every recipe (space is a valuable commodity in these pages), add salt in increments, not just at the end of cooking. It is wise to salt meat, poultry, and fish before they are put on to cook as well; it helps to develop their flavor. And when I say "salt," I mean kosher salt or sea salt, rather than regular table salt, which I find has a chemical taste. Also, I prefer freshly ground black pepper, rather than white pepper. To my palate, the latter is hot and not as flavorful.

Except for the occasional use of dried oregano and bay, all the herbs in the recipes are fresh. If parsley, basil, or mint is used in the initial *battuto* (chopped-vegetable base), it is a good idea to add some of the freshly chopped herb at the end of cooking for additional brightness. Rosemary and sage usually hold their own, rather than fade, but if you think they have lost presence, add a little more during the last ten minutes of cooking. They need to cook a bit longer and should not be a last-minute sprinkle like the others. Mint and basil bruise and turn black when chopped, so instead stack the leaves, roll up the stack lengthwise, and then cut crosswise into narrow strips. This will keep them from discoloring. Also, in most of the source recipes, that is, the recipes on which I based my adaptations, herbs are used sparingly, probably because they and the other ingredients are of such stellar quality. You may, of course, be more generous in your use.

If possible, use only free-range or kosher poultry. Look for labels that indicate the birds are free of antibiotics, or ask your butcher. Meat for stewing or braising should be marbled with some fat. If the meat is too lean, the stew or braise will be dry. A moderate amount of fat adds needed moisture and carries flavor in slow and savory cooking, and, as part of a balanced diet, will not be harmful to your health.

How to Judge Doneness

Every stove is slightly different. You know yours and I know mine. I teach in many cooking schools and prepare charity dinners in people's homes or restaurants, so wherever I am, I need to ask about the efficiency of the stove top or guesstimate the accuracy of the oven. An oven thermometer is helpful, but it does not tell me about hot spots, weak burners, or inaccurate timers. A bad oven can be ruinous to that perfect rare rib roast, but, fortunately, for most slow cooking, timing nuances are not critical.

Your nose will give you the first clue that the food is almost ready. Usually you can smell the dish as it nears completion, but your mouth is the best test for doneness. You bite the meats or vegetables or grains and decide if the food is tender enough, or if it needs to cook a little longer. If the dish is ready and the pan juices are too thin, you can reduce them. If there are not enough pan juices, you can add broth or water.

Slow cooking is commonsense cooking. The timing given in each recipe is only a guideline, so you use your senses to judge when a dish is ready.

Follow the lead of the Italians and be a fussy and discerning shopper, without, of course, being a pain to your purveyors. If possible, try to establish a relationship with a butcher and a fishmonger and make your needs known. They will value your standards and your patronage. Skimp on laundry soap or paper towels, but not on good food. Buy the best cheeses—*Parmigiano-Reggiano, Fontina Val d'Aosta,* fresh mozzarella, fresh ricotta—extra virgin olive oil, unsalted butter, organic produce.

In many places, there is a growing artisanal cheese industry, a choice of fine domestic olive oil, and an abundance of superb wines. Of course, we should enjoy them, and with pride. But for a first culinary frame of reference, try to use Italian products: extra virgin olive oils, balsamic vinegar, olives, salted capers, *farro,* cheeses, and cured meats.

Cooking wines should be drinkable wines. In other words, use a good-quality wine, a wine that you would drink at the table. When it comes time to choose the table wine, you can pour the same one or another reputable vintage. If you live near a wine shop that carries a selection of Italian wines, be adventurous. Sample as many as possible while you cook from this book. Regional pairings are usually harmonious, and will give you a sense of *terroir* (territory). In his book *Slow Food: The Case for Taste,* Slow Food founder Carlo Petrini defines territory as "the combination of natural factors (soil, water, slope, height above sea level, vegetation, microclimate) and human ones (tradition and practice of cultivation) that give a unique character to each small agricultural locality and the food grown, raised, made, and cooked there." In other words, if you are preparing a recipe from Apulia, why not drink Salice Salentino? If you are cooking a dish from the Abruzzo, pour a Montepulciano d'Abruzzo. Of course, there are wines from other regions, and other countries, that are excellent counterparts, but the first time around, try the wine from the region, or do a side-by-side pairing of a regional Italian wine and a similar varietal from another *paese.*

The Italian Meal

The classic Italian restaurant meal begins with the antipasto, which is followed by the *primo piatto,* the *secondo,* and the *contorno,* then *frutta, formaggio,* and, for the tourist or on special occasions, a *dolce,* or "dessert." The antipasto might be a special house-cured sausage or local prosciutto, an assortment of *salumi* (cured meats), a seafood salad, assorted *crostini* or *bruschette,* or a seasonal vegetable specialty like white asparagus. Piedmont is a paradise for antipasto aficionados, with the largest assortment of these small plates. You might be served as many as ten before you formally begin your meal!

The *primo piatto,* or first course, can be pasta, risotto, or soup. The pasta portion is small, maybe three to four ounces, and usually lightly sauced. (Granted, in poor families, it might be the entire meal, but we are talking about traditional restaurant service here.) The *secondo* could be a piece of grilled or baked fish, a few tiny rib lamb chops or a veal chop (probably accompanied with potatoes, but often arriving alone on the plate), slices of boiled beef with *salsa verde,* or lamb or veal stew. These portions are not large either, usually no more than five or six ounces. Seldom are the *secondi* mixtures of vegetables and meats, but on occasion you might be served a plate of sautéed artichokes and sweetbreads or shrimp and artichokes, dishes that could eaten as *primi* as well. *Contorni*—asparagus or spinach with olive oil and lemon, a stuffed artichoke, peas and prosciutto, or a green salad—can be served as *secondi,* too. To an Italian, that plate of garden-fresh spring peas flecked with prosciutto is as appealing as a grilled veal chop! *Primo* and *secondo* hold equal weight. They are not first (a minor beginning) and main (the primary attraction). Instead, their titles come from their sequence in the meal. In other words, when you cook Italian food, every plate is important.

I know that most of you will not be serving multiple courses in the customary Italian restaurant sequence, and that you might want to serve a few things simultaneously. In that spirit, I have suggested harmonious accompanying side dishes, or *contorni,* for some of the recipes in this book. You can serve them on platters, *all'italiana,* or on the dinner plates, *all'americana.*

A Sense of Taste and Regional Flavors

In the early 1980s, Italian cooking began to move beyond the country's borders in ways it had not spread before. Suddenly, Italian food, prepared at home or eaten in every type of place from a top-end eatery to a chain restaurant, had become daily fare in the United States and elsewhere. Some home cooks were serving imported artisanal pasta tossed with imported *Parmigiano-Reggiano* cheese, while others simply defrosted a frozen pasta dinner. Not surprisingly, children everywhere were happy to join the Italian revolution. Indeed, I have never met a child who did not love pasta.

As the passion for Italian food and nearly everything else Italian has grown, the number of Italian cookbooks on the market has increased exponentially. But certain parts of the country seem to have captured the public's fancy more than others. Culinarily rich regions such as Emilia-Romagna, Apulia, Liguria, Friuli, the Abruzzo, the Marches, Umbria, Calabria, and Lazio, all of which are included in general anthologies of Italian cooking, have been the focus of only a few excellent studies. The romance of Venice and the aura of Sicily, however, are powerful in their appeal, and have inspired numerous cookbooks as a result. And then there is the phenomenon of Tuscany. It has become an industry—and an obsession—in itself, with a deluge of magazine articles, cookbooks, lifestyle books, and travel journals, as well as a flood of food products and wine. Even the collective dream vacation has become renting a villa in the Tuscan countryside.

But the Italian kitchen and table have always had a strong sense of place. In other words, each region has its signature flavors—ingredients, dishes, wines—and the best Italian cooking and eating respect these distinctions.

Piedmont

Main Cities: Alba, Asti, Biella, Cuneo, Novara, Turin, Vercelli

Cuisine: The Piedmont is the most French—in richness, not in recipes—of all the Italian regions. Butter, cream, and other dairy products reign supreme, as evidenced in part by the Piedmont's many cheeses, including *Bra, toma, Raschera, testun, Castelmagno, robiola,* Gorgonzola from Novara and Vercelli, and

bross, a cheese fermented with grappa. *Fonduta* (page 102) is a typical dish, enhanced by the renowned white truffles of Alba and elsewhere, hunted from October through December. Many dishes are based on rice, polenta, potato gnocchi, *tajarin* (egg noodles), *agnolotti* (ravioli), and excellent *brodo* (broth), and large sweet red peppers, mushrooms, cardoons, hazelnuts, and chestnuts are highly prized local ingredients. The Piedmont is also the home of *grissini* (breadsticks), *bollito misto* (page 180), *fritto misto* (mixed fried meats, such as liver, sweetbreads, brains, and seasonal vegetables), *bue brasato al Barolo* (page 166), *stracotto* (braised beef or veal), and *carne cruda* (raw meat); condiments such as *cognà, mostarda di frutta, bagnèt verd,* and *bagnet ross* (page 180); and *bagna cauda* (anchovy-and-garlic-infused oil dip for vegetables).

Wine Regions: Langhe, Monferrato

Red Wines: Barbaresco, Barbera, Barolo, Dolcetto, Freisa, Gattinara, Ghemme, Grignolino

White Wines: Asti Spumante, Brachetto, Chardonnay, Cortese di Gavi, Moscato d'Asti, Roero Arneis

Fortified Wine: Vermouth

Wineries: Albino Rocca, Altare, Bartolo, Cascina Ca' Rossa, Ceretto, Clerico, Correggia, Einaudi, Gaja, Mascarello, Michele Chiarlo, Moccagatta, Pio Cesare, Prunotto, Renato Ratti, Rocche dei Manzoni, Vietti, Villa Sparina, Voerzio

Aosta Valley

Main Cities: Aosta, Cogne

Cuisine: Local cooks in this mountainous area turn out hearty fare centered around rice, chestnuts, polenta, buckwheat, potatoes, cabbage, and apples. *Salumerie* carry the region's cured meats, such as *carne salata* (salted beef), *speck* (smoked pork), and *lardo di Arnad* (page 211), and bakers make rye loaves. Along with excellent cream and butter, the Aosta Valley is known for regional cheeses, including Fontina, *toma,* and *tomini,* and for cheese dishes such as *fonduta* (page 102).

Wines: Most local wines are in small production and are not exported. The exceptions are the outstanding wines from Les Crêtes, which produces fine Chardonnay and Syrah.

Lombardy

Main Cities: Bergamo, Brescia, Cremona, Mantua, Milan, Pavia

Cuisine: The region boasts a rustic and rich cuisine based on butter and cream, rice, polenta and *polenta taragna* (page 90), chestnuts, wild mushrooms, potatoes, asparagus, walnuts, and some truffles. *Tortelli, casonsei, agnolini,* and other filled pastas are popular, as are *pizzoccheri* (buckwheat and wheat noodles layered with potatoes and leeks or sometimes cabbage and cheese) and squash and potato gnocchi. Lombards are meat eaters, enjoying *ossobuco alla milanese* (page 185), *cotoletta alla milanese* (breaded veal chop), beef roasts and braises, and cured meats such as *bresaola* (air-cured beef) and *carne salata* (salted beef). They also take pride in their mostly cow's milk cheeses, including *bel paese, bitto, crescenza,* Gorgonzola, *grana padano,* mascarpone, *robiola, stracchino,* and *Taleggio.* A four-spice mixture of clove, nutmeg, white pepper, and cinnamon is a favorite seasoning, as is saffron, and local condiments include *mostarda di frutta* (page 180) and *gremolata* (garlic, parsley, and lemon zest). Milan is home of mildly bitter, rose-scarlet Campari, first marketed in the nineteenth century.

Wine Regions: Erbusco, Franciacorta, Oltrepò Pavese

Red Whites: Barbera, Cortese, Franciacorta, Lambrusco, Pinot Nero

White Wines: Chardonnay, Garganega, Pinot Bianco, Riesling

Wineries: Bellavista, Ca' del Bosco, Cavalleri d'Erbusco, Gancia *(spumante),* Martilde, Negri, Rainoldi, Salis, Triacca, Uberti

Trentino and Alto Adige

Main Cities: Bolzano, Trento

Cuisine: Two styles of cooking, both hearty, prevail in these cold, mountainous regions, Tyrolean or Germanic in the Bolzano area, and a cross between the tables of Lombardy and the Veneto in the Trento area. Look for *polenta taragna* (page 90), buckwheat, barley, *canederli* (dumplings), cabbage, potatoes, mushrooms, dark bread, game, *gulasch di manzo* (beef goulash), sauerbraten, and cured meats such as *carne salata* (salted beef), *bresaola* (air-cured beef), *speck* (smoked pork), and various sausages. Common

seasonings are cumin, poppy, and caraway seeds; a delicate olive oil is made around Lake Garda; and the local *malga* cheese is traditionally made in alpine huts.

White Wines: Chardonnay, Gewürztraminer, Müller-Thurgau, Pinot Bianco, Pinot Grigio, Sauvignon Blanc, *spumante*

Red Wines: Cabernet, Lagrein, Marzemino, Merlot, Teroldego

Wineries: Alois Lageder, Colterenzio, Elena Walch, Foradori, Hofstatter, Pojer & Sandri, Santa Maddalena, Tiefenbrunner, Zeni

Veneto

Main Cities: Padua, Venice, Verona, Vicenza

Cuisine: This is seafood heaven, with all manner of fish and shellfish—crab, scampi, cuttlefish, salt cod, octopus, eel—cooked into dishes from *broèto di pesce* (fish stew) to *baccalà mantecato* (salt cod whipped with olive oil, milk, and garlic). The locals are not serious meat eaters, but they do enjoy turkey, duck, pigeon (squab), quail, and other small game birds. They like white polenta, rice, *bigoli* (whole-wheat pasta), artichokes, speckled *Lamon* beans (especially in the regional *pasta e fagioli*), white asparagus, pumpkin, gnocchi, chestnuts, radicchio, fish prepared *in saor* (sweet and sour), pine nuts, raisins, pomegranate, and spices such as cinnamon and cloves. Among the best-known cheeses are Asiago, *Monte Veronese,* and *ricotta affumicata.*

Wine Regions: Colli Berici, Colli Euganei

White Wines: Bianco di Custoza, Cortese di Gavi, Garganega, Pinot Bianco, Pinot Grigio, *prosecco,* Recioto di Soave, Roero Arneis, Soave, Tocai

Red Wines: Amarone, Bardolino, Breganze, Cabernet, Corvina, Fratta blend, Merlot, Recioto di Valpolicella, Valpolicella

Wineries: Allegrini, Anselmi, Bertani, Bolla, Gini Inama, Maculan, Masi, Pieropan, Quintarelli, Zenato, Zonin

Friuli–Venezia Giulia

Main Cities: Gorizia, Trieste, Udine

Cuisine: Influences from the Slavic table (sauerkraut, sausages, game), Tyrolean and Austrian dishes and ingredients (*speck,* poppy seeds, *gulasch,* dumplings, paprika, cumin, horseradish, mustard, Sacher torte, and apple strudel), and Venetian foods are all found here. The region is known for its fine prosciutto from San Daniele and for its speck (smoked pork but not necessarily "prosciutto"), *montasio* cheese, *frico* (crisp cheese fritter), gnocchi, stuffed cabbage (page 228) garnished with *ricotta affumicata* (smoked ricotta), pork dishes, cured meats, *brodetto* and other seafood stews, *sclupit* (greens), *bruscandoli* (hops), white asparagus, potatoes, beans and bean soups, polenta, and *cialzons* (stuffed pasta). Paprika, marjoram, cumin, cloves, pepper, nutmeg, cinnamon, horseradish, mustard, and dill are signature seasonings.

Wine Regions: Colli Orientali del Friuli, Collio, Grave del Friuli, Isonzo

White Wines: Müller-Thurgau, Picolit, Pinot Bianco, Pinot Grigio, Ribolla Gialla, Riesling, Sauvignon, Terre Alte, Tocai Friulano, Verduzzo, Vintage Tunina

Red Wines: Cabernet Franc, Cabernet Sauvignon, Merlot, Refosco, Schioppettino

Wineries: Dorigo, Jermann, Lis Neris, Livio Felluga, Livon, Marco Felluga, Ronchi di Manzano, Ronco del Gnemiz, Ruzzis Superiore, Scarbolo, Schiopetto, Venica & Venica, Vie di Romans, Villa Russiz

Liguria

Main Cities: Genoa, Camogli, Imperia, La Spezia, Lerici, Rapallo, San Remo, Savona

Cuisine: Much of Ligurian cooking is defined by its narrow, rather mountainous strip of coastline that includes the Riviera di Ponente and Riveria di Levante. Little meat is consumed here, but the seafood is abundant, with fish soups and stews such as *burrida* (page 129) and *ciuppin* (page 39), dishes made with *baccalà* (salt cod), *calamari all'inzimino* (page 127), and *sardenaira* (pizza with anchovies) all popular. So, too, are double-crusted and multilayered *torte,* focaccia, *farinata* (chickpea flour pancake), rice dishes, polenta and bean dishes, gnocchi, *pansôti con tocco di noxe* (triangular ravioli with walnut sauce), *trenette* and *piccage* (ribbon pastas), *tocco di carne* (meat sauce), stuffed vegetables, chestnuts, and wild mushrooms. Dishes are assembled with *prescinseua* cheese (similar to a tart, creamy ricotta), fruity olive oil, and generous additions of herbs, especially basil,

marjoram, and *preboggion,* a mixture of five herbs and greens, including borage and dandelion.

White Wines: Bianco delle Cinque Terre, Pigato, Trebbiano, Vermentino

Red Wines: Ciliegiolo, Ormeasco, Rossese di Dolceacqua, Sciacchetrà

Wineries: Bisson, La Columbiera, Terre Bianche

Emilia-Romagna

Main Cities: Bologna, Cremona, Ferrara, Modena, Parma, Piacenza, Ravenna, Reggio Emilia, Rimini

Cuisine: The so-called big three foods are from this region: *Parmigiano-Reggiano* cheese, *prosciutto di Parma,* and balsamic vinegar. Other cured meats and sausages are specialties of the area as well, including *culatello* (pork rump), *mortadella, cotechino,* and *zampone* (sausage-stuffed pig's trotter). Local cooks use butter and cream, and meat—*ragù alla bolognese* (page 50), *stracotto* (braised beef)—fills menus. Egg-rich pasta doughs are shaped into *pappardelle,* fettuccine, *garganelli* (page 62), *paglia e fieno* ("straw and hay," a mixture of spinach and egg pastas), *tortellini,* and *tortelloni,* and there are polenta and bean dishes, a savory pie of greens, cheese, and eggs called *erbazzone,* and *piadina,* a griddle bread. In addition to its famed *Parmigiano-Reggiano,* Emilia-Romagna is proud of its cave-aged *formaggio di fossa* and its creamy mascarpone.

White Wines: Albana, Pignoletto, Trebbiano

Red Wines: Cabernet Sauvignon, Lambrusco, Sangiovese di Romagna

Wineries: Castelluccio, Cesari, Conti, Drei Donà, Fattoria Zerbina, La Stoppa, Riunite, Tre Monti, Vallona

Tuscany

Main Cities: Cortona, Florence, Livorno, Lucca, Pisa, Siena

Cuisine: Simple and unpretentious, Tuscan cuisine is rich with beans, in soups, salads, and side dishes. Indeed, other Italians have nicknamed the Tuscans *mangiafagioli,* or "bean eaters." The region is also known for its crusty saltless bread, which is used in such classic local dishes as *panzanella* (bread salad) and various bread-thickened soups; *farro* (page 79); *tagliatelle, pappardelle, necci* (chestnut flour pancakes); chicken liver–topped *crostini;* and *finocchiona* salami. Game is popular—wild boar, birds, hare—as are pigeon (squab), rabbit, *pollo alla diavola* (chicken with black pepper), and *pollo al mattone* (chicken cooked under a brick). Many meats are roasted, grilled, or braised—*bistecca alla fiorentina, arista* (page 212), *porchetta* (roast pig), *ragù*—and are often paired with wild mushrooms, tomatoes, artichokes, fennel, or kale. Fish is not forgotten, with *cacciucco* (page 130) from Livorno, *calamari all'inzimino* (squid with greens; page 127), and tuna and white beans. Dishes are seasoned with sage, rosemary, *nepitella* (similar to mint), black pepper, and the region's peppery olive oil, and nearly every town has its own *pecorino toscano* cheese.

Wine Regions: Bolgheri (the Maremma), Chianti, Montalcino, Montepulciano

White Wines: Trebbiano, Vermentino, Vernaccia

Red Wines: Brunello di Montalcino, Carmignano, Chianti Classico, Morellino di Scansano, Vino Nobile di Montepulciano; Super Tuscans, including Cepparello, Fontalloro, Grattamacco, Luce, Ornellaia, Saffredi, Sassicaia, Solaia, Summus, Tenuta Guado al Tasso, Tignanello

Dessert Wine: Vin santo

Wineries: Antinori, Avignonesi, Banfi, Biondi Santi, Bolgheri, Capezzana, Col d'Orcia, Coltibuono, Fattoria dei Barbi, Fonterutoli, Fontodi, Frescobaldi, Isole e Olena, Le Pupille, Moris Farms, Poliziano, Querciabella, Selvapiana

Umbria

Main Cities: Assisi, Foligno, Norcia, Orvieto, Perugia, Spoleto

Cuisine: The Umbrian table draws on black truffles, wild mushrooms, celery, chicory, chard, fava beans, lentils, *farro* (page 79), and excellent dried pastas. The pig is prized here, in the form of pancetta and other cured pork products, as well as *porchetta* (pig roasted with fennel, rosemary, and other aromatics) and other pork dishes, and various birds—pheasants, pigeon (squab), duck, guinea fowl—are cooked with grapes or olives. The region's olive oil is fragrant and deep green, and the cheeses are primarily made of sheep's milk.

White Wines: Chardonnay, Grecchetto, Orvieto, Trebbiano

Red Wines: Rosso di Montefalco, Sagrantino di Montefalco, Sangiovese, Torgiano

Wineries: Arnaldo Caprai, Castello della Sala, La Fiorita-Lamborghini, Lungarotti, Palazzone, Paolo Bea

The Marches

Main Cities: Ancona, Macerata, Pesaro, Urbino

Cuisine: The kitchens of the Marches look to the sea, with saffron-seasoned *brodetto* (page 132), baked sardines, and *pesce crudo* (raw fish) regularly on menus. Rabbit, suckling pig, poultry, and game are prepared in *porchetta* (flavored with rosemary, garlic, and fennel). Among the other classic foods of the region are dried and stuffed pastas, fried stuffed olives, black truffles, *prosciutto di Carpegna, formaggio di fossa* (cave-ripened sheep's milk cheese), and *casciotta,* a cheese made from part cow's milk and part sheep's milk.

White Wines: Trebbiano, Verdicchio

Red Wines: Lacrima, Montepulciano, Rosso Conero, Rosso Piceno

Wineries: Bucci, Ercole Velenosi, Le Terrazze, Lanari, Moroder, Saladini Pilastri, Sartarelli, Tenuta Cocci Grifoni, Umani Ronchi

Lazio

Main Cities: Frosinone, Rieti, Rome, Viterbo

Cuisine: This is a pastoral cuisine based in large part on sheep, in the form of cheese (*pecorino romano,* ricotta) and lamb, and on pigs, from pancetta to *guanciale* (page 211) to *porchetta* (roast pig). Many local pasta sauces—*all'amatriciana, alla carbonara, cacio e pepe, alla gricia*—rely on these sheep and/or pork products. Artichokes, peas, asparagus, favas, *puntarelle* (wild chicory), and celery are among the superb local vegetables. Favorite antipasti include *supplì al telefono* (fried rice balls stuffed with mozzarella) and *bruschetta* (toasted country bread rubbed with garlic and drizzled with fruity olive oil), while *saltimbocca* (veal scallop with sage and prosciutto), *coda alla vaccinara* (page 190), and *fritto misto alla romana* (fried mixed meats, innards, and a few vegetables) are among the best-known *secondi*.

White Wines: Colli Albani, Est! Est!! Est!!!, Frascati, Malvasia, Trebbiano

Wineries: Colle Picchioni, Falesco, Fontana Candida

Abruzzo and Molise

Main Cities: Avezzano, Chieti, L'Aquila, Pescara, Sulmona, Teramo

Cuisine: Like Lazio, these regions offer a pastoral cuisine, with delicious lamb stews and lamb pasta sauces. Pecorino cheeses are made here, but some of most famous *formaggi* are made from cow's milk, including *caciocavallo* and *scamorza,* the latter a type of mozzarella that is often grilled (*scamorza ai ferri*). Cured meats and fresh sausages are a specialty of both regions, with *soppressata,* spicy *capocollo,* fennel sausages, and spicy or sweet liver sausages among the most lauded. Dried semolina pasta is especially good here, with two well-regarded brands, De Cecco and Del Verde, based in Abruzzo, while *maccheroni alla chitarra* (page 61) is a classic fresh pasta of the same region. The area around Avezzano is famous for its potatoes, sweet red bell peppers and celery grown in market gardens near the coast, and saffron, from near the town of Navelli in the Abruzzo, rivals the best in Europe. The seaside also yields the makings for clams with polenta and for *brodetto,* a fish stew of the Adriatic flavored with garlic, chile, and olive oil. Hearty soups and stews call for locally cultivated lentils and other beans and *farro* (page 79).

White Wine: Trebbiano

Red Wines: Cerasuolo, Montepulciano d'Abruzzo

Wineries: Illuminati, Masciarelli, Valentini

Campania

Main Cities: Benevento, Capri, Caserta, Naples, Salerno

Cuisine: The long Campanian coastline guarantees plenty of seafood stews and salads, and bowls of peppery clams and mussels. *Mozzarella di bufala* and San Marzano tomatoes are signature ingredients of the region, and local factories make some of the country's best dried pastas, including *ziti, maccheroni,* spaghetti, and vermicelli. Stuffed vegetables—peppers, eggplants, tomatoes, zucchini— are traditional here, and so too, of course, is pizza, born in Naples. Seafood *fritto misto, braciole* (stuffed rolled meats), and meats served with a *pizzaiola* sauce (page 179) are typical main courses, while *sopressata* and other cured meats show up on antipasto platters. *Limoncello,* served both as an aperitif and an after-dinner drink, is made from the abundant local lemons.

White Wines: Fiano d'Avellino, Greco di Tufo, Lacrima Christi

Red Wines: Aglianico, Falerno, Taurasi

Wineries: Caggiano, Feudi San Gregorio, Mastroberardino, Terredora, Villa Matilde

Calabria and Basilicata

Main Cities: Catanzaro, Cosenza, Matera, Potenza, Reggio

Cuisine: Calabrian cooks use the bounty of the sea to make *zuppa di pesce* (fish soup) and dozens of swordfish and tuna dishes. Mountainous Basilicata, in contrast, is known for its *lucanica* (spiced pork sausage), lamb stews, and soups and pastas with beans and vegetables. *'Nduja,* a soft pork sausage highly seasoned with chile, and *capocollo* (lightly cured pork sausage) are often on Calabrian antipasto platters, and both regions make excellent versions of *sopressata. Melanzana alla parmigiana* (eggplant with tomatoes and mozzarella) and *pitta* (a single- or double-crusted pizza) are everyday dishes in Calabria, while *millecosedde* (vegetable, bean, and pasta soup) is primarily, though not exclusively, a dish found in Basilicata. *Caciocavallo, burrata,* mozzarella, and provolone cheeses span both regions, as do garlic and chiles—often to season broccoli rabe or other greens—and oregano.

Red Wine: Aglianico del Vulture

Wineries: Paternoster, Librandi

Apulia

Main Cities: Altamura, Bari, Brindisi, Foggia, Lecce, Otranto, Taranto

Cuisine: Wheat is grown in Apulia, and the big, crusty loaves of Altamura and the olive bread, or *puccia,* of Lecce are well known throughout Italy. Bakers also make *taralli,* round, pretzel-like crackers, and cooks regularly use bread to thicken soups. Local pastas include *orecchiette* (little ears), often tossed with broccoli rabe; *ciceri e tria* (fresh and fried pasta with chickpeas); and *cavatelli.* The fertile soil of the region produces fennel, *lampascioni* (page 234), favas, wild greens, broccoli rabe, cauliflower, eggplants, peppers, and tomatoes, while the sea puts mussels, seafood stews, and *pesce crudo* (raw fish) on local tables. Lamb and pork—and their grilled innards—are eaten in Apulia, and olive oil and table olives, almonds, and *cotognata* (quince paste) are important local products. *Cacioricotta* (aged ricotta), *burrata* (rich cow's milk cheese with a creamy center), *caciocavallo,* and provolone are among the region's fine *formaggi.*

White Wines: Bombino Bianco, Chardonnay, Verdeca

Red Wines: Aleatico di Puglia, Malvasia Nera, Negroamaro, Primitivo, Salice Salentino

Wineries: A Mano, Calò, Felline, Sinfarossa, Taurino

Sicily

Main Cities: Agrigento, Catania, Messina, Palermo, Syracuse, Taormina

Cuisine: Sicilian cuisine has been richly influenced by the Arabic kitchen, as evidenced in the use of pine nuts and raisins and the popularity of sweet-and-sour sauces. Vegetables are central to the table, with wild fennel, tomatoes, peppers, broccoli, zucchini, cauliflower, onions, and garlic used bountifully, but the eggplant is the star of the market gardens, showcased in *pasta alla Norma, caponata* (sweet-and-sour vegetable relish), and *melanzana alla parmigiana,* among other dishes. A large population of fisherman has contributed to a tradition of big seafood stews and *cùscusu* (couscous with seafood) and to swordfish, tuna, sardines, octopus, sea urchins, mussels, and clams prepared in myriad ways. *Arancini* (fried rice balls concealing a heart of meat and vegetables) and *panelle* (chickpea fritters), two traditional snacks, and *farsu magru* (page 174) and *pasta con le sarde* (pasta with sardines and wild fennel) are all signature dishes. Salt-packed capers and anchovies, oregano, and olives are standard flavorings, tomato and red wine sauces are typically used for braising meats, and *salmoriglio,* a condiment of olive oil, parsley, oregano,

garlic, and lemon juice, is a common accompaniment to grilled fish. Classic cheeses include *ragusano* (cow's milk cheese from Ragusa), *canestrato* (sheep milk's cheese shaped in a basket), *caciocavallo,* and *majorchino* (pepper-studded pecorino). Citrus orchards—lemons, mandarins, oranges, blood oranges, citrons—thrive on the island, and their harvests, along with almonds, pistachios, and candied fruits, flavor many of the celebrated desserts.

White Wines: Chardonnay, Catarratto and Inzolia blends

Red Wines: Cerasuolo di Vittoria, Nerello, Nero d'Avola

Fortified and Dessert Wines: Malvasia di Pantelleria, Marsala, Moscato di Pantelleria

Wineries: Abbazia Sant'Anastasia, Cos, DeBartoli, Donnafugata, Duca di Salaparuta, Hauner, Planeta, Regaleali

Sardinia

Main Cities: Cagliari, Nuoro, Olbia, Sassari

Cuisine: Sun-dried tomatoes, mint, saffron, and bay leaves flavor the rustic dishes of the island. Among the distinctive pastas are *fregola* (page 30), *malloreddus* (narrow, ridged semolina dumplings), and *culingiones* (cheese- or potato-stuffed pasta). *Bottarga* (salted and dried tuna or red mullet eggs), seafood *cassola* (stew), lobster, and red mullet are prized offerings from the sea, while *impanada* (meat-stuffed pie) and *porceddu* (spit-roasted suckling pig) and lamb with wild fennel are inland traditions. *Carta da musica,* a thin, crisp flat bread that was originally the *pane* of the shepherds, is now commonplace in the city and the countryside, and the local sheep's milk cheeses, including ricotta and *pecorino sardo,* are among the best in Italy. Almonds; *sapa,* a syrup made by reducing wine must; and honey flavor many of the island's desserts.

White Wines: Vermentino di Gallura, Vermentino di Sardegna, Vernaccia di Oristano

Red Wine: Cannonau

Wineries: Argiolas, Contini, Sella & Mosca

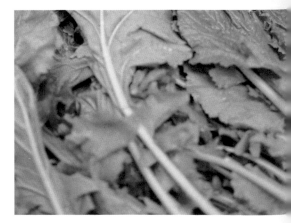

SOUPS

In Italy, soup is a *primo piatto,* or first course, but many of the *zuppe* that follow are so substantial and satisfying that they can be served as main courses, accompanied with only a salad, bread, and maybe a piece of cheese to complete the meal. Indeed, many modern Italians, faced with contemporary time constraints, have reduced the frequency of the traditional multicourse meal.

Several of the soups included here are based on beans or legumes, such as lentils, chickpeas, white beans, and dried favas, or on grains, such as polenta, rice, or *farro.* Some are enriched with bread or with eggs and cheese. All of these additions add to the general heartiness of the dishes. Stocks—meat, poultry, fish—are sometimes used, but often the cooking liquid is water, especially for vegetable soups that benefit from its clarity of flavor. All of the soups can be prepared well ahead of serving time and reheated easily, although care must be taken that they do not burn. Regular stirring will prevent ingredients from sinking to the bottom, where they can scorch.

To many people outside of Italy, soup is simply soup, but the Italians employ a variety of names to distinguish a wealth of types. A *brodo* is a broth. If it includes rice or pasta, it may be called a *minestra in brodo. Minestra* alone is a soup with rice or pasta and is heartier than a *brodo.* The word *minestrone* refers to a big soup with many ingredients, while a *zuppa* is a thick, full-bodied soup—a meal in a bowl—often ladled over toasted or grilled bread. A *farinata* is a soup thickened with polenta, and a *pancotto* is a soup thickened with bread. A *passato* is a purée, and a *crema* is a purée usually enriched with milk or cream; both may be garnished with croutons.

Ordinarily, you would not go out of your way to pair wine with soup, as both are liquids. But because many of these soups are quite substantial, and can be served as meals, I have made one or more wine suggestions with each recipe.

Zuppa di lenticchie agli aromi dell'orto
Lentil Soup with Garden Vegetables

SERVES 4 TO 6

Umbria is known for its tiny green lentils, cultivated near the towns of Castelluccio, Sostino, Colfiorito, and Sellano. This recipe is from Salvatore Denaro, the esteemed proprietor of Il Bacco Felice, an *enoteca* in the town of Foligno. He uses water rather than stock so that the special taste of the local lentils shines, and he ladles the soup over toasted bread. The classic lentil soup of the Madonie, the mountainous region of central Sicily, includes chopped tomatoes, macaroni, and grated *caciocavallo* cheese, while cooks in the Abruzzo like to add crumbled cooked chestnuts, tomato paste, marjoram, basil, and bay to their lentil soup. If you cannot find tiny lentils of Umbria, look for small French green lentils from the area around Le Puy, in the Auvergne.

2 tablespoons extra virgin olive oil, plus more for serving

1 bunch fresh flat-leaf parsley, minced

1 celery heart with leaves, finely chopped

2 olive oil–packed anchovy fillets, minced

1 pound (about 2 1/2 cups) small green lentils (see recipe introduction), picked over and rinsed

1 cup cooked white rice (optional)

1 cup sliced or crumbled cooked sweet sausage (optional)

1 cup crumbled cooked chestnuts (optional)

Salt and freshly ground black pepper

4 to 6 thick slices coarse country bread, toasted

In a large saucepan, heat the 2 tablespoons olive oil over medium heat. Add the parsley, celery, and anchovies and sauté until the vegetables are soft, about 8 minutes. Add the lentils and water to cover by 2 inches and bring to a gentle boil. Reduce the heat to low, cover, and simmer until the lentils are tender, 40 to 60 minutes.

Add the rice, sausage, or chestnuts, if using, and heat to serving temperature. Season to taste with salt and pepper. (You may not need any salt, as the anchovies are salty.) Put a slice of toasted bread in each bowl and ladle the soup over the top. Drizzle with olive oil and serve at once.

WINE: *If you have added sausage or rice, you could sip a Nebbiolo d'Alba or Gattinara from the Piedmont, or an Umbrian Sagrantino di Montefalco. And even if you have not added sausage or rice, a light red will work nicely.*

Minestrone di ceci e costine di maiale
Chickpea Soup with Pork Ribs

SERVES 6

In the dead of winter, nothing is more warming than this hearty soup from the Piedmontese town of Casale Monferrato. Milanese cooks prepare a similar soup called *cisrà*, originally made with a pig's head and traditionally served on November I, the Day of the Dead. Pork skin, or rind, is used in this soup, an exotic ingredient for many cooks outside Italy. Called *cotenna* or *cotica*, it is the outer skin of the pig, and although it is not essential, you might try to talk your butcher into setting some aside for you. It will add to the flavor of the soup. You can freeze the skin, so you will have it on hand when you need it. Although this recipe is from a Parmesan cheese region, I think that pecorino adds just the right note of tart and salt.

2 pounds meaty pork spareribs or country-style ribs

Salt and freshly ground black pepper

1 pound chickpeas, picked over, rinsed, and soaked overnight

2 quarts boiling salted water

Piece of pork skin, 3 by 6 inches (see recipe introduction; optional)

2 yellow onions, chopped

8 cloves garlic, chopped

8 fresh sage leaves, chopped

1 small bunch fresh flat-leaf parsley, chopped

Pinch of chile pepper flakes (optional)

1 cup Rich Tomato Sauce (page 69), Tomato Sauce (page 69), or canned tomato sauce

2 or 3 russet potatoes, peeled

Extra virgin olive oil for drizzling

6 slices coarse country bread, toasted

Grated pecorino cheese for serving

Season the pork ribs with salt and a generous amount of black pepper and set aside.

Drain the chickpeas, transfer to a Dutch oven, and add water to cover by about 3 inches. Bring to a gentle boil over medium heat, reduce the heat to low, and add 2 teaspoons salt. Simmer, uncovered, until the chickpeas start to become tender, 35 to 40 minutes. They should still be somewhat firm in the center.

Drain the chickpeas and return them to the pot. Add the boiling salted water, pork skin (if using), onions, garlic, sage, parsley, chile pepper flakes (if using), tomato sauce, ribs, potatoes, and a generous drizzle of olive oil. Bring the soup to a gentle boil over medium heat, reduce the heat to low, cover, and simmer until the chickpeas are soft, the ribs are tender, and the potatoes are falling apart and have thickened the soup, about 1 1/2 hours.

Remove the ribs and set them aside until they are cool enough to handle. Season the soup with salt and pepper. Remove the meat from the pork bones, cut up any large pieces, and return the meat to the pot. Reheat the soup to serving temperature.

Place a slice of bread in the bottom of each warmed bowl. Ladle in the soup, sprinkle generously with cheese, and serve.

WINE: *For a local red, drink Barbera. A hearty red from Apulia or Campania, such as Salice Salentino or Taurasi, respectively, would also be a fine foil for this equally hearty soup.*

Parmesan, *Grana Padano,* and Pecorino Cheeses

Parmesan, *grana padano,* and pecorino are Italy's most common grating cheeses. Each carries a label indicating it has received the national government's *denominazione d'origine protetto* (DOP), which limits its production to a "protected designation of origin" and to certain specific practices, regulations designed to ensure consistent quality.

Grana is a general term used for all hard grating cheeses that were first produced in the Po Valley. The most famous of the grana cheeses is Parmesan or *Parmigiano-Reggiano,* an ivory-white cow's milk cheese that is aged for at least twelve months *(giovane)* and for up to four years *(stravecchione),* with most wheels sold at two years. It is produced primarily in the provinces of Modena, Reggio-Emilia, and Parma.

Grana padano is made in some two dozen provinces. It, too, is a cow's milk cheese and is usually aged from twelve to twenty-four months and sometimes longer. While not as prestigious as Parmesan, this straw-gold cheese is still excellent for grating.

Pecorino romano, a sheep's milk cheese, was once made in great quantities around Rome, but the grazing lands have been replaced with housing and industry. Most of the pecorino sold today is *pecorino sardo* from Sardinia. It is used at various stages of ripening, and must be aged for eight to ten months for grating. Do not confuse *pecorino toscano,* a table cheese, with either of these grating cheeses.

Parmesan and *grana padano,* both of which have a slightly nutty flavor, are generally used in northern Italy, where they are added to dishes sauced with cream or butter. Pecorino is tart and salty. It is used more often with the olive oil, garlic, and tomato dishes of the south. This does not mean that you cannot combine them with dishes that do not fit these geographic profiles. I try to pair them with foods of their regions of production, but every now and again I find that I want the sharp tartness of a pecorino when the milder Parmesan would be geographically "correct."

Zuppa di fagioli e cozze
White Bean Soup with Mussels

Beans with shellfish is a magical combination. This Tuscan soup, which is served at the Locanda dell'Amorosa in Sinalunga, in Siena Province, is flavored with a little fresh tarragon, a favorite herb of Sienese cooks. Another version calls for chile pepper flakes instead of the licorice-scented *dragoncello*.

SERVES 6

FOR THE BEANS

1 pound large dried white beans, picked over, rinsed, and soaked overnight (or see page 240 for quick-soak method)

2 yellow onions, chopped

5 cloves garlic, smashed

1 bay leaf

2 cups peeled, seeded, and chopped tomatoes

Salt

1/4 cup olive oil

2 yellow onions, chopped

4 cloves garlic, minced

1/2 teaspoon chile pepper flakes (optional)

2/3 cup dry white wine

36 mussels, well scrubbed and debearded

Fish stock, if needed

1 to 2 tablespoons chopped fresh tarragon

Salt and freshly ground black pepper

2 tablespoons chopped fresh flat-leaf parsley

To prepare the beans, drain them, transfer to a large saucepan, and add water to cover by about 3 inches. Add the onions, garlic, bay leaf, and tomatoes and bring to a gentle boil over medium heat. Reduce the heat to low, add 2 teaspoons salt, and simmer gently, uncovered, until the beans are tender, about 1 hour. Start checking for doneness after 45 minutes and monitor the cooking carefully, as you do not want them to be mushy. At this point, you may remove the beans from the heat and set them aside for a few hours at room temperature or refrigerate them overnight before continuing.

In a wide sauté pan, heat the olive oil over medium heat. Add the onions and sauté until softened, about 8 minutes. Add the garlic and the chile pepper flakes (if using) and cook for 2 minutes longer. Pour in the wine, add the mussels, raise the heat to high, and bring to a boil. Cover and cook until the mussels open, which should take only a few minutes. Remove the pan from the heat and lift the mussels from the pan, reserving the contents of the pan. Discard any mussels that failed to open. When the mussels are cool enough to handle, remove them from their shells, holding them over a bowl as you work to catch all of the juices.

Reheat the beans to serving temperature. Add the mussels, the onion mixture in which they were cooked, and the captured juices to the beans and stir to mix. If the soup is too thick, add a little fish stock. Simmer for a few minutes to heat all the ingredients thoroughly.

Add the tarragon to taste, and season with salt and pepper. Ladle the soup into warmed bowls, sprinkle evenly with the parsley, and serve at once.

WINE: *Pour a Chardonnay, a Sauvignon Blanc, or a lean white Cortese.*

Minestra di vongole alla sarda
Sardinian Clam Soup with Fregola

SERVES 8

Fregola (sometimes spelled *fregula*) is a type of semolina pasta that looks like large, irregularly shaped couscous. It is a signature ingredient of Sardinian cuisine, and although I have seen it for sale at my Italian specialty market, it is not widely available. The more frequently stocked *moughrabiye,* better known as Israeli couscous, is a suitable substitute, or, in a pinch, you can use orzo or tiny pasta shells. Do not use regular couscous, however, as it is too fine. The sun-dried tomatoes add an extra level of richness to this satisfying soup.

3 pounds littleneck clams, well scrubbed

1/2 cup dry white wine

1/4 cup extra virgin olive oil

1 yellow onion, finely chopped

2 cloves garlic, minced

1/4 cup chopped fresh flat-leaf parsley

1 1/2 cups fregola or Israeli couscous (see recipe introduction)

1/3 cup drained, chopped olive oil–packed sun-dried tomatoes

6 cups fish stock or water, or as needed

Salt and freshly ground black pepper

Chopped fresh flat-leaf parsley or finely shredded fresh basil or mint leaves for garnish

In a saucepan, combine the clams and wine, cover, place over high heat, bring to a boil, and steam the clams until they open, just a few minutes. Remove the pan from the heat and lift the clams from the liquid, reserving the liquid. Discard any clams that failed to open. When the clams are cool enough to handle, remove them from their shells, chop coarsely, and set aside. Strain the steaming liquid through a cheesecloth-lined sieve and reserve.

In a large saucepan, heat the olive oil over medium heat. Add the onion, garlic, and 1/4 cup parsley and sauté until tender, about 10 minutes. Add the *fregola* or couscous and toss in the oil for a few minutes. Add the sun-dried tomatoes, the strained clam liquid, and enough stock or water to cover the pasta. Bring to a simmer, reduce the heat to medium-low, cover, and cook until the pasta is soft, about 20 minutes.

Add the clams and simmer gently for 5 minutes longer to heat through and blend flavors. Season to taste with salt (clams are salty, so you may not need any) and pepper. Ladle into warmed bowls and garnish with the herb of choice. Serve at once.

WINE: *Salty, briny clams are difficult to pair with wine, but Greco di Tufo, Gavi di Gavi, or a tart Sauvignon Blanc is usually a good choice.*

Zuppa di farro con carciofi
Farro *and Artichoke Soup*

SERVES 4

Spring, when artichokes first come to market, would be an ideal time to make this surprisingly sweet and delicate soup from Ristorante Gio Arte e Vini in the charming Umbrian city of Perugia. Sardinian cooks put together a similar soup, with potatoes replacing the *farro* and a slice of toasted bread in the bottom of each bowl.

1 lemon, halved

5 large artichokes

1/4 cup extra virgin olive oil, plus more for serving

1 yellow onion, chopped

2 cloves garlic, minced

1 cup farro (page 79)

5 cups vegetable stock, or as needed

Salt and freshly ground black pepper

1/4 cup chopped fresh flat-leaf parsley or mint

Squeeze the juice from the lemon halves into a bowl of cold water. Working with 1 artichoke at a time, remove all of the leaves, then trim away any dark green parts from the base and the stem. If the stem seems tough, cut it off flush with the base. Scoop out the prickly choke with a spoon, or cut it out with a paring knife. Cut the base vertically into 1/2-inch-thick slices. As each artichoke is trimmed, add the slices to the lemon water and leave them in the water until ready to cook.

In a saucepan, heat the 1/4 cup olive oil over medium heat. Drain the artichokes, add to the saucepan along with the onion and garlic, and sauté until the artichokes and onion are lightly golden, 10 to 15 minutes. Add the *farro* and mix well with a wooden spoon, then pour in the stock to cover. Raise the heat to high and bring to a boil. Reduce the heat to low, cover, and simmer until the *farro* is tender, about 30 minutes, adding more stock if needed to keep the artichokes and *farro* covered.

Season to taste with salt and pepper. Ladle the soup into warmed bowls and top each serving with the parsley or mint and a drizzle of olive oil.

WINE: *Artichokes are a challenge for wine. But in this case, because of the presence of the* farro, *you can safely pour a Sauvignon Blanc or Pinot Grigio.*

Le virtù

Farro *and Bean Soup from the Abruzzo*

SERVES 6 TO 8

This is an abridged version of the famous—and very complex—soup known as *le virtù*, a signature dish of the town of Teramo in the Abruzzo. The classic version combines seven beans, seven vegetables, and seven cuts of meat, mostly from the pig, plus *farro* or dried small pasta. One story says that the soup symbolizes the virtue of kitchen thriftiness for which Abruzzese women are known. Another tale contends that the soup is the result of a contest to see which virtuous woman would devote the time to a dish requiring so many steps. Few of us are that virtuous today, however, so I have simplified the recipe in the hope that you will be tempted to prepare it. My version is inspired by a soup that I ate at a small family-run restaurant in the Abruzzese town of Rocca di Calascio. It was made with four kinds of legumes—lentils, white beans, black-eyed peas, and red beans—along with *farro* and pancetta. You can prepare it ahead of time and reheat it, but if you are a fanatic about texture, do not add the *farro* until you reheat the soup, and then simmer the beans and grain together for the final 10 to 15 minutes.

2 to 2 1/2 cups assorted dried beans such as chickpeas, cannellini, small white beans, borlotti, and lentils, picked over and rinsed

1/4 cup olive oil

1/2 cup chopped pancetta or prosciutto

1 large yellow onion, chopped

2 carrots, peeled and chopped

2 celery stalks, chopped

4 large cloves garlic, minced

1 tablespoon chopped fresh sage

1 tablespoon chopped fresh marjoram

1 tablespoon chopped fresh mint

1 tablespoon chopped fresh thyme

Soak all the beans except the lentils overnight (or use the quick-soak method on page 240), then drain.

In a saucepan, heat the olive oil over medium heat. Add the pancetta or prosciutto and sauté, stirring often, until the fat is released, about 5 minutes. Add the onion, carrots, celery, garlic, and all the chopped herbs and sauté, stirring often, until the vegetables begin to soften, about 5 minutes. Add the drained beans and lentils, tomatoes, water or stock, and 2 teaspoons salt, raise the heat to high, and bring to a boil. Reduce the heat to low, cover, and simmer until the beans are tender, about 1 hour. Season to taste with salt and pepper. (If you want a creamier soup, scoop out 1 cup of the bean mixture, purée it in a blender or food processor, and return it to the pan.)

Meanwhile, bring a second saucepan three-fourths full of salted water to a boil over high heat. Add the *farro*, reduce the heat to medium, and cook until the *farro* is al dente, 25 to 30 minutes. Drain it and add it to the beans when they are tender.

1¹/₂ *cups diced canned plum tomatoes*

2 *quarts water or chicken stock, or as needed*

Salt and freshly ground black pepper

³/₄ *cup* farro

Extra virgin olive oil and grated Parmesan cheese for serving

Simmer the beans and *farro* together for 10 to 15 minutes, stirring often to prevent scorching. Ladle the soup into warmed bowls and top each serving with a thread of extra virgin olive oil, some grated Parmesan, and a liberal dusting of pepper.

WINE: *Accompany this filling soup with the local Montepulciano d'Abruzzo.*

Bean and Grain Soups

Le virtù is only one of many Italian soups that combine beans and *farro,* an ancient wheat strain cultivated primarily in Tuscany and Umbria. The Tuscan *zuppa di farro con cavolo nero,* also known as *granfarro,* calls for adding 2 bunches of *cavolo nero* (page 247), chopped and cooked, to the beans along with the *farro* during the last 10 to 15 minutes of cooking. Other versions add spinach, broccoli rabe, or beet greens.

Mesc-ciùa, dialect for *mescolanza,* or "mixture," is a simple *farro* and bean soup from the Ligurian town of La Spezia. No pancetta, no tomatoes, no *battuto* of vegetables. It combines equal parts (2 cups) dried chickpeas and *cannellini* beans with 1 cup *farro,* buckwheat (kasha), or wheat berries, and cooks them in salted water until very tender. This rather stoic soup is garnished with a generous drizzle of extra virgin olive oil.

Finally, *millecosedde*—"a thousand things"—is a hearty soup from Basilicata and Calabria that resembles *le virtù* in that it is a mixture of many beans and vegetables, but it uses short macaroni in place of the *farro.*

Farro *in Pork Broth with Citrus and Herbs*

The original recipe from the Marches called for half a pig's head to make the rich broth. To simplify, I have used country-style ribs. You may want to add a spritz of lemon or orange juice at the end of cooking.

SERVES 8

FOR THE BROTH AND MEAT

4 quarts water

Salt

4 large, meaty country-style pork ribs, 2 to 3 pounds total weight

2 celery stalks, chopped

2 carrots, peeled and chopped

2 yellow onions, chopped

1 or 2 cinnamon sticks

2 cups farro

Grated zest of 1 lemon

Grated zest of 1 orange

1/4 to 1/3 cup mixed fresh herb sprigs such as sage, mint, marjoram, and thyme, in any combination, finely chopped

Salt and freshly ground black pepper

Fresh lemon or orange juice (optional)

1/4 cup grated Parmesan cheese

1/4 cup grated pecorino cheese

To prepare the broth and meat, bring the water to a boil in a large saucepan. Salt the water lightly and add the pork, celery, carrots, onions, and cinnamon stick(s). When the water returns to a boil, reduce the heat to low, cover partially, and simmer, skimming off any scum from the surface from time to time, until the broth is flavorful and the pork is tender, about 1 1/2 hours. Remove the pork ribs from the broth and set them aside until they are cool enough to handle. Pour the broth through a fine-mesh sieve. You should have about 8 cups. Remove the pork from the bones and cut or tear it into small pieces. Set aside.

In a saucepan, bring the pork broth to a boil over high heat. Add the *farro,* reduce the heat to low, and simmer for 15 minutes. Add the lemon and orange zests and chopped herbs to the pan and continue cooking until the *farro* is tender, 15 to 20 minutes longer.

Add the reserved pieces of pork to the pan and heat through. Season to taste with salt and pepper and with a little lemon or orange juice, if desired. Ladle the soup into warmed bowls, and pass the grated cheeses at the table.

WINE: *Serve a light red, a Riesling, a Vernaccia, or the local Verdicchio.*

Riso in brodo con piselli

Pea Broth with Rice and Peas

If you like it thick, you have the Venetian *risi e bisi*. If you like it thin and brothy, you have a beautiful pale green soup with rice. Simply steam the rice and blanch the peas in two separate steps and add them both to the pea broth, thereby eliminating the extra work of cooking the soup in the manner of risotto.

SERVES 6

3 pounds English peas in the pod

2 yellow onions, chopped

2 celery stalks, chopped

2 large carrots, peeled and chopped

Vegetable stock or water as needed

2 tablespoons olive oil

2/3 cup chopped fresh flat-leaf parsley

1 1/2 cups Arborio rice

Salt and freshly ground black pepper

Grated Parmesan cheese for serving (optional)

Shell the peas. You should have 3 to 3 1/2 cups peas; set them aside. Put all of the pea pods, 1 of the chopped onions, the celery, and the carrots in a large saucepan and add stock or water to cover. Bring to a gentle boil over medium-high heat, reduce the heat to low, and simmer, uncovered, until the pods are very tender, 40 to 50 minutes.

Remove from the heat. Working in batches, purée the vegetables, pea pods, and cooking liquid in a blender until smooth. If the purée is fibrous, pass it through a food mill. Measure the purée and add vegetable stock or water to total 8 cups. The liquid must be thin enough to be easily absorbed by the rice.

Pour the 8 cups broth into a saucepan and bring to a simmer over medium heat. Adjust the heat to maintain a gentle simmer. In a large sauté pan with high sides, heat the olive oil over medium heat. Add the remaining chopped onion and half of the parsley and sauté until the onion is softened, about 8 minutes. Add the rice and stir until opaque, about 3 minutes. Add a ladleful (about 1 cup) of the simmering broth, and stir until the liquid is absorbed, 3 to 4 minutes. Continue to add broth a ladleful at a time, always waiting until the liquid is absorbed before adding more, until the rice kernels are al dente at the center and creamy on the outside, 18 to 20 minutes in all. You may not need all of the broth. Add the shelled peas midway during the cooking (just before the final 2 additions of broth).

Thin with additional stock or water, or any remaining broth, as needed to achieve the desired consistency, then season to taste with salt and pepper. Ladle soup into warmed bowls and sprinkle with the remaining parsley and Parmesan, if using. Serve immediately.

WINE: *Sip the local Soave.*

Although *maritata* means "married," this soup has nothing to do with weddings. What is celebrated here is the marriage of two basic ingredients: rich meats and lean greens. Despite the relatively large amount of meat, this is not a heavy soup, as the broth and greens balance it nicely. Because of the time involved, and the abundance of ingredients, this soup is not an everyday occurrence at the Neapolitan table, nor at Casa Goldstein. But it is worth the effort and will provide you more than one good meal. *Minestra maritata* is an old recipe, predating the arrival of tomatoes in the Campanian kitchen. Jeanne Caròla Francesconi, in her *La cucina napoletana,* gives two different versions of this soup, the traditional and the modern. This is the more traditional one.

SERVES 8 TO 10
(WITH LEFTOVERS)

FOR THE BROTH AND MEATS

*4 large, meaty country-style pork ribs,
2 to 3 pounds total weight*

1/2 pound salami, in one piece

1/2 pound sweet sausages with or without fennel

1/2 pound piece sopressata *(cured pork sausage),
in one piece*

1/4 pound pancetta or lardo *(page 211),
in one piece*

1 prosciutto bone

2-by-4-inch piece prosciutto fat

*1 each fresh rosemary, thyme, sage, and parsley
sprig, tied in a cheesecloth sachet*

5 quarts water

To prepare the broth and meats, combine all the meats and the prosciutto bone and fat in a large soup pot. Add the herb sachet and water and place over medium-high heat. Bring to a gentle boil, skim off any scum from the surface, reduce the heat to low, cover, and simmer until the meats are tender and falling apart and the broth is flavorful, about 3 hours.

Remove from the heat and remove and discard the herb sachet. Lift the meats out of the broth, place them in a large bowl, and refrigerate. Strain the broth through a fine-mesh sieve, let cool, and refrigerate until well chilled. When the meats are cold, remove and discard any bones and cut the meats into bite-sized pieces. When the broth is well chilled, lift off and discard the layer of fat from the surface.

To prepare the greens, bring a huge pot—the bigger, the better—three-fourths full of water to a boil. Lightly salt the water, then, working in batches, add the greens and boil just until wilted. Each batch should take 3 to 5 minutes. As each batch is ready, use a slotted spoon or tongs to transfer it to a colander. Refresh with cold water and drain again.

Pour the broth into the cleaned soup pot and place over high heat. Bring to a boil and add the drained greens, cheese rind (if using), *caciocavallo* or provolone cheese (if using), and the chile pepper flakes. Reduce the heat to low and simmer until the greens are tender to the bite, about 20 minutes. Add the reserved meats and

FOR THE GREENS

Salt

1 head escarole, coarsely chopped

1 bunch kale, tough stems discarded and coarsely chopped

2 heads curly endive (chicory), coarsely chopped

1 bunch Swiss chard, thick stems discarded and coarsely chopped

1 small head Savoy cabbage, coarsely chopped (optional)

3-inch piece Parmesan cheese rind (optional)

¹/₄ pound aged cacio cavallo or provolone cheese, cut into small pieces (optional)

Pinch of chile pepper flakes

Salt and freshly ground black pepper

Grated Parmesan cheese for serving

simmer for 10 minutes longer to blend the flavors. Season to taste with salt—it may not need any—and pepper.

Discard the cheese rind. Ladle the soup into warmed bowls and pass the Parmesan at the table.

WINE: *A red from Campania is the local choice, but you could also try a leafy red such as Cabernet Franc.*

Variations on the Marriage Theme

Ippolito Cavalcanti, in his 1837 *Cucina teorico-pratica,* a cookbook written for the kitchens of the Neapolitan nobility, offers an even more elaborate version of this bountiful soup. He replaces the pork ribs with chicken and beef and adds chopped carrots, celery, and onion to the meats. In the city of Padua, a chicken and its giblets replaces all of the meats, while in the region of Apulia, the ingredients are layered—greens, meats, diced cheese, olive oil, broth—and baked in a hot oven for nearly an hour.

Cooks in Emilia-Romagna prepare a soup called *malmaritata,* or "badly married," in which beans are braised with a bit of tomato and then combined with *maltagliati* ("badly cut" fresh egg pasta) in broth. No meats, no greens.

Zuppa di baccalà, ceci e cavolo nero
Lenten Soup with Salt Cod, Chickpeas, and Kale

In the days before refrigeration, *baccalà* (salt cod) was the only fish regularly available to Italians who lived away from the seaside or from a lake or river. It is still popular in several regions of Italy, even in those with substantial coastlines. For example, the Veneto, and especially water-surrounded Venice, has at least thirty traditional ways of preparing salt cod.

SERVES 6

1/2 pound salt cod fillets

1 1/2 cups dried chickpeas, picked over, rinsed, and soaked overnight

1 fresh thyme sprig

1 fresh rosemary sprig

Salt

1 pound cavolo nero (page 247), tough stems discarded and chopped

1/3 cup extra virgin olive oil, plus more for serving

1 yellow onion, finely chopped

3 cloves garlic, minced

1/4 cup chopped fresh flat-leaf parsley

6 plum tomatoes, peeled and chopped

1/2 teaspoon chile pepper flakes

Freshly ground black pepper

Place the salt cod in a large bowl, add water to cover, and refrigerate for at least 24 hours, changing the water 3 times. Drain the salt cod and cut into spoon-sized pieces, discarding any errant bones and skin. Refrigerate until needed.

Drain the chickpeas, transfer to a large saucepan, and add water to cover by about 3 inches. Add the thyme and rosemary sprigs, place over medium-high heat, and bring to a gentle boil. Reduce the heat to low, add 1 teaspoon salt, cover, and simmer until the chickpeas are tender, about 1 hour.

Meanwhile, bring a large saucepan three-fourths full of water to a boil. Salt the water lightly, add the *cavolo nero,* and cook until tender, about 15 minutes. Drain and set aside.

When the chickpeas are ready, remove from the heat, let cool slightly, and scoop out half of the cooked chickpeas with a little of the liquid. In a blender or food processor, process the removed chickpeas to a smooth purée and set aside. Reserve the remaining whole chickpeas and all the cooking liquid.

In a saucepan, heat the 1/3 cup olive oil over medium heat. Add the onion, garlic, and parsley and cook, stirring, until softened, about 10 minutes. Add the tomatoes and chile pepper flakes and simmer for 10 minutes to blend the flavors. Add the salt cod and add hot water just to cover. Simmer gently—do not boil or the cod will toughen—until the cod is tender, about 15 minutes.

Add the *cavolo nero,* the chickpeas and their liquid, and the chickpea purée and simmer for 10 minutes longer, stirring to prevent scorching. Taste and adjust the seasoning with salt, ladle the soup into warmed bowls, and top with black pepper and a drizzle of olive oil.

WINE: *Pour a Soave from the Veneto or a tart Pinot Bianco from Friuli.*

Ciuppin

Fish Soup from Liguria

The name is similar, but this is not cioppino, the well-known San Francisco fish stew, although the appellation of the latter is most likely derived from this Ligurian fish soup. *Ciuppin* is a fish purée, much like the *soupe de poisson* served just across the border in Nice. This recipe can be used to make a true *ciuppin,* a thick soup that needs only toasted bread to make it complete, or to make a stock for use as a base for cooking other fish soups (see note). For a purer fish flavor, do not add the tomatoes. The amount of chile heat is up to you.

SERVES 8
(MAKES ABOUT 2 QUARTS STOCK)

1/4 cup extra virgin olive oil

2 yellow onions, chopped

2 celery stalks, chopped

4 or 5 cloves garlic

1 teaspoon chile pepper flakes, or less to taste

3 pounds mild white fish steaks such as halibut or black cod

2 bay leaves

Handful of fresh flat-leaf parsley sprigs

1 tablespoon black peppercorns

1 can (28 ounces) plum tomatoes, drained and chopped (optional)

2 cups dry white wine

8 to 10 cups water

FOR THE SOUP
Salt

8 slices coarse country bread, toasted

1/2 cup grated Parmesan cheese (optional)

In a stockpot, heat the olive oil over medium heat. Add the onions and celery and sauté until softened, about 8 minutes. Add the garlic, the chile pepper flakes, and the fish steaks and toss in the oil for a minute or two. Add the bay leaves, parsley, peppercorns, tomatoes (if using), wine, and water to cover. Bring to a gentle boil over medium-high heat, reduce the heat to low, and simmer, uncovered, for 1 hour. Remove from the heat.

To make the soup, scoop out all the fish steaks and, when cool enough to handle, remove and discard all the bones and any skin. Working in batches, process the fish and the ingredients remaining in the pot in a food processor to form a smooth purée or pass the fish and other ingredients through a food mill fitted with the medium disk.

Return the purée to a clean saucepan, thin with remaining broth, and reheat to serving temperature. Season to taste with salt. Put a slice of toasted bread in each warmed bowl and ladle the soup over the top. If you like, pass the Parmesan at the table.

WINE: *Drink Vermentino with the rich fish purée served atop toasted bread.*

NOTE: To make a fish stock, strain the contents of the stockpot through a fine-mesh sieve, pressing down on the solids to extract as much liquid as possible. Discard the solids. Use immediately, refrigerate it for up to 2 days, or freeze it for up to 3 months.

Crema di asparagi allo zafferano
Asparagus Soup with Saffron

SERVES 6

When you see saffron, you know the dish is for a festive occasion. In fact, this is a Passover soup from the Veneto. You will notice that no onion is used. I find that onion masks the pure and delicate flavors of the asparagus. Although the soup is called a *crema*, you can omit the cream or milk at the end in favor of maintaining the pure asparagus flavor. Calabrian cooks omit the costly saffron in their asparagus and enrich the soup with beaten eggs and cheese and sometimes croutons. The Milanese also prepare a similar soup without the saffron, relying on a rich meat stock in place of the vegetable stock to add the touch of luxury.

4 1/2 to 5 cups vegetable stock

1/4 teaspoon saffron threads, crushed

3 1/2 to 4 pounds asparagus

4 tablespoons unsalted butter

1 large russet potato, peeled and diced

1/2 cup heavy cream or milk (optional)

Salt and freshly ground black pepper

1/4 cup chopped fresh flat-leaf parsley

1 1/2 cups small croutons, each about 1/2 inch square (optional)

In a small saucepan, bring 1/2 cup of the stock to a boil over high heat. Add the saffron, remove from the heat, and let steep for 15 minutes.

Trim off the tough stem ends from the asparagus, then cut each spear into 2-inch lengths. In a large saucepan, melt the butter over medium heat. Add the asparagus pieces and cook, stirring, for 3 minutes. Add the potato, saffron infusion, and 4 cups of the stock. Bring to a gentle boil over medium heat, reduce the heat to low, and simmer, uncovered, until the asparagus and potato are very soft, 30 to 40 minutes.

Remove from the heat and let cool slightly. Working in batches, purée the soup in a blender until smooth. Return the purée to the pan and reheat gently to serving temperature. Add the cream or milk (if using) and season to taste with salt and pepper. Add the remaining 1/2 cup stock if the soup is too thick.

Ladle the soup into warmed bowls. Top each serving with an equal amount of the parsley and with the croutons, if desired. Serve at once.

WINE: *Pairing wine with asparagus is difficult. Tocai Friulano should work here if you add a generous measure of croutons.*

Zuppa alla santé
"Health" Soup with Meatballs and Greens

SERVES 8

The name of this southern soup is a bit of an affectation, as *santé* is the French word for health. It uses meat stock, a sign of prosperity, so the hand of the *monzù*, or imported French chef, is probably behind this creation. As advertised, the soup is nourishing, filling, and somewhat extravagant. The meatballs can be made with veal or beef and are usually poached directly in the soup. The eggs and cheese are rich additions.

FOR THE MEATBALLS

1/2 pound ground beef, veal, or lamb

2 or 3 tablespoons grated yellow onion (optional)

1/2 cup dried bread crumbs

1 egg, lightly beaten

3 tablespoons grated pecorino cheese

2 tablespoons chopped fresh flat-leaf parsley

1 clove garlic, finely minced (optional)

Salt and freshly ground black pepper

To make the meatballs, combine all of the ingredients, including a good sprinkling of salt and pepper, in a bowl and mix well. Fry a small nugget of the mixture, taste, and adjust the seasoning. Form the mixture into about 40 small meatballs, each about the size of an unshelled hazelnut (about 1/2 inch in diameter), and set these aside to poach in the soup.

To make the soup, in a large soup pot, heat the olive oil over medium heat. Add the onion and celery and sauté until softened, about 8 minutes. Add the stock and tomatoes and bring to a boil over high heat. Reduce the heat to very low and simmer, uncovered, for about 30 minutes to develop the flavor.

Meanwhile, bring a large saucepan three-fourths full of water to a boil. Salt the water lightly, add the greens, and cook until almost tender, about 5 minutes. Drain well.

When the stock has simmered for 30 minutes, add the greens and the meatballs and continue to simmer over very low heat until the meatballs are cooked through, about 20 minutes. Add the cooked pasta (if using) and simmer for 5 minutes.

FOR THE SOUP

3 tablespoons olive oil

1 cup chopped yellow onion

1/2 cup chopped celery

2 quarts meat stock

4 cups chopped, peeled plum tomatoes

Salt

*2 pounds greens such as escarole or curly endive
(chicory), tough stems discarded and chopped
(about 8 cups)*

1 1/2 cups cooked pasta such as ditalini *or
small shells (optional)*

*3 eggs, lightly beaten with 1/2 cup grated
Parmesan cheese, or 2 hard-boiled eggs,
chopped, and 1/2 cup diced* scamorza *or
caciocavallo cheese*

*3 tablespoons chopped fresh flat-leaf parsley,
if using beaten eggs*

1 cup croutons, if using hard-boiled eggs (optional)

If you are using the beaten eggs and grated cheese, stir the mixture into the soup until the eggs are just set in long strands, then ladle the soup into warmed bowls, sprinkle evenly with the parsley, and serve at once. If you are using the hard-boiled eggs and diced cheese, ladle the soup into warmed bowls and sprinkle with the chopped eggs, diced cheese, and the croutons (if desired), then serve.

WINE: *Serve a red from Apulia or Campania.*

Soups for Good Health

This same nourishing soup takes on different guises in different regions. In Apulia and the Abruzzo, the meatballs are flavored with grated pecorino cheese and thickened with bread crumbs and egg. The cheese enrichment is diced *scamorza,* and the eggs are hard boiled and chopped. In Campania, the meatballs contain no cheese, but the soup is enriched with beaten eggs and cheese at the end, in the manner of a *stracciatella.* The stock varies, too. In the Abruzzo, it is a poultry stock enhanced with giblets; in Campania and Apulia, it is a meat stock.

Wild Fennel and Bread Soup

SERVES 4 TO 6

Fennel grows wild in Sicily and Sardinia, and even in California. It's unlikely, however, that you are going to find enough wild fennel for this recipe. But you do not have to abandon the idea of making this delicious soup. Cultivated fennel, also called sweet anise, is widely available at markets. (If you want to garnish the soup with fennel fronds, you may have to ask your produce person to save them for you, as many markets trim off the leafy tops.)

2 pounds fennel bulbs

6 cups water or vegetable or chicken stock, or as needed

Salt

1 teaspoon fennel seeds, toasted in a dry pan and ground in a mortar

Freshly ground black pepper

6 tablespoons unsalted butter

2 tablespoons olive oil

8 to 12 slices coarse country bread

1/2 pound ricotta or sheep's milk feta cheese

Cut off the stalks and fronds from the fennel bulbs. Reserve the fronds for garnish, if desired. Cut the fennel bulbs in half and cut out the tough core from each half. Peel off any discolored outer leaves, then thickly slice the fennel lengthwise.

In a large saucepan, bring the water or stock to a boil over high heat. If using water, salt it lightly. Add the fennel and fennel seeds, reduce the heat to low, and simmer, uncovered, until tender, 15 to 20 minutes. Remove from the heat. Season with salt and pepper.

Preheat the oven to 350°F. In a large sauté pan, melt 2 tablespoons of the butter and 1 tablespoon of the olive oil over medium heat. Add half of the bread slices and fry on both sides until golden, about 5 minutes total. Transfer to a cutting board. Repeat with the remaining slices, 2 tablespoons of the butter, and the remaining 1 tablespoon oil. Cut each slice into 2-inch squares.

Using a slotted spoon, remove the fennel slices from the fennel broth, reserving the broth. In a large earthenware baking dish or 4 to 6 ovenproof soup bowls or ramekins, arrange a layer of bread. Top with a layer of cheese, applying dollops of the ricotta or crumbling the feta. Add a layer of fennel slices, and sprinkle with the fennel broth. Repeat until all the ingredients are used, ending with a layer of fennel. Cut the remaining 2 tablespoons butter into small pieces and dot the top layer.

Bake until golden, about 30 to 35 minutes for the large dish and 20 minutes for the small dishes. If you have used a large dish, scoop out into warmed bowls with a large spoon. Chop some of the fennel fronds and garnish each serving, if desired. Serve immediately.

WINE: *Drink a Vermentino from Sardinia or Greco di Tufo from Campania.*

Farinata con cavolo nero
Polenta and Kale Soup

This Tuscan recipe could just as easily be in the grains chapter among the many polenta dishes enriched with beans or greens, such as *polenta incatenata* (page 100). Because this mixture is thinner, however, it falls into the soup category. In Friuli, a similar soup, made with cooked spinach, is called *paparot*.

SERVES 4 TO 6

6 quarts water

Salt

2 bunches cavolo nero (page 247) or Swiss chard, tough stems discarded

1 cup polenta

2 tablespoons extra virgin olive oil, plus more for serving

4 cloves garlic, minced

Freshly ground black pepper

In a large pot, bring the water to a boil over high heat. Salt lightly, then add the *cavolo nero* or Swiss chard and cook until tender. The *cavolo nero* will take almost 30 minutes, while the chard will take only about 15 minutes. Remove the greens with a slotted spoon or tongs to a colander, reserving the cooking water (those thrifty Tuscans!). Rinse the greens with cold water to set the color, then drain well. Chop the greens coarsely.

Measure out 7 cups of the reserved cooking water into a saucepan; reserve the remainder. Stir in the polenta, place over medium heat, and bring slowly to a boil, stirring often to prevent lumping. As soon as it boils, reduce the heat to low. When the mixture has thickened, after about 15 minutes, add the greens and continue to cook over very low heat, adding additional cooking water as needed to achieve a thick, soupy consistency, until the polenta is no longer grainy on the tongue, 20 to 30 minutes longer.

Meanwhile, in a small sauté pan, heat the 2 tablespoons olive oil over low heat. Add the garlic and cook until softened, just a few minutes. Remove from the heat.

When the soup is ready, stir in the garlic. Ladle into warmed bowls, sprinkle with pepper, and drizzle with olive oil. Serve immediately.

WINE: *If you want a red, pour a Ghemme. If you prefer a white, serve a Vernaccia.*

VARIATIONS: Add 1 cup peeled, seeded, and chopped tomatoes with the greens. Alternatively, sauté 1 yellow onion, finely chopped, until tender and then add with the garlic.

SAUCES FOR PASTA AND POLENTA

Stories of Italian grandmothers simmering their tomato sauces for hours are familiar but probably untrue. Tomatoes that are cooked for too long lose their sweetness, and the resulting sauce tastes old and tired. Most likely those beloved *nonne* were actually cooking a *ragù* or *sugo,* that is, a meat sauce, which may or may not have included tomatoes.

Meat sauces generally call for beef, veal, pork, or a combination, although lamb, rabbit, or duck is common in some Italian regions. Sometimes sausage or chicken giblets are also included for extra richness, and although tomatoes enter the picture, they are typically in the form of *pelati* (canned plum or San Marzano tomatoes), tomato purée, tomato paste, or tomato sauce. Broth along with red or white wine might be added for liquid and taste, while dried porcini often contribute an earthy flavor.

Most such sauces begin with a *battuto* (from *battere,* "to beat") of chopped onion, carrot, and celery. The mixture is cooked slowly in oil, butter, lard *(strutto),* or pancetta fat, possibly with the addition of finely chopped garlic and herbs, at which point it becomes a *soffritto,* meaning "under fried" *(sottofriggere).* Then the sauce, whether a *ragù,* a *sugo,* or another type, is built on this flavorful base.

The outsider quickly discovers that no tidy distinctions exist among the names used for these pasta sauces. A *ragù,* for example (from the French *ragoût,* or "stew"), can be either chopped meat cooked and served in the sauce, or a single large piece of meat braised in the sauce to flavor it and then served as a separate course following the pasta. The term *sugo* is used for a sauce, a gravy, pan juices (the result of cooking a roast), or even just juice, while *tocco* is what the Genoese call a *sugo. Intingolo* also means gravy or pan juices, but it is used for something you can dip bread into or sometimes for a stew, plus it is synonymous with both *ragù* and *sugo. Salsa* is "sauce," as in *salsa di pomodoro,* or "tomato sauce," although a tomato sauce can be a *sugo* as well.

The subject of what constitutes a *ragù* arouses perhaps the greatest passion, however. There is no single correct way to make a *ragù,* and recipes for it vary wildly within regions, towns, and even families. In this chapter, I have included a selection of some of the best-known *ragùs* along with some lesser-known meat-based sauces. Some are used to dress fresh pasta, such as *pappardelle* or fettuccine; some are layered in a lasagna or with polenta; some are tossed with dried pasta; and still others are spooned over polenta or gnocchi. I have also slipped in a few sauces based on vegetables and fish, among them a simple tomato sauce that simmers just long enough to thicken, but not so long that it becomes bitter, and a "fast" tomato sauce that can be used in place of canned in slow and savory dishes.

Most of these sauces can be stored for three to five days in the refrigerator, and the meat sauces can even be frozen. This gives you the best of both worlds: a slow and savory sauce that becomes fast and easy when all you need to do is reheat it with a little additional liquid.

Ragù alla napoletana
Meat Sauce from Naples

SERVES 6

While the *ragù* from Bologna has meat and barely any tomato, this version from Naples is tomato sauce flavored with only a little meat. Most Neapolitans cook the meat in the sauce, remove it, and serve it after the pasta. But if you want the meat in the sauce, you can start with chopped meat, or you can chop the meat after it has been cooked and return it to the sauce as many Italian Americans do. Neapolitans usually serve this sauce over *ziti*, but you can also use rigatoni or *fusilli*.

1/3 cup olive oil

1 1/2 pounds beef brisket or chuck, in one piece

1/2 pound boneless veal shoulder, in one piece

1/2 pound boneless pork shoulder, in one piece

Salt

1 yellow onion, chopped

1/2 cup dry red wine

2 cans (28 ounces each) plum tomatoes with juice, chopped or pulsed in a food processor

Pinch of chile pepper flakes (optional)

Meat stock, if needed

Freshly ground black pepper

FOR SERVING
1 pound dried ziti, cooked

Grated pecorino cheese

In a large Dutch oven or deep skillet, heat the olive oil over high heat. Add all the meats and sprinkle with salt. When the meats have given up their juices, after about 15 minutes, add the onion and stir well. Reduce the heat to medium and cook, stirring occasionally, until the meats are browned and the onion is golden. This might take as long as 15 minutes.

Add the wine and cook until it is absorbed into the meats, about 10 minutes. Add the tomatoes and the chile pepper flakes (if using) and stir well. Cover partially and simmer, stirring often, for 2 1/2 hours. Check from time to time to see if more liquid is needed, adding stock or water if necessary to prevent scorching. At this point, the sauce should be thick and the juices should coat a spoon.

Using a slotted spoon, remove the meat and reserve for another dish, or chop it and return it to the sauce. Season the sauce to taste with salt and pepper. Toss the sauce with the pasta and serve. Pass the cheese at the table.

WINE: *Stay local with an Aglianico from Campania. Look for Taurasi from Mastroberardino or Feudi San Gregorio.*

You can use a knife—my preference—or kitchen scissors to chop the meat, or you can use the pulse function on a food processor, though you run the risk of the meat becoming too fine before you stop. I like to use brisket for *ragù alla bolognese* because it has a particularly rich flavor. It makes a good alternative to the traditional combination of beef and pork.

SERVES 6

3 tablespoons unsalted butter

3 tablespoons extra virgin olive oil

1 celery stalk, chopped

1 carrot, peeled and chopped

1 yellow onion, chopped

1/2 pound boneless beef chuck or brisket, chopped

1/2 pound boneless pork shoulder, chopped

2 ounces prosciutto, chopped

2 ounces pancetta, chopped

2 tablespoons tomato paste diluted in 1/2 cup water

1/4 cup tomato purée (optional)

1 cup dry red wine

1 cup meat stock, or as needed

1 cup milk (optional)

Salt and freshly ground black pepper

FOR SERVING

1 pound fresh tagliatelle (fettuccine) or pappardelle, *cooked*

Unsalted butter (optional) and Parmesan cheese

In a large sauté pan, melt the butter with the olive oil over medium heat. Add the celery, carrot, and onion and sauté until softened and lightly golden, about 15 minutes. Add the beef, pork, prosciutto, and pancetta and sauté, stirring often, until the meats lose their redness, about 10 minutes. Stir in the tomato paste, tomato purée (if using), and wine and cook until the wine is absorbed into the meats, about 10 to 15 minutes. Add the 1 cup stock and the milk (if using), cover, reduce the heat to the lowest setting, and simmer gently for about 2 1/2 hours. Check from time to time to see if more liquid is needed, adding more stock if necessary to prevent scorching. At this point, you should have a rich, concentrated sauce. Season with salt and pepper.

Toss the sauce with the pasta. Top each serving with a pat of butter, if desired, and some grated Parmesan.

WINE: *Sangiovese di Romagna is the local wine. Good producers are Castelluccio, Tre Monti, Fattoria Zerbina, and Fattoria Paradiso. If you cannot find these, opt for a Nebbiolo, Barbera d'Alba, or Merlot.*

———————

VARIATIONS: Some versions of this sauce do not use any wine, but increase the amount of stock, or they leave out the pork shoulder and replace it with an additional 1/2 pound of beef. Tuscan cooks may add a few chicken livers (up to 1/2 pound) to a similar *ragù*, use pork sausage in place of the chopped pork, and never add the milk. Still other versions add 1/2 ounce dried porcini mushrooms, soaked in hot water for 30 minutes, drained, and chopped, after the *battuto* is sautéed.

Ragù alla triestina
Meat Sauce from Trieste

SERVES 6

This sauce is traditionally used to dress *strucolo* (page 273) or potato gnocchi, but it would also be excellent with a robust pasta such as *pappardelle* or penne. The sauce can be prepared ahead of time and refrigerated for up to 5 days or frozen.

4 tablespoons unsalted butter

2 tablespoons olive oil

1 yellow onion, chopped

1 carrot, peeled and chopped

1 celery stalk, chopped

1/2 pound ground veal or beef

1/2 pound ground pork

1/4 cup tomato paste diluted in 1/2 cup water

1/2 cup dry red wine

1 teaspoon chopped fresh thyme

2 teaspoons chopped fresh marjoram

4 to 6 cups meat stock, or as needed

Salt and freshly ground black pepper

FOR SERVING

Strucolo *(page 273)* or 1 pound fresh pappardelle *or dried penne, cooked*

Grated Parmesan cheese

In a large sauté pan, melt the butter with the olive oil over medium heat. Add the onion, carrot, and celery and sauté until softened, about 8 minutes. Add the ground meats and sauté, breaking them up with a fork, until they lose their redness, about 8 minutes. Add the tomato paste and wine and cook until the liquids are absorbed into the meat, 5 to 8 minutes longer.

Add the thyme and marjoram and stock to cover, reduce the heat to low, cover partially, and simmer for about 2 hours. Check from time to time to see if more liquid is needed, adding more stock if necessary to prevent scorching. At this point, you should have a rich, concentrated sauce. Season with salt and pepper.

Toss the sauce with the pasta and serve. Pass the cheese at the table.

WINE: *Refosco is the big red of the region. The best producers are Dorigo, Scarbolo, and Venica & Venica. Your next best option is a Côte du Rhône, a California Rhône, or a peppery, rich Zinfandel.*

Pasta and Sauce

Fresh and dried pastas are of equal importance in the Italian kitchen, although distinctions do exist. In general, most fresh pasta is served in the north, while most dried pasta is eaten from Rome and the Abruzzo south into Sicily. One is not better than the other, of course, but because they are different, they take different kinds of sauces.

Fresh pasta, which is typically made at home or bought in small specialty shops, is inherently soft because it is made with the Italian equivalent of all-purpose flour and eggs, or sometimes just egg yolks. Therefore, it must be cooked until tender, rather than al dente. It is highly porous and absorbent, which means it marries well with sauces based on butter and cream, as well as with many of the *ragù* and *sugo* recipes in this chapter.

Dried pasta, which is made in factories, is produced by kneading hard-wheat (durum) semolina flour with water. The best dried pasta is extruded under great pressure through bronze dies and then air-dried slowly. Because the extrusion process is slow, the dies form minute ridges along the surface of the noodle that trap the sauce. Cheaper mass-produced dried pastas are extruded quickly through Teflon dies, which results in a slick surface, and then dried with heat. The sauce, rather than clinging to the pasta, easily rolls off of it. Recommended brands of semolina pasta include Martelli, Latini, Rustichella d'Abruzzo, Benedetto Cavalleri, and the De Cecco products processed in its plant in the Abruzzo.

Dried semolina pasta should be cooked al dente, that is, firm to the bite. Look for the white dot in the center when you bite into a test strand. It will give you an indication of doneness. When the dot is tiny, the pasta is ready. Dried pasta is usually dressed with tomato sauce or olive oil and vegetables or seafood.

Dried pasta may be used in place of fresh with some of the sauces in this chapter, and I have indicated when substitutions are possible. But some basic rules always apply: a substantial noodle calls for a heavy sauce, and a delicate or thin noodle needs a light sauce. Finally, certain sauces are traditionally paired with certain pastas, and for a good reason: balance.

Sugo di coniglio alla toscana
Rabbit Sauce from Tuscany

SERVES 4 TO 6

The classic Tuscan *sugo di lepre* is rich, dark pasta sauce made with wild hare. This gamier meat is not always readily available elsewhere, but rabbit does nicely in its place. In Siena, a little chopped fresh tarragon might be added to the sauce. Because this sauce is so rich, you need a wide noodle to balance it. Ideally, the *pappardelle* are fresh and handmade, but dried will work, too. The sauce can be prepared a few days ahead of time and refrigerated. As with most rich meat sauces, you will need to add some stock when reheating.

1 rabbit with liver, about 3 pounds

1/4 cup extra virgin olive oil

Salt and freshly ground black pepper

1 yellow onion, chopped

1 carrot, peeled and chopped

1 celery stalk, chopped

3 cloves garlic, minced

1 tablespoon finely chopped fresh rosemary, or to taste

1 cup dry red wine

2 tablespoons tomato paste diluted in 1/4 cup water or chicken stock

2 cups chicken stock, or as needed

1 ounce dried porcini mushrooms

FOR SERVING

1 pound fresh or dried pappardelle, *cooked*

Grated Parmesan cheese (optional)

Cut the rabbit into small pieces, rinse, and pat dry. Reserve the liver whole.

In a large saucepan or Dutch oven, heat the olive oil over medium-high heat. Add the rabbit pieces and brown on all sides until golden, sprinkling them with salt and pepper. This should take about 10 minutes. Using a slotted spoon, transfer the rabbit pieces to a plate and set aside.

Return the pan to medium heat, add the onion, carrot, and celery, and sauté until softened, 8 to 10 minutes. Add the garlic and rosemary and sauté for 2 minutes longer. Add the wine and cook until reduced by half, about 10 minutes. Return the rabbit to the pan, add the tomato paste and 2 cups stock, and bring to a gentle boil. Reduce the heat to low, cover, and simmer for 1 to 1 1/2 hours. (You may also cook the sauce in a 350°F oven for the same amount of time; be sure use an ovenproof pan.) Check from time to time to see if more liquid is needed, adding more stock if necessary to prevent scorching.

Meanwhile, soak the porcini in hot water to cover for 30 minutes. Drain, reserving the soaking liquid, and chop finely. Pour the liquid through a fine-mesh sieve lined with cheesecloth. Set the mushrooms and liquid aside.

When the meat is very tender, lift the rabbit pieces from the pan juices and let cool until they can be handled, then remove the meat from the bones.

Add the porcini and their soaking liquid to the pan juices. Chop the rabbit liver finely and add to the pan juices along with the rabbit meat. Simmer the sauce over medium heat until it is thick and rich, about 15 minutes. If the sauce seems too thick, add more stock. Taste and adjust the seasoning with salt and pepper. You may want a bit more rosemary, too.

Add the *pappardelle* to the sauce, toss well to coat, and simmer for a minute or two, then serve. Some cooks top this pasta with a bit of Parmesan.

WINE: *Choose a full-bodied Sangiovese such as Rosso di Montalcino, or Brunello di Montalcino.*

VARIATION: Add $^1/_2$ cup pitted Gaeta olives in place of, or in addition to, the porcini.

SERVES 4 TO 6

This sauce of duck and aromatic vegetables is a specialty of the Veneto. In Vicenza, it is tossed with *bigoli,* a thick whole-wheat noodle that is extruded though a pasta machine called a *bigolaro.* In Venice, the same sauce, augmented with tomatoes, is served over gnocchi. No one will stop you from putting it over fettuccine, but the noodle is not typical of the Veneto. Its use depends on how much of a purist you want to be. :: Traditionally, the duck is skinned and boned, and the meat is cut into walnut-sized pieces and cooked along with the vegetables and wine. Perhaps your poultry butcher will handle the boning and skinning, or you can try it on your own. The pieces do not need to be pretty; rustic chunks are fine. You can also cut the duck into eighths, remove as much of the skin as possible, and cook the bone-in pieces along with the vegetables and wine. Once the meat is tender, remove the duck pieces from the sauce, cut the meat from the bones, add it back to the sauce, and then carefully skim away any fat from the surface.

2 tablespoons olive oil or unsalted butter

1 large yellow onion, chopped

1 carrot, peeled and chopped

1 celery stalk, chopped

3 cloves garlic, minced

1/4 cup finely chopped fresh flat-leaf parsley

1 duck, about 5 pounds, cut into 8 pieces and most of the skin removed or boned and skinned and the meat cut into small pieces

2 bay leaves

4 fresh sage leaves

3 whole cloves

3 cups dry white wine

1 cup tomato sauce (optional)

In a large sauté pan, heat the olive oil or butter over medium heat. Add the onion, carrot, celery, garlic, and parsley and sauté until softened and golden, about 15 minutes. Add the duck pieces, bay leaves, sage, cloves, wine, tomato sauce (if using), and 2 cups stock and season with salt and pepper. Bring to a gentle boil, reduce the heat to low, and simmer, uncovered, until the duck meat is very tender, 1 to 1 1/2 hours. Check from time to time to see if more liquid is needed, adding more stock if necessary to prevent scorching.

If you used bone-in duck pieces, remove them from the sauce with a slotted spoon. When they are cool enough to handle, cut away the meat from the bones and return the meat to the pan. Add the cinnamon (if using), then taste and adjust the seasoning. You may need to add a bit of stock if it is too thick.

Toss the sauce with the pasta and pass the cheese at the table.

WINE: *Pour a Valpolicella from the Veneto. Among the best producers are Allegrini, Tenuta di Sant'Antonio, Masi, and Quintarelli.*

2 cups poultry stock, or as needed

Salt and freshly ground black pepper

$1/2$ teaspoon ground cinnamon, or to taste (optional)

FOR SERVING

1 pound fresh or dried bigoli *or other whole-wheat pasta or gnocchi, cooked*

Grated Parmesan or grana padano *cheese*

Other Duck Sauces

In one recipe from the Marches, chicken, duck, or turkey giblets are added to the sauce with the duck, and cloves are used instead of cinnamon. In another sauce from the same region, chopped prosciutto goes in with the duck pieces, giving the sauce a slightly sweeter tone. Some Lombardian cooks add pieces of cooked sausage to their duck sauces, providing additional textural contrast and a more complex flavor.

SERVES 6

A *sugo* made with poultry giblets is sometimes called *alla romana*, but its popularity is not confined to Lazio. In the Marches, cooks combine the giblets with a *ragù* of chopped meats for an even richer sauce. *Sugo di rigaglie* (sometimes spelled *regaglie*) is great on *pappardelle*, but would work on potato gnocchi as well. In general, no cheese is used with this pasta sauce.

1 ounce dried porcini mushrooms

3/4 pound chicken giblets (gizzards, hearts, and livers), trimmed of any fat, connective tissue, and gristle, then gizzards and livers cut into large bite-size pieces

3 tablespoons olive oil or lard, plus 2 tablespoons olive oil for sautéing livers

1 yellow onion, chopped

1 carrot, peeled and chopped

1 small celery stalk, chopped

2 cloves garlic, minced

2 cups dry white wine

2 cups chicken stock, or as needed

2 cups peeled, seeded, and diced canned tomatoes

Salt and freshly ground black pepper

FOR SERVING

1 pound fresh pappardelle *or fettuccine, cooked*

Soak the porcini mushrooms in hot water to cover for 30 minutes. Drain, reserving the soaking liquid, and chop finely. Pour the liquid through a fine-mesh sieve lined with cheesecloth. Set the mushrooms and liquid aside. Set the gizzards and hearts aside together and refrigerate the livers.

In a large sauté pan, heat the 3 tablespoons olive oil or lard over medium heat. Add the onion, carrot, and celery and sauté until softened, about 8 minutes. Add the garlic, gizzards, and hearts and sauté until coated with oil, about 5 minutes. Add the wine and cook until reduced by half, about 10 minutes. Add the porcini and their soaking liquid and enough stock just to cover the gizzards and hearts. Reduce the heat to low, cover, and simmer until the gizzards and hearts are very tender, about 1 hour. Using a slotted spoon, transfer the giblets to a cutting board and chop coarsely. Pour the pan juices into a bowl and set the giblets and pan juices aside.

Wipe out the sauté pan, place over high heat, and add the 2 tablespoons olive oil. When it is hot, add the livers and brown on all sides, 5 to 7 minutes. Return the giblets and their juices to the pan, add the tomatoes, and simmer for 10 minutes to blend the flavors and heat through. If the sauce seems dry, add a bit of stock or water. Taste and adjust the seasoning with salt and pepper.

Toss the sauce with the pasta and serve.

WINE: *To stay local, try a Sangiovese-Montepulciano blend such as Rosso Piceno Superiore from Tenuta Cocci Grifoni or Ercole Velenosi, or a Rosso Conero from Umani Ronchi, Moroder, or Le Terrazze. If these are not available, your favorite Chianti will do nicely.*

Bruscitt con polenta
Chopped Meat Sauce for Polenta

SERVES 6 TO 8

When I first read a recipe for this Lombardian sauce, I wondered about it. Would the fennel flavor penetrate the meat? What holds the sauce together? When I cooked it, I discovered that it is more of a stew than a sauce, with tiny pieces of meat that become tender, but do not break down. The fennel truly does perfume the meat, and the additional butter rounds out the pan juices.

1/2 cup unsalted butter, plus more for serving

1 1/2 pounds boneless beef brisket or chuck, cut into pieces 1/3 to 1/2 inch square

6 pancetta slices, chopped or diced

Salt and freshly ground black pepper

20 fennel seeds, tied in a cheesecloth sachet

A few juniper berries, crushed (optional)

2 cups dry red wine, or as needed

FOR SERVING

2 cups polenta, cooked in salted water with 2 cloves garlic, smashed (see Basic Polenta, page 89)

Grated Parmesan cheese

In a large saucepan with a tight-fitting lid, melt 4 tablespoons of the butter over medium heat. Add the beef and pancetta and sauté until lightly browned, about 10 minutes. Sprinkle with salt and pepper, add the sachet of fennel seeds, the juniper berries (if using), and 1/2 cup of the wine. Reduce the heat to very low, cover, and simmer for 2 to 3 hours, adding more wine every half hour or so as needed to keep the meat moist. At this point, the sauce should be dense and aromatic. Discard the sachet and season with salt and pepper.

Stir the remaining 4 tablespoons butter into the sauce. Ladle the sauce atop soft polenta in warmed individual bowls, top with more butter and some Parmesan, and serve.

WINE: *The best choice is a wine from the Valtellina, such as a Nebbiolo DOC from Rainoldi or Negri. In its absence, stay with the grape and pour a Ghemme or Gattinara from the Piedmont. Dessilani and Nervi are reliable producers.*

A Specialty of Busto Arsizio

The Lombardian town of Busto Arsizio is the home of this unusual meat sauce for polenta. According to written recipes, the beef is cut into pieces the size of "small cherries" or "dried beans" and then cooked in butter in a tightly sealed terra-cotta casserole, along with a sachet of fennel seeds. In some versions, strips of pancetta are placed on top of the chopped beef; in others, the pancetta is chopped and mixed with the beef. Traditionally, the sauce is ladled over soft polenta cooked with smashed garlic cloves for flavor.

Tocco alla genovese
Meat Sauce from Genoa

SERVES 4 TO 6

Tocco is Genoese dialect for "sauce," and the ample use of dried porcini, which adds an earthiness and depth of flavor, is a signature of this classic Genoese *sugo*. Here, you have two options: you can make the sauce with large pieces of meat, remove them, and use them for another course, or you can make it in the manner of *ragù alla bolognese,* with chopped meat. In the old days, a *tocco* was typically prepared with beef marrow for extra richness. Today, it is not always easy to find a butcher who carries marrowbones, so the marrow has been omitted here. Some Genoese cooks add a few tablespoons of crushed pine nuts with the porcini, or use white wine in place of the red. The sauce is traditionally used to dress *piccage,* which is Genoese dialect for ribbons and is used for the Ligurian equivalent of fettuccine or tagliatelle.

2 ounces dried porcini mushrooms

2 tablespoons olive oil

1 yellow onion, chopped

2 carrots, peeled and chopped

2 celery stalks, chopped

1 pound boneless beef brisket or chuck or veal shoulder, cut into large pieces or chopped

1 cup dry red wine

1 clove garlic, minced

3 tablespoons chopped fresh flat-leaf parsley

2 to 3 cups light meat stock, or as needed

Salt and freshly ground black pepper

FOR SERVING

1 pound fresh piccage or fettuccine, cooked

Grated Parmesan cheese

Soak the mushrooms in hot water to cover for 30 minutes. Drain, reserving the liquid, and chop finely. Pour the liquid through a fine-mesh sieve lined with cheesecloth. Set the mushrooms and liquid aside.

In a large sauté pan, heat the olive oil over medium heat. Add the onion, carrots, and celery and sauté until softened, about 8 minutes. Add the meat and brown on all sides; the timing will depend on the size of the pieces. Add the wine and and cook until the liquid is absorbed into the meat, about 10 minutes. Add the garlic and parsley and then add the porcini and their soaking liquid and enough stock to just cover the meat. Bring to a gentle boil, reduce the heat to low, cover partially, and simmer gently for 2 hours or longer, until meat is tender, adding more stock as needed to prevent scorching. At this point, the sauce should be thick and the juices should coat a spoon. Season to taste with salt and pepper.

If you have used large pieces of meat, remove them with a slotted spoon and pass the rest of the sauce through a food mill. Serve the meat as another course and toss the sauce with the pasta, or chop the meat, stir it into the sauce, and then toss the sauce with the pasta. If you started with chopped meat, simply serve the *tocco* tossed with the pasta. Pass the cheese at the table.

WINE: *Because Liguria does not have a red wine of note, look for a hearty Barbera from Vietti, Bartolo Mascarello, or Aldo Conterno, or from other, lesser-known producers, such as Oberto or Bocchino.*

Sugo di castrato
Lamb Sauce with Tomatoes and Hot Pepper

SERVES 6

This rich lamb sauce from the Abruzzo is traditionally served over *pasta alla chitarra,* which is shaped on a *chitarra,* a wooden frame strung with wires that calls to mind a guitar, thus the name. The pasta dough is rolled into a thin sheet, the sheet is laid over the wires, and then a rolling pin is used to push the dough through the wires, producing thin strands. *Sugo di castrato* may also be served over cheese-filled ravioli or layered in lasagna. If this sauce is made with *ciavarre,* a sheep that has not yet given birth, it is called *guazzetto di ciavarre.*

3 tablespoons chopped lardo *(page 211) or pancetta*

1 large yellow onion, chopped

2 tablespoons chopped fresh rosemary

1 pound ground lamb

1 cup dry white wine

2 cups peeled, seeded, and chopped tomatoes (fresh or canned), or 1/4 cup tomato paste diluted in 1/2 cup water

1/2 teaspoon chile pepper flakes, plus a tiny pinch (optional)

Light meat stock or water if needed

Salt and freshly ground black pepper

FOR SERVING

1 pound fresh pasta alla chitarra, *fettuccine, or cheese ravioli, cooked*

Grated pecorino cheese

In a large sauté pan, combine the *lardo* or pancetta, onion, and rosemary over medium heat and sauté until the *lardo* has rendered its fat and the onion is softened, 8 to 10 minutes. Add the lamb and sauté, breaking it up with a fork, until it loses its red color and starts to brown, about 10 minutes. Add the wine and cook until the liquid is absorbed into the meat, about 10 minutes. Add the tomatoes or tomato paste and the 1/2 teaspoon chile pepper flakes (if using), reduce the heat to low, cover, and simmer for 1 1/2 to 2 hours. Check from time to time to see if more liquid is needed, adding a little stock or water if necessary to prevent scorching. At this point, the sauce should be thick and the juices should coat a spoon. Season to taste with salt and black pepper. Some cooks add a tiny pinch of chile pepper flakes at the end.

Toss the sauce with the pasta and pass the pecorino at the table.

WINE: *Locally, look for a Montepulciano d'Abruzzo from Illuminati, Masciarelli, or Agriverde. Or, move to neighboring Molise for a reasonable Sangiovese called Di Majo Norante.*

VARIATION: To make *ragù d'agnello e peperoni,* add 1 clove garlic, minced, and 2 red bell peppers, seeded and sliced, with the tomatoes.

Sugo di salsicce
Sausage Sauce for Polenta or Pasta

SERVES 6

Simple and rich, this sauce from the Piedmont can be layered with polenta and cheese for *polenta pasticciata* (page 75), or tossed with fresh or dried egg pasta such as fettuccine or *garganelli,* a short, tubular, ridged pasta that is a specialty of Romagna and sometimes flavored with nutmeg. The sauce is essential to *polenta di Natale,* or the Christmas polenta of Mantua, where 1/2 cup red wine is added to it early on and cream is stirred in toward the end of cooking. The polenta itself is cooked with part milk and part water, and mixed with both egg yolks and beaten egg whites to produce a particularly festive dish.

4 tablespoons unsalted butter

1 large yellow onion, chopped

1/2 pound ground pork

6 sweet sausages with or without fennel, casings removed and meat crumbled

1 1/2 cups Rich Tomato Sauce (page 69)

1/2 cup milk or heavy cream, or as needed

Salt and freshly ground black pepper

Light meat stock if needed

FOR SERVING

1 pound fresh or dried fettuccine or garganelli, cooked

Grated Parmesan cheese

In a heavy skillet, melt the butter over medium heat. Add the onion and sauté until beginning to soften, about 5 minutes. Add the ground pork and pork sausage and cook, stirring often to break up the meats, until the meat loses its pink color, about 10 minutes. Pour in the tomato sauce, reduce the heat to very low, cover, and simmer for about 1 1/2 hours. As the sauce simmers, add the milk or cream a spoonful or two at a time to prevent scorching. At this point, the sauce should be thick and the juices should coat a spoon. Season to taste with salt and pepper. If the sauce is too thick, add a little meat stock to thin.

Toss the sauce with the pasta and pass the cheese at the table.

WINE: *Dolcetto, Dolcetto, Dolcetto. Look for Dolcetto d'Alba wines from Vietti or Cigliotto, Dolcetto d'Aqui from Villa Spanna, or Dolcetto Dogliani from Abbona.*

VARIATION: Add 1 pound fresh mushrooms such as cremini or porcini, wiped clean, sliced, and sautéed in 4 tablespoons unsalted butter until tender, to the sauce during the last 30 minutes of cooking. Alternatively, add 1 ounce dried porcini mushrooms, soaked in hot water for 30 minutes, drained, and finely chopped, with the tomato sauce. You can also omit the milk or cream.

Pesto di triglie
Fish Sauce for Pasta

SERVES 4

Wherever there is a coastline teeming with seafood, a fish-based pasta sauce is certain to evolve. This recipe is from the Marches, a region that borders the Adriatic, and it calls for highly prized red mullet, but you can use any delicately flavored small fish or tender fillets. In the Abruzzo, cooks make a similar fish sauce with trout, while the *ragù di pesce* from Tuscany adds basil leaves to the sauce and omits the garlic. In the Veneto, *pasta alla buranella* combines this fish sauce with a light cream sauce made with fish stock, and uses it to dress either fresh tagliatelle or a pasta gratin called *pasticcio di pesce*. :: If the juice in which the tomatoes are packed is tasty, add it along with the tomatoes. While rigatoni is the usual pasta, penne or even another dried short pasta will work as well. And no one will sneer if you pass grated cheese at the table. It is recommended with this dish.

2 1/2 pounds red mullet (about 4), cleaned, or 1 1/2 pounds mild fish fillets such as rockfish, snapper, sole, cod, or trout

1/4 cup extra virgin olive oil

1 celery stalk, chopped

1 yellow onion, chopped

2 cloves garlic, minced

3 tablespoons chopped fresh flat-leaf parsley

Salt

1/2 cup dry white wine

2 1/2 pounds chopped canned tomatoes

1 teaspoon tomato paste, if needed

Freshly ground black pepper

FOR SERVING

1 pound rigatoni, penne, or other dried short pasta, cooked

Grated pecorino cheese

If using whole red mullet, rinse well, fillet the fish and skin the fillets, and chop the fillets coarsely. If using fish fillets, chop them coarsely.

In a large sauté pan, heat the olive oil over medium heat. Add the celery, onion, garlic, and parsley and sauté until softened, 8 to 10 minutes. Add the fish, sprinkle with salt, and sauté until lightly colored, 8 to 10 minutes. Add the white wine and cook until it is absorbed by the fish, about 8 minutes. Add the tomatoes, reduce the heat to low, and simmer, uncovered, until thickened, about 30 minutes. Taste the sauce, and if the tomato flavor is weak, add the tomato paste. Season to taste with salt and pepper.

Toss the sauce with the pasta and pass the pecorino at the table.

WINE: *When you think of white wine in the Marches, the first thought is Verdicchio. Try Verdicchio dei Castelli di Jesi or Verdicchio di Matelica. Noted producers are Umani Ronchi, Sartarelli, Fattoria San Lorenzo, and Bucci.*

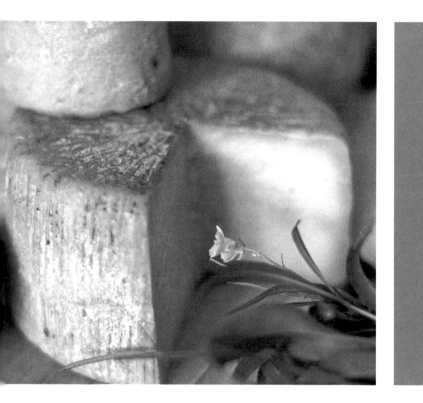

Fish and Cheese

First-time tourists to Italy are often surprised by the reaction to their requests for cheese to sprinkle on *linguine con vongole* or another seafood pasta. The waiter typically shrugs, looks askance, and then delivers the cheese to the table. Most of the country is governed by an unwritten rule of no cheese with fish or shellfish, but certainly not all of Italy. This recipe for *pesto di triglie* is just one example of that break with tradition. So is the stuffed squid recipe (page 124) in the Fish and Shellfish chapter. I do not know if the exceptions are because the influence of the *monzù* (French-inspired chef) trickled up from Naples or Palermo, or because of the legacy of the Greeks or Normans, but in the case of this pasta, you can sprinkle cheese without any guilt.

Sugo di carciofi alla ligure
Artichoke Sauce from Liguria

You can use this Genoese sauce on pasta, of course, but it can also be spooned over cooked meat or fish. I like it a bit chunky, although it is sometimes puréed. If you want it smooth, use a food mill; if you want to maintain a bit of texture, use the pulse function on a food processor. Note the typical Ligurian addition of dried porcini, which boosts the overall flavor of the sauce.

SERVES 4

1 ounce dried porcini mushrooms

1 lemon, halved

4 large artichokes

3 tablespoons olive oil

1 yellow onion, chopped

1 clove garlic, minced

3 tablespoons chopped fresh flat-leaf parsley

Salt

1 tablespoon all-purpose flour

1/2 cup Rich Tomato Sauce (page 69), Tomato Sauce (page 69), or canned tomato sauce

1/2 cup dry white wine

3 tablespoons unsalted butter

FOR SERVING

1 pound fresh egg pasta such as pappardelle, fettuccine, piccage (page 60), or garganelli (page 62), cooked

Grated Parmesan cheese (optional)

Soak the mushrooms in hot water to cover for 30 minutes. Drain, reserving the liquid, and chop finely. Pour the liquid through a fine-mesh sieve lined with cheesecloth. Set the mushrooms and liquid aside.

Squeeze the juice of the lemon into a large bowl filled with water. Working with 1 artichoke at a time, remove all of the leaves and trim away any dark green parts from the base and the stem. If the stem seems tough, cut it off flush with the base. Scoop out the prickly choke with a spoon, or cut it out with a paring knife. Cut the base into 6 or 8 wedges or into thick slices. As each artichoke is trimmed, add the pieces to the lemon water.

In a large sauté pan, heat the olive oil over medium heat. Add the onion, garlic, parsley, and porcini and sauté until the onion is softened and translucent, about 10 minutes. Drain the artichokes and add them to the pan along with some salt and the mushroom soaking liquid and cook, stirring often, until the artichokes are well coated with the vegetable mixture and start to soften, about 10 minutes. Reduce the heat to low, stir in the flour and tomato sauce, and simmer for 10 minutes longer to blend the tomato sauce and vegetables. Pour in the wine and cook until it is absorbed by the artichokes, 8 to 10 minutes. Continue to cook, stirring often, until the artichokes are very tender, 10 to 15 minutes longer. Stir in the butter, then taste and adjust the seasoning with salt.

Toss the sauce with the pasta and serve. If desired, pass the cheese at the table.

WINE: *Vermentino, a minerally, aromatic white from Liguria, is an ideal wine for the pasta. If you can find a bottle of Colle dei Bardellini, grab it. If not, look for whites from the Cinque Terre.*

Sugo di funghi alla Valtellina
Mushroom Sauce from Lombardy

SERVES 6

This is the classic Lombardian mushroom sauce used for *polenta pasticciata* (page 75), but it would be delicious on fresh egg pasta or gnocchi as well. Seek out an assortment of fresh mushrooms for the most complex, and therefore satisfying, flavor. This sauce can be thinned with stock or cream if you want to serve it with *sformati* (vegetable flans).

1 ounce dried porcini mushrooms

4 to 5 tablespoons unsalted butter

2 tablespoons olive oil

1 yellow onion, chopped

1 1/2 pounds assorted fresh mushrooms such as cremini, chanterelle, porcini, oyster, hen of the woods, and lobster, in any combination, wiped clean and thinly sliced

1 cup vegetable or meat stock

2 cloves garlic, minced (optional)

1/4 cup chopped fresh flat-leaf parsley

2 tablespoons chopped fresh thyme

Salt and freshly ground black pepper

FOR SERVING

1 pound fresh pappardelle, fettuccine, or gnocchi, cooked

Soak the porcini mushrooms in hot water to cover for 30 minutes. Drain, reserving the soaking liquid, and chop finely. Pour the liquid through a fine-mesh sieve lined with cheesecloth. Set the mushrooms and liquid aside.

In a large sauté pan, melt 2 tablespoons of the butter with the oil over medium heat. Add the onion and sauté until softened, about 8 minutes. Add the sliced mushrooms and sauté until tender, about 10 minutes. Add the stock, the chopped porcini and their soaking liquid, and the garlic (if using) and simmer for 20 minutes longer to blend the flavors. Add the parsley and thyme and season with salt and pepper.

Toss the sauce with the pasta and serve.

WINE: *Your best local choice would be a Valtellina DOC wine from Rainoldi in Lombardy. Failing that, pour a Barbera from the Piedmont.*

Other Regional Mushroom Sauces

The Ligurians, who love their porcini, make their local *sugo, intingolo di funghi porcini,* by sautéing a pound of sliced fresh mushrooms with a couple cloves of garlic and some chopped rosemary in butter and oil. The Tuscans typically use a generous measure of fresh porcini in their mushroom sauces as well, and often season them with *nepitella,* a minty herb that grows wild in the region.

Sugo di pomodoro ricco
Rich Tomato Sauce

I could fill a chapter with tomato sauce recipes. This one is all-purpose, good both for pasta and for cooking in general. It is sometimes called *sugo finto,* or "false sauce," because the chopped vegetables give it the texture of a meat sauce.

MAKES ABOUT 3 CUPS

3 tablespoons olive oil

1 carrot, peeled and chopped

1 celery stalk, chopped

1/2 yellow onion, chopped

1 clove garlic, minced (optional)

1/4 cup chopped fresh flat-leaf parsley

5 large fresh basil leaves, chopped (optional)

Salt and freshly ground black pepper

1/2 cup dry white wine

1 can (28 ounces) plum tomatoes with juice, coarsely chopped

3 tablespoons unsalted butter (optional)

In a large saucepan, heat the olive oil over medium heat. Add the carrot, celery, onion, garlic (if using), parsley, and basil (if using) and season with salt and pepper. Sauté until the vegetables are pale gold, about 12 minutes. Add the wine and cook until it evaporates, about 5 minutes. Add the tomatoes with their juice, stir well, and simmer gently, uncovered, until thickened, about 40 minutes. Adjust the seasoning, and pass through a food mill if you want a smoother texture. Stir in the butter, if desired.

WINE: *Sangiovese is the answer here. Try Carmignano from Capezzana, or Morellino di Scansano from Le Pupille.*

Tomato Sauce

Sometimes you need a tomato sauce that does not fit the slow and savory profile. This quick and simple recipe will yield a practical sauce that can be used whenever tomato sauce is called for: In a food processor, process 1 can (28 ounces) plum tomatoes with juice until finely chopped but not liquefied. Transfer to a heavy saucepan, stir in 1/2 cup tomato purée, and place over low heat. Bring to a simmer and cook, stirring often, until slightly thickened, about 10 minutes. Season to taste with salt and freshly ground black pepper. If desired, stir in 2 tablespoons unsalted butter or 2 tablespoons extra virgin olive oil. You can also add a pinch of sugar, or 6 fresh basil leaves, chopped, to balance the flavor. If you want a richer, sweeter, thinner sauce, stir in 1/2 to 3/4 cup heavy cream. Makes about 3 cups.

Tomatoes

Italian cooks were slow to adopt tomatoes. They arrived from the New World by way of Spain in the 1500s, but were not used in cooking until some three hundred years later. The first published recipe for tomato sauce for pasta appeared in the 1839 appendix to *Cucina teorico-practica,* written by Neapolitan nobleman Ippolito Cavalcanti in 1837. Today, Italian food without tomatoes is unimaginable.

Because Italian cooking is based on using only the best-quality ingredients, Italians avoid using fresh tomatoes out of season. Even when tomatoes are in season, some years are better than others, some tomatoes are more flavorful than others. I shop at farmers' markets and know that not every heirloom tomato delivers what it promises, no matter how good it looks and how romantic or whimsical its name. You have to taste to know which are the richest in flavor, which have a good balance between sweetness and acidity.

In Italy in the summertime, tomatoes are used for salads and sauces. Some sauces are uncooked, that is, the tomatoes are simply chopped and tossed with warm pasta. Other sauces are cooked, but not for too long, as overcooking makes tomatoes bitter. During the abundance of the summer harvest, families put up jars and jars of tomato sauce, enough to last through the winter. Some southern Italian households, especially in Apulia, hang bunches of small cluster tomatoes in the sun to dry, where they develop an intense flavor; others dry tomatoes in the oven or in the sun and then pack them in extra virgin olive oil. Commercial operations can whole tomatoes in juice or purée or transform them into sauce and paste.

So how do you know which tomatoes to use for the recipes in this book? Think like an Italian. When tomatoes are in season, full flavored and ripe, use them in sauces and other recipes. Always store your fresh tomatoes at room temperature. Cold is the enemy of the tomato. Refrigerate it and you have killed it.

Whether you need to peel and seed a tomato depends on the tomato and the recipe. Taste the tomatoes before you decide. If the skin seems bitter, remove it. If you cook tomatoes with their skins and seeds, and you believe that they detract from the texture of the sauce, pass the sauce through a food mill to eliminate them. Sometimes, when the pieces are small and tender, the skin is not a problem.

Most Italian recipes that call for canned tomatoes recommend San Marzano, a meaty, plum-shaped tomato variety grown around Naples. Many labels promise San Marzano, but only a few of them hold the real thing. Two reliable Italian brands are di Nola and one simply labeled San Marzano, with a picture of red plum tomatoes on a white background. Both are free of any metallic flavor and are neither bitter nor excessively salty. Among brands sold in the United States, I have found organic Muir Glen to be excellent, as are Hunt's and Contadina and the diced tomatoes from Del Monte. For most recipes, it does not matter whether the tomatoes are a plum or a round variety. When deciding whether to use the juice or purée in which the tomatoes are packed, taste it. If it is neither too salty nor sour or metallic, use it. Taste is what is important.

Tomatoes are also used in three other forms, paste, sauce, and dried. Because you typically need only a few tablespoons tomato paste for any recipe, it is best to buy it in tubes—look for an Italian brand—rather than cans, and, once opened, store it in the refrigerator. It will keep for a long time. As with whole tomatoes, choose a canned tomato sauce based on how it tastes: full flavored, not metallic, not too salty. When you have time, make your own (page 69). Most Italians cooks use sun-dried tomatoes only occasionally, with Sardinians seeming to use them most often. Pick the best-tasting commercial ones, of course, or you can roast your own in a low oven (page 262).

Salsa besciamella
Basic Cream Sauce

MAKES 2 GENEROUS CUPS

Many of the sauces in this chapter can be used in lasagna or other baked pasta dishes, often along with a cream sauce. This is an everyday cream sauce for those preparations. It is often used to soften the density of a rich meat sauce, adding a creamy texture. It turns up as a topping for a simple gratin or *pasta al forno,* forms alternating layers in the making of lasagna, and helps to bind vegetable gratins and *sformati* (vegetable flans). Use the sauce as soon as possible after making it, as it thickens if it is left standing. If it is not used immediately, thin it with a little milk.

4 tablespoons unsalted butter

¹/4 cup all-purpose flour

2 cups milk or light cream, heated

Salt and freshly ground black pepper

Freshly grated nutmeg

In a small saucepan, melt the butter over low heat. Add the flour and cook, stirring, until it is well incorporated with the butter, about 3 minutes; do not let the mixture color. Slowly whisk in the hot milk or cream and bring almost to a boil. Reduce the heat to low and cook, stirring often, until the sauce is quite thick and the flour has lost all of its raw taste, about 8 minutes. Remove from the heat and season to taste with salt, pepper, and nutmeg.

Pasta al forno
Oven-Baked Pasta

SERVES 6

Simple pasta gratins such as this one are popular in the south, from Campania to Sicily. Cooked tubular pasta is tossed with a rich meat sauce and then put into an oiled or buttered baking dish. Some are topped with sliced hard-boiled eggs; others call for spooning the sauced pasta over a layer of cooked eggplant slices. The dish is then topped with cream sauce and grated cheese and baked. The beauty of this dish is that it can be assembled ahead of time and refrigerated for up to 2 days before baking.

1 pound dried pasta such penne, ziti, rigatoni, *or other tubular pasta, cooked*

3 to 4 cups ragù or sugo *of choice*

1¹/2 to 2 cups Basic Cream Sauce (page 71)

About ¹/2 cup grated Parmesan cheese

Preheat the oven to 350°F. Oil or butter a 2-quart gratin dish.

Toss the pasta with the *ragù* or *sugo* and spoon into the prepared dish. Spread the cream sauce evenly over the top, and sprinkle with the Parmesan. Bake until hot and golden, 25 to 30 minutes. Serve directly from the dish.

WINE: *Pick the wine recommended for the* ragù *or* sugo.

Lasagne al forno
Basic Lasagna

Once you have made the sauces, you can easily assemble an elegant and satisfying lasagna. Although this recipe may look like a good deal of work, once the elements are in the dish, the lasagna may be refrigerated for up to a day before baking. Once baked, it also reheats successfully in a moderate oven. Use only fresh lasagna noodles; they must meld with the sauce. I find that dried ones are too leaden.

SERVES 8 AS MAIN COURSE
(12 AS A FIRST COURSE)

Double recipe Meat Sauce from Bologna (page 50), Meat Sauce from Naples (page 49), Giblet Sauce (page 58), Duck Sauce (page 56), Rabbit Sauce from Tuscany (page 54), or Artichoke Sauce from Liguria (page 66)

1 pound fresh lasagna noodles, parboiled, drained, and laid flat on kitchen towels

Double recipe Basic Cream Sauce (page 71)

1 cup grated Parmesan cheese

Unsalted butter, at room temperature and cut into bits, for topping

Preheat the oven to 350°F. Butter a 9-by-12-by-3-inch or a 10-by-13-by-3-inch baking dish.

Spread a thin layer of sauce on the bottom of the prepared dish. Add a layer of noodles, overlapping them slightly, top with another layer of sauce, and then a layer of cream sauce. Sprinkle with some Parmesan. Repeat the layers, beginning with noodles, until all of the sauces, noodles, and cheese are used and ending with a layer of noodles. Dot the top with butter.

Bake until heated through and bubbling at the edges, 45 to 60 minutes. Remove from the oven and let rest for 10 minutes, then cut into squares to serve.

WINE: *Look to the sauce for the wine choice.*

Lasagne di carnevale
Holiday Lasagna

More elaborate than the basic lasagna of *sugo* and *besciamella,* and served on holidays and for special events, this is the baroque lasagna of the Italian south, prevalent in Campania, where it is called *sagna chiena;* in Calabria, where it is known as *sagna chine;* and in Basilicata. In this festive dish, meatballs and/or cooked sausage, pieces of salami, cooked peas, artichokes or mushrooms, and sometimes hard-boiled eggs are added along with ricotta, mozzarella, and Parmesan. In Naples, one pound *ziti* or *maccheroni,* parboiled, rinsed, and tossed with olive oil, is used in place of the flat noodles. The pasta is tossed with some of the *sugo* and arranged in two or three layers alternately with the meatballs and cheese.

SERVES 8 AS MAIN COURSE
(12 AS A FIRST COURSE)

4 cups sugo *from braising a large piece of meat such as Rolled Pork Shoulder from Calabria (page 214) or Sicilian Stuffed Beef Roll with Tomatoes and Red Wine (page 174)*

1 pound fresh lasagna noodles, parboiled, drained, and laid on kitchen towels

2 pounds ricotta cheese

1 pound small meatballs, such as double recipe meatballs for "Health" Soup with Meatballs and Greens (page 42) or Meatballs from Sardinia (page 225), cooked, or 1 pound sweet sausages with or without fennel, cooked and cut into 1/2-inch pieces

2 cups cooked shelled English peas (optional)

2 cups sautéed sliced mushrooms (optional)

4 hard-boiled eggs, sliced (optional)

1 pound fresh mozzarella cheese, sliced

1 1/2 cups grated Parmesan cheese

Unsalted butter, at room temperature and cut into bits, for topping

Preheat the oven to 350°F. Butter a 9-by-12-by-3-inch or a 10-by-13-by-3-inch baking dish.

Spread a layer of *sugo* on the bottom of the prepared dish. Add a layer of one-fifth of the noodles, overlapping them slightly, then top with one-fourth each of the ricotta, the meatballs and/or sausages, the peas (if using), the mushrooms (if using), or the eggs (if using), the mozzarella, and the Parmesan. Repeat the layers, beginning with noodles, until all of the ingredients are used, and ending with a layer of noodles. Dot the top with butter.

Bake until heated through and bubbling at the edges, about 1 hour. Remove from the oven and let rest for 10 minutes, then cut into squares to serve.

WINE: *Pour an Aglianico from Taurasi, a Sangiovese, or Sagrantino di Montefalco.*

Polenta pasticciata
Baked Polenta with Sauce and Cheese

SERVES 8

To assemble *polenta pasticciata* (sometimes spelled *pastizzada*), in which layers of cooked polenta are alternated with *sugo* in the manner of some baked pastas, you do not need a cream sauce, as you do for lasagna, but you do need cheese, which can be either shredded, as is the case here, or thinly sliced. While this dish looks like lots of work, you can cook the polenta up to I day in advance and the sauce up to 3 days ahead of time. Also, the dish can be fully assembled and refrigerated for up to 2 days before you bake it. It is hearty, too, so that all you need to round out the meal is some cooked greens or a salad. For a particularly festive dish, cook the polenta in equal amounts milk and water.

FOR THE POLENTA

2 cups coarse-grind polenta

8 cups water, or 4 cups each water and milk

1 tablespoon salt

4 tablespoons unsalted butter

1/4 cup grated Parmesan cheese

3 egg yolks, lightly beaten (optional)

1 1/2 cups shredded Fontina cheese

Double recipe Meat Sauce from Bologna (page 50), Sausage Sauce for Pasta or Polenta (page 62), or Mushroom Sauce from Lombardy (page 68)

1 1/2 cups grated Parmesan cheese

Unsalted butter, at room temperature and cut into bits, for topping

To make the polenta, whisk together the polenta, water or water and milk, and salt in a large saucepan. Place over medium heat and gradually bring to a low boil, stirring from time to time. Reduce the heat to low and simmer, stirring often, until the polenta is thick and no longer feels grainy on the tongue, about 30 minutes. Add the butter, cheese, and the egg yolks (if using) and stir until the butter is melted. Pour onto an oiled rimmed baking sheet and refrigerate to chill until firm.

Preheat the oven to 375°F. Butter or oil a 9-by-12-by-3-inch or a 10-by-13-by-3-inch baking dish.

Cut the chilled polenta into rectangles measuring 2 1/2 to 3 by 4 inches. Using half of the rectangles, arrange a layer of the polenta on the bottom of the prepared dish, cutting as needed to cover completely. Top evenly with half of the Fontina cheese. Spoon on half of the sauce, and then sprinkle evenly with half of the Parmesan. Repeat the layers, beginning with the polenta and ending with the Parmesan. Dot the top with butter.

Bake until the top is golden, about 40 minutes. Remove from the oven and let rest for 10 minutes, then cut into squares to serve.

WINE: *Look to the sauce for the wine choice. You can also try Aglianico del Vulture or a California Cabernet Franc.*

GRAINS

In Italy in the past, many of the grain dishes in this chapter would have been served in smallish portions, as a *primo piatto,* or first course, followed by a *secondo piatto* of meat, poultry, or fish. But nowadays, as I have already noted, daily multi-course meals at home are vanishing. Thus, many of these recipes, all of them based on *farro,* polenta, or rice, are substantial enough for a main meal. In most cases, a simple salad or a cooked vegetable and a loaf of good bread will be all you need for a satisfying supper.

Farro

Farro seems newly fashionable, but, in fact, it is an ancient grain. Originally served as cereal and called *puls,* it nourished the soldiers and others of the Roman Empire. It was difficult to grow, however, and produced only small yields. As newer wheat varieties emerged and proved more rewarding to harvest, the cultivation of *farro* gradually faded. It never disappeared fully from the Italian table, but it was little seen outside Tuscany and the Abruzzo until the mid-1980s, when a number of farmers in the two regions recognized its nutritional and culinary merits and began growing it on a larger scale.

An early variety of wheat, *farro* is sometimes erroneously labeled spelt. While it is related to spelt, or *Triticum speltum,* it is actually *T. dicoccum*. It is primarily cultivated near the Tuscan town of Lucca, in an area known as the Garfagnana, and in the Abruzzo, and is semipearled, that is, some of the outer hull still remains after a few abrasions. Lighter in mouth-feel than wheat berries, it has a nutty taste and texture that resembles barley more than wheat.

Most old-time recipes for *farro* tell you to clean the grain carefully, removing debris and stones; soak it overnight in water; and then cook it for a couple of hours. After cooking many brands of *farro,* I can tell you that this is unnecessary, as today's product is well cleaned and quite tender. The kernels from the Garfagnana are slightly rounder than the Abruzzo variety, and they cook more quickly because more of their outer hull has been removed. The pearled Garfagnana *farro* cooks in about 25 minutes, while the sturdier, browner *farro* from the Abruzzo is ready in about 35 minutes, although soaking it for 30 minutes will reduce the cooking time slightly.

Cook *farro* in a generous measure of salted boiling water—use 3 cups water for every 1 cup *farro*—and start testing for doneness after 20 minutes. You want it to be al dente—

tender but chewy. Drain it the moment it has achieved the proper texture; it will have doubled in volume. You can store cooked *farro* in the refrigerator for up to 5 days, and then reheat it in stock or water.

You can also cook *farro* as you would cook risotto, in other words as a *farrotto,* adding ladles of hot stock until it is tender. This will take longer, about 40 minutes, and will work especially well if you have soaked the *farro* for an hour in advance. It is easier to precook the *farro* and then reheat it in stock, gradually adding as much liquid as you need for the degree of soupiness you desire, but it is not as slow as cooking it *farrotto* style.

In the Abruzzo, at a farm called Gioie di Fattoria near the small town of Torano Nuovo, I purchased a bag of ground *farro,* labeled *puls* (shades of the Roman legions), and another labeled *farricello,* which was more coarsely ground. Both are prepared like polenta. They are nourishing and delicious, but not widely available. To achieve similar textures, you can grind whole *farro* in a spice mill or blender. The finer grind speeds up the cooking and produces a kind of whole-wheat polenta. Of course, the texture is quite different from the whole-kernel *farro,* more like cereal instead of chewy like wheat berries or barley.

If you cannot find *farro* in your local Italian shop or you are unable to purchase it online, you can use spelt, kamut, soft-wheat berries, or barley as a substitute. Spelt tastes wheatier than *farro* and is a darker color, and it takes about an hour to cook. Kamut, a large-grain, high-protein wheat, is golden and also takes about 1 hour to soften. Wheat berries should be soaked to reduce cooking time; if they are not soaked, they can take up to 2 hours to become tender. Pearl barley takes about 30 minutes.

Farro con la zucca o la barbabietola gialla
Farro *with Butternut Squash or Golden Beets*

SERVES 6

Squash and *farro* form a rich combination, ideal for a fall or winter supper. The flesh of the Italian pumpkin is a bit redder than that of butternut squash, but its texture—firm and meaty— is close to butternut or kabocha squash. To make this Tuscan dish more festive, you can add cooked chestnuts. You can also use golden beets in place of the squash. They make a lovely addition to *farro* and do not bleed color into the grain. I do not think they pair well with chestnuts, however, but you can add some toasted walnuts for contrasting texture and taste. Sage is harmonious both with squash and beets.

2 cups farro

6 cups water if making pilaf, or 7 to 8 cups vegetable or chicken stock if making farrotto

Salt

1 butternut squash, 1 1/2 pounds, halved, seeded, peeled, and cut into 1/2-inch dice (about 3 cups), or 1 bunch golden beets, about 1 1/4 pounds total weight

4 tablespoons unsalted butter, plus more for finishing

1 yellow onion, chopped

1 cup crumbled cooked chestnuts, if using squash (optional)

1/2 cup walnuts, toasted and coarsely chopped, if using beets (optional)

2 tablespoons chopped fresh sage

Freshly grated nutmeg

1 cup vegetable or chicken stock, or as needed, if making pilaf

Freshly ground black pepper

To cook this as a pilaf, in a saucepan, combine the *farro* and the water and bring to a boil over high heat. Add 1 1/2 teaspoons salt, reduce the heat to low, cover, and simmer until tender but still chewy at the center. Start checking for doneness after 20 minutes. A bit of water may remain unabsorbed, but that is fine, as you need to reheat the cooked vegetables with the grain. If the *farro* is too wet, drain it in a sieve. Set aside.

If you are using the squash, bring a saucepan three-fourths full of water to a boil. Salt lightly, add the squash, and cook until barely tender, 5 to 8 minutes. It will cook to final tenderness later on, so do not let it become too soft. Drain and set aside.

If you are using the beets, trim away the greens if they are still attached, leaving 1 inch of the stem intact. Combine the beets with water to cover in a saucepan, bring to a gentle boil over medium heat, reduce the heat to low, and simmer until tender, 30 to 45 minutes, depending on size. Drain and, when cool enough to handle, peel and cut into 1/2-inch pieces. Alternatively, put the beets in a baking pan with 1/2 inch water, cover with aluminum foil, and bake in a 350°F oven until tender, about 1 hour. Let cool, then peel and cut as for boiled beets. You should have about 3 cups. Set aside.

cont'd

In a sauté pan, melt the 4 tablespoons butter over medium heat. Add the onion and sauté until translucent and tender, 8 to 10 minutes. Add the squash or beets, the chestnuts or walnuts (if using), the sage, a little nutmeg, and the 1 cup stock and cook for about 5 minutes to blend the flavors. Fold in the cooked *farro,* reduce the heat to very low, and simmer, uncovered, for 10 minutes longer. All the ingredients should be tender and the flavors well married. Season with salt and pepper and add a little butter for richness, if desired. Add more stock if you want a soupier consistency. (You can even add lots of stock and turn this dish into a hearty soup.) Serve at once.

To cook this as a *farrotto,* pour the 7 to 8 cups stock into a saucepan, place over high heat, and bring to a boil. Reduce the heat to low and keep the stock at a bare simmer. In a large, deep sauté pan, melt the 4 tablespoons butter over medium heat. Add the onion and sage and sauté until the onion is translucent and tender, 8 to 10 minutes. Add the *farro* and stir well to coat with the butter. Add 1 cup of the simmering stock and cook, stirring a few times, until the stock is almost absorbed. Then continue to add the stock 1 cup at a time, always allowing it to be almost fully absorbed before adding more. Add the cooked squash or beets when about half the stock has been added. Add the chestnuts or walnuts (if using) during the last 5 minutes of cooking. The *farro* is ready when it is tender but still chewy at the center. You may not need all of the stock. The whole process, beginning with sautéing the onion, should take about 40 minutes. Season to taste with nutmeg, salt, and pepper and stir in a little butter for richness, if desired. Serve at once.

WINE: *With the butternut squash, try a rich white such as Vermentino di Gallura or a full-flavored rosato. For the beets, drink an earthy Friuli white such as Verduzzo, Tocai, or a Vintage Tunina from Jermann. Verdicchio will also harmonize.*

Farrotto con funghi e nocciole
Farro *with Mushrooms and Hazelnuts*

SERVES 6

The Piedmont is famous for the cultivation of hazelnuts, especially the superb variety known as *tonda gentile* that is grown in the Langhe region, an area south of Asti celebrated for its red wines. The combination of mushrooms and hazelnuts is typical of the Piedmont, where now a few farmers are cultivating *farro*.

FOR THE MUSHROOMS

1 ounce dried porcini mushrooms

2 tablespoons unsalted butter

2 tablespoons olive oil

1 1/2 pounds assorted fresh mushrooms such as cremini, chanterelle, porcini, and portobello, in any combination, wiped clean and sliced 1/4 inch thick

Salt and freshly ground black pepper

7 to 8 cups vegetable or chicken stock

3 tablespoons unsalted butter or olive oil

1 small yellow onion, finely chopped

Salt

2 cups farro

1/2 cup hazelnuts, toasted and coarsely chopped

1/4 cup chopped fresh flat-leaf parsley

Freshly ground black pepper

Unsalted butter for finishing

To prepare the mushrooms, soak the dried porcini in hot water to cover for 30 minutes. Drain, reserving the soaking liquid, and chop finely. Pour the liquid through a fine-mesh sieve lined with cheese-cloth. Set the mushrooms and liquid aside.

In a large sauté pan, melt the butter with the oil over high heat. Add the fresh mushrooms and sauté until they release some of their liquid, about 5 minutes. Stir in the chopped porcini and their soaking liquid. Season to taste with salt and pepper and set aside.

Pour the stock into a saucepan, place over high heat, and bring to a boil. Reduce the heat to low and keep the stock at a bare simmer. In a large, deep sauté pan, heat the 3 tablespoons butter or olive oil over medium heat. Add the onion and sauté until translucent and tender, 8 to 10 minutes. Add 2 teaspoons salt and the *farro* and stir well to coat the *farro* with the butter or oil. Add 1 cup of the simmering stock and cook, stirring a few times, until the stock is almost absorbed. Then continue to add the liquid 1 cup at a time, always allowing it to be almost fully absorbed before adding more. Add the mushrooms and the hazelnuts with the last addition of stock and cook, stirring occasionally, for about 10 minutes to absorb the stock and combine the flavors. The *farro* is ready when it is tender but still chewy at the center. You may not need all of the stock. The whole process, beginning with sautéing the onion, should take about 40 minutes.

Stir in the parsley, season to taste with salt and pepper, and stir in a little butter for richness. Serve at once.

WINE: *If you want to serve a white, try a Soave or Franciacorta. For a red, pour a Barbera d'Asti, Barbera d'Alba, Barbera del Monferrato, or a Merlot.*

Farrotto con scampi e spinaci
Farro *with Shrimp and Spinach*

SERVES 4

You do not need to have scampi, the small, slim, long-clawed relative of the lobster that lives in the waters off Europe, to enjoy this delicious dish from the Marches. Shrimp will do nicely. If you do not have fish stock, you can make a lovely stock with the shrimp shells, or you can use chicken or vegetable stock. You may substitute arugula or another full-flavored green for the milder spinach.

5 to 6 cups fish, chicken, or vegetable stock

3 tablespoons olive oil

1 yellow onion, finely chopped

1 clove garlic, minced

1 1/2 cups farro

1/2 cup dry white wine

1 pound medium-sized shrimp, peeled and deveined

1 pound spinach, stems discarded and leaves cut into 1-inch-wide strips

Salt and freshly ground black pepper

2 tablespoons finely shredded fresh basil

2 tablespoons chopped fresh flat-leaf parsley

1 tablespoon grated lemon zest (optional)

Pour the stock into a saucepan, place over high heat, and bring to a boil. Reduce the heat to low and keep the stock at a bare simmer.

In a large, deep sauté pan, heat the olive oil over medium heat. Add the onion and garlic and cook until tender and translucent, 8 to 10 minutes. Add the *farro* and stir well to coat with the oil. Add the wine and let it bubble up and be absorbed. Then add 1 cup of the simmering stock and cook, stirring from time to time, until the stock is almost absorbed. Continue to add the stock 1 cup at a time, always allowing it to be almost fully absorbed before adding more. Add the shrimp and spinach with the last addition of stock and cook, stirring occasionally, until the shrimp are pink and opaque throughout, the spinach is wilted, and the stock is absorbed, about 5 minutes. The *farro* is ready when it is tender but still chewy at the center. You may not need all of the stock. The whole process, beginning with sautéing the onion, should take about 40 minutes.

Season to taste with salt and pepper and sprinkle with the basil and parsley and with the lemon zest, if using. Serve at once.

WINE: *Verdicchio is the perfect regional choice. Look for wines from the two DOCs, Verdicchio dei Castelli di Jesi and Verdicchio di Matelica.*

***

VARIATION: Add a few chopped olive oil–packed sun-dried tomatoes or 1 cup peeled, seeded, and chopped tomatoes (fresh or canned) with the last addition of stock.

This is a traditional recipe from the Garfagnana region of Tuscany. It is an elegant first course, but it could be a main course if accompanied with a salad. While some versions use a simple bread-crumb crust, others call for a pastry crust.

SERVES 6

FOR THE PASTRY

1 1/2 cups all-purpose flour

Pinch of salt

1/2 cup unsalted butter, cut into 1-inch pieces

1 egg, lightly beaten

1 tablespoon cold water, or as needed

FOR THE FILLING

2 cups cooked farro (page 79)

1 1/4 cups ricotta cheese

1/4 cup grated Parmesan cheese

3 eggs, lightly beaten

1/4 teaspoon freshly grated nutmeg

2 tablespoons chopped fresh flat-leaf parsley

2 tablespoons chopped fresh marjoram

Salt and freshly ground black pepper

To make the pastry, stir together the flour and salt in a bowl. Scatter the butter pieces over the flour mixture and, using a pastry blender, cut in the butter until the mixture resembles cornmeal. Add the egg and 1 tablespoon water and stir and toss with a fork until the dough is evenly moistened and comes together in a mass. If the dough is too dry, add more water a spoonful at a time. Gather the dough together into a ball, then flatten it into a disk. Wrap in plastic wrap and refrigerate for 1 hour.

Preheat the oven to 325°F. Butter a 9-inch tart pan with a removable bottom or an 8-inch springform pan.

Place the dough disk between 2 sheets of baker's parchment and roll it out into a round about 11 inches in diameter and 1/8 inch thick. (You can also roll it out on a lightly floured work surface.) Fit it into the prepared pan. Roll the rolling pin across the top to trim the pastry edges even with the pan rim. Alternatively, press the dough into the pan, rather than roll it out. Pat some of the dough evenly onto the bottom of the pan, making it no more than 1/8 inch thick. Make a long rope with the remaining dough, lay it around the bottom of the pan against the sides, and then push upward to cover the sides evenly.

To make the filling, in a bowl combine the *farro,* cheeses, eggs, nutmeg, parsley, marjoram, and a little salt and pepper and mix well. Spoon the filling into the prepared pan.

Bake the tart until set, about 40 minutes. Transfer to a wire rack, let cool to lukewarm, and remove the pan sides. Cut into wedges and serve.

WINE: *Drink a Pinot Grigio from the Friuli or Veneto region; a Vermentino from Cima, Tenuta Guado al Tasso, or Grattamacco; or a Vernaccia di San Gimignano. Or for a Chardonnay blend, look for Batàr from Querciabella.*

———————————

VARIATION: To use a bread-crumb crust in place of the pastry crust, butter an 8-inch square baking dish or an 8-inch springform pan with 2 tablespoons unsalted butter and sprinkle the bottom and sides with 1/3 cup fine dried bread crumbs, lightly toasted.

Polenta

The word *polenta* means "porridge." Today, it is usually associated with a hearty peasant dish made from cornmeal, although the same dish is also made—albeit more rarely—with flour milled from chickpeas, chestnuts, buckwheat, *farro,* or wheat berries.

Corn was introduced to Europe from Mexico in the sixteenth century, and some northern Italians quickly adopted it. It was first planted in the Veneto about 1530, and by the early seventeenth century its cultivation extended north to the Po River delta and Friuli and as far south as Lazio and Campania. The corn grew easily in soil that had previously produced meager crops. The Italians considered the grain exotic, so they called it *granoturco,* or "Turkish grain," because, in their minds, exotic things inevitably came from Asia or the Middle East.

Italians, long accustomed to eating porridges made from *farro,* buckwheat, barley, chickpeas, and chestnuts, readily introduced *polenta di mais* (corn porridge) to their tables. Many poor people became totally dependent on cornmeal for sustenance, but it proved detrimental to their health, as it was lacking in niacin and other amino acids, causing many of them to develop pellagra. This nutritional failing was eventually remedied with the addition of beans and other sources of niacin to the diet, which complete the protein needed for good health. Polenta eventually became the basis for an entire repertory of recipes, moving from peasant food to gourmet cuisine within a few centuries. While it can be a dish in itself, it also serves as an accompaniment to numerous hearty stews, grilled meats and poultry, fish and shellfish dishes, game birds, and sausage.

Most cornmeal polenta is golden yellow. The white polenta much loved by the Venetians is blander and sweeter, with less corn flavor. *Polenta taragna,* a mixture of stone-ground cornmeal and buckwheat, is favored in the mountain regions of Trentino and the Valtellina. Buckwheat, known as *grano saraceno,* originated in Central Asia and has been in eaten in Italy for over three thousand years. It is finely ground into flour, which is sometimes used for making pasta. Coarse-grind buckwheat is also available.

The best cornmeal for polenta is hulled and stone ground. It comes in fine, medium, and coarse grinds. I prefer the medium grind, as I think it makes the most full-flavored polenta and I like the subtle crunch. It can be cooked in water (remember, this was poor people's food), broth, or milk, or a combination. The corn flavor is most intense if the cooking liquid is water, while milk is usually added for special-occasion polentas. The cooked grain is often enriched with butter and cheese just before serving.

Polenta also comes in instant form, but I find it too soft and lacking in interesting texture. The best stone-ground cornmeal brands for polenta are Golden Pheasant, Giusto's, and Molino Sobrino from La Morra. For *polenta taragna,* look for Moretti, Molino Sobrino, and Il Saraceno, the last produced by Giancarlo and Paolo Sala. When shopping for polenta, remember that fresh is best. Flavor fades over time.

Basic Polenta

Most recipes for polenta instruct to bring salted water to a boil—4 cups water for each 1 cup cornmeal—and to add the cornmeal in a thin stream while stirring constantly to prevent lumps. Once all the cornmeal is in the pan, the heat is reduced to low and simmered slowly, stirring every 5 minutes or so, until the polenta is cooked, 25 to 45 minutes. I have found that whisking together the cold water, salt, and cornmeal, bringing it to a gradual boil over medium heat, and then whisking from time to time as it cooks, is foolproof, producing lump-free polenta. As soon as it boils, I reduce the heat to low and simmer it, stirring every so often, until the polenta is creamy, rather than grainy, on the tongue. This usually takes 30 to 40 minutes. I then stir in the butter and Parmesan.

Some cooks prefer to simmer the polenta in a double boiler to prevent scorching, but I do not think it is necessary. Another method, which requires virtually no stirring, calls for whisking together the cornmeal, water, salt, and butter, pouring it into a well-buttered deep baking dish or saucepan, and then baking it in a 350°F oven for 1 hour and 20 minutes. Stir it once, taste and adjust the seasoning, and continue to bake for 10 minutes longer.

Cooked polenta can be kept soft and flowing in a saucepan or in the top of a double boiler by adding small amounts of hot water at regular intervals. It will take as much water as you add and keep on drinking. When you are ready to serve, you can fold in a creamy, good-melting cheese, such as mascarpone, Gorgonzola, *robiola,* or Fontina. You can also add chopped herbs like chives or sage, or fold in chopped cooked vegetables such as spinach or broccoli or mashed butternut squash. If you do not want it soft, pour it onto a wet or oiled rimmed baking sheet and refrigerate until set. You can then cut it into strips or squares, and bake, fry, or grill the pieces.

Smacafàm

Buckwheat-Polenta Pie with Sausage

SERVES 6 AS MAIN COURSE

(8 TO 10 AS A FIRST COURSE)

Smaccare means "to shame," and *fame* means "hunger." *Smàcco* loosely translates as a mortification or slap in the face. *Smacafàm* is a hearty, rustic pizza or pancake from the Trentino that will banish your hunger. It is enhanced with onion and sausage and makes for a filling meal, best accompanied with a simple green salad, or cut into small wedges and served as an appetizer. The Trentino and the Valtellina are mountainous northern regions where coarsely milled buckwheat, known as *polenta taragna, polenta nera,* or *grano saraceno,* is used in many recipes, alone or in combination with cornmeal. Many people find buckwheat alone too intense, however. Packaged *polenta taragna* comes with the buckwheat premixed with cornmeal. If you cannot find *polenta taragna,* you can make this dish with regular cornmeal polenta. Use Fontina cheese from the Aosta Valley, which is far superior to imitators made elsewhere.

4 tablespoons lard or olive oil

2 yellow onions, sliced

1/2 pound sweet sausages with or without fennel

4 cups milk

1 1/2 cups polenta taragna or cornmeal polenta

Salt and freshly ground black pepper

3 ounces Fontina cheese, thinly sliced or shredded

Preheat the oven to 350°F. Butter a 2-quart baking dish, an 8-by-11-inch gratin dish (or one slightly larger), or a 12-inch pie dish.

In a sauté pan, heat the lard or olive oil over medium heat. Add the onions and sauté until golden, 10 to 15 minutes. Remove from the heat and set aside.

To cook the sausages, prick them with a fork and place them in a sauté pan with water to a depth of about 1/3 inch. Place over medium heat and cook, turning once, until the water evaporates and the sausages start to brown, about 15 minutes. Remove the sausages from the pan, let cool, remove the casings, and cut into 1/2-inch-thick slices.

Pour the milk into a saucepan, place over medium heat, and heat just until small bubbles appear along the edges of the pan. Stir in the polenta, then continue to stir until creamy and smooth, about 5 minutes. Add the onions to the polenta mixture, and season with salt and pepper.

Pour half of the polenta into the prepared baking dish in a smooth, even layer. Top with half of the sausage slices. Pour in the remaining polenta and top with the remaining sausage slices. Top evenly with the cheese.

Bake the pie until it is set and the surface is golden, 30 to 35 minutes. To serve, cut into squares or wedges.

WINE: *This dish calls for Lagrein, a great red wine from the Alto Adige. Try to pick up a bottle from Alois Lageder, Colterenzio, Santa Maddalena, or Cantina Terlano. Other suitable regional wines are Teroldego and Pinot Nero.*

Italy's Other Polenta Pies

Salami is sometimes used instead of sausage in a polenta pie, or cooked *pancetta affumicata* (smoked bacon) is added along with the sausage. The polenta can also be cooked in stock instead of milk. In Naples, pork cracklings are layered with polenta and pecorino in a dish called *migliaccio con i ciccioli*. In the Molise, local cooks prepare a dish call *macche,* in which polenta is layered with sausage or pork *ragù* and topped with warm honey or *mosto d'uva* (grape must).

Pastuccia, a polenta pie baked with sausages and raisins, is a specialty of the town of Teramo in the Abruzzo. After testing this recipe, I decided to increase the amount of raisins because their texture and sweetness are a wonderful contrast to the meaty sausages, and they heighten the sweetness of the cornmeal. *Pastuccia* is rather filling if served as a *primo piatto,* but makes a satisfying meal accompanied with a salad or green vegetable.

SERVES 6 AS MAIN COURSE

(8 TO 10 AS A FIRST COURSE)

2 tablespoons olive oil or lard, plus more olive oil for drizzling

1/4 pound pancetta, diced

3/4 pound sweet sausages with or without fennel, casings removed and meat crumbled

2 cups polenta

Salt

About 4 cups boiling water

1 cup golden raisins, plumped in hot water and drained

3 egg yolks

Freshly ground black pepper

Preheat the oven to 375°F. Oil or butter a gratin dish 10 inches long, a 12-inch pie dish, or a 9-by-12-inch baking dish.

In a large sauté pan, heat the olive oil or lard over medium heat. Add the pancetta and sausage and sauté until cooked through but not crisp, 7 to 8 minutes. Remove from the heat.

In a large bowl, combine the polenta and 1 teaspoon salt. Gradually whisk in enough boiling water to make a very thick batter. Add the raisins, three-fourths of the pancetta and sausage, the egg yolks, and some pepper and mix well. Pour into the prepared dish. Top evenly with the remaining pancetta and sausage, and drizzle with a little olive oil.

Bake the pie until the top is golden and the pancetta and sausage are crisp, about 40 minutes. Transfer to a rack and let cool for 10 minutes, then serve.

WINE: *For a red, choose Montepulciano d'Abruzzo or Dolcetto. If you prefer an aromatic white, try a Trebbiano d'Abruzzo from Valentini, Illuminati, or Masciarelli, or a Fiano d'Avellino from Campania.*

SERVES 6

AS A RICH FIRST COURSE

A *ciotola* is a rustic wooden bowl, and this recipe is remarkable in its understated simplicity. There is one catch, however. You need white truffles for this hunter's bowl. They transform a rather plain dish of polenta, Fontina cheese, and egg into something quite elegant. If you cannot obtain a fresh white truffle, use truffle oil to create the illusion. This Piedmontese recipe is from chef Pina Fassi of the very chic Gener Neuv restaurant in Asti.

1 1/2 *cups polenta*

1 *tablespoon all-purpose flour*

2 *to 3 teaspoons salt*

6 *cups water*

7 *ounces Fontina cheese, diced*

6 *egg yolks*

Grated Parmigiano-Reggiano *cheese*

1 *white truffle, cut into thin shavings, or a little white truffle oil*

In a heavy saucepan, whisk together the polenta, flour, 2 teaspoons salt, and water. Bring slowly to a boil over medium heat, then reduce the heat to low and simmer uncovered, stirring occasionally, until the mixture is soft and smooth and no longer tastes grainy, about 45 minutes. Taste and adjust with more salt if needed. Remove from the heat.

Divide the Fontina cheese evenly among 6 warmed bowls. Spoon the warm polenta on top, again dividing evenly. Carefully place an egg yolk on each serving. If using a fresh truffle, scatter a little grated cheese over the top and then some truffle shavings. If using truffle oil, drizzle a little of the oil over each egg yolk and then top with the grated cheese. Cover the bowls immediately and let the flavors infuse for a few minutes. Bring to the table and uncover so that everyone gets a whiff of the truffle perfume.

WINE: *Stay with Piedmont reds. Splurge on a Barolo or Barbaresco, or perhaps a blend of Barbera and Nebbiolo, such as the Bricco Manzoni from Rocche dei Manzoni or the Suo di Giacomo from Eugenio Bocchino.*

————————

VARIATION: The chef at Ristorante I Bologna, in the Piedmontese town of Rocchetta Tanaro, mixes soft, warm polenta with a mixture of soft, ripe *robiola di Roccaverano* and ricotta cheeses, and then tops each dish with black truffle shavings. For this amount of polenta, or 6 servings, use 9 ounces *robiola* and 1 pound ricotta. Rich!

Soufflé di polenta alla piemontese
Polenta Soufflé from the Piedmont

While this rich soufflé does not need a sauce, in the spirit of Piedmontese voluptuousness, you might want to serve it with a cream-enriched tomato sauce; a creamy purée of green vegetables such as broccoli, spinach, or peas; or sautéed wild mushrooms.

SERVES 6

2/3 cup polenta

1 teaspoon salt, or to taste

3 cups milk

4 tablespoons unsalted butter

1/2 cup plus 2 tablespoons grated Parmesan cheese

5 eggs

Preheat the oven to 350°F. Butter a 1-quart soufflé dish. Cut a strip of aluminum foil about 2 inches longer than the circumference of the dish and about 6 inches wide. Fold it in half lengthwise and butter one side well. Position the strip, buttered side facing in, around the top of the prepared dish so that it rises about 2 inches above the rim, and secure it in place with kitchen string.

In a heavy saucepan, whisk together the polenta, salt, and milk. Bring to a gradual boil over medium heat, then reduce the heat to low and simmer uncovered, stirring occasionally, until the mixture is soft and smooth, about 25 minutes. Remove from the heat and stir in the butter and 1/2 cup of the cheese. Let cool for about 5 minutes. Separate 3 of the eggs, and stir 2 whole eggs and 3 egg yolks into the polenta mixture.

Using an electric mixer, beat the 3 egg whites until they hold firm peaks. Fold the egg whites into the polenta mixture. Pour into the prepared dish and sprinkle with the remaining 2 tablespoons cheese.

Bake the soufflé until lightly set and golden, about 35 minutes. Serve at once.

WINE: *To match the richness, choose a juicy Dolcetto from Abbona, Villa Sparina, or Seghesio or a bright Barbera from Vietti, Bartolo Mascarello, Prunotto, or Cascina Ca' Rossa. A light Sangiovese could also work. If you added a green vegetable, try a Chardonnay, Greco di Tufo, or Vernaccia di San Gimignano.*

Polenta Cakes with Wild Greens

SERVES 8

It was snowing in the tiny mountain village of Caprafico, near the town of Guardiagrele in the Abruzzo. I was a guest at the *agriturismo* of Giacomo Santoleri, a sophisticated and charming artisan-farmer who cultivates *farro,* barley, and lentils; makes pasta; and bottles his own wonderful olive oil. Giacomo's wife cooked this classic Abruzzese polenta cake in a wood-burning oven. It was crisp and crunchy from the coarse texture of the cornmeal, and the intensely flavored wild greens were gathered in the neighboring fields. The hearty dish was accompanied with a glass of Montepulciano d'Abruzzo made by Giacomo's sister-in-law. It was a memorable meal.

Salt

2 1/2 pounds assorted greens such as curly endive (chicory), Swiss chard, beet greens, dandelion greens, mustard greens, kale, and/or broccoli rabe, in any combination, tough stems discarded and cut into 2-inch pieces

1/2 to 2/3 cup extra virgin olive oil

5 cloves garlic, minced

1 teaspoon chile pepper flakes

2 medium-sized waxy potatoes such as Yukon Gold, Yellow Finn, or Bintje, boiled, peeled, if desired, and diced (optional)

Freshly ground black pepper

2 cups coarse- or medium-grind polenta

4 cups water

Bring a large pot three-fourths full of water to a boil. Salt lightly, add the greens, and boil until tender, about 10 minutes. (You may have to do this in batches.) Using a slotted spoon, transfer the greens to a colander to drain.

In a large sauté pan, heat the olive oil over medium heat. Add the garlic and chile pepper flakes and sauté until the garlic is softened, 3 to 4 minutes. Add the drained greens and the cooked potatoes (if using) and heat through, stirring to coat with the hot oil. Sprinkle with salt and black pepper. Remove from the heat. (You can make this dish up to this point 6 hours in advance and reheat it before continuing.)

Preheat the oven to 400°F. Liberally oil a 12-inch cast-iron skillet or round ovenproof baking dish and place in the oven for a few minutes to heat.

In a heavy saucepan, whisk together the polenta and water. Bring to a gradual boil over medium heat, then reduce the heat to low and simmer uncovered, stirring occasionally, for just a few minutes until smooth. Season with salt and black pepper. Pour the polenta into the warm prepared skillet or dish.

Bake the polenta cake until it pulls away from the sides of the pan and is lightly golden, 30 to 40 minutes. The cake will be rather crisp. Just before it is ready, reheat the greens.

cont'd

Remove the cake from the oven and unmold onto a cutting board. Cut into wedges. Place the wedges on warmed individual plates and serve with the greens.

WINE: *I enjoyed a Montepulciano d'Abruzzo with this dish, but you could also go white to match the greens and drink a Sauvignon Blanc or Pinot Grigio.*

VARIATION: To make *broccoletti brodosi con pizza di granoturco,* cook 2 1/2 pounds broccoli rabe in the salted water until very tender, 15 to 20 minutes. With tongs, remove the greens from the water and drain well. Measure out 4 cups of the broccoli rabe cooking water, mix it with the polenta on the stove top as directed, and then bake as directed. Sauté the broccoli rabe in the extra virgin olive oil with the garlic and chile pepper flakes as directed for the assorted greens. Serve the polenta cake with the broccoli rabe.

The Tradition of the *Agriturismo*

Staying in an *agriturismo* in the Italian countryside offers the traveler a special experience. An *agriturismo* is a farm that accommodates guests and serves and sells food raised on the premises. The Italian government gives tax breaks to farmers who take in paying guests, plus it allows them to sell their products directly to the consumer, thus sidestepping some of the European Union laws governing food distribution. Most important, *agriturismo* guests who are accustomed to city life have the opportunity to experience the more rustic environment of *la vita contadina,* or "peasant living."

SERVES 8 HUNGRY PEOPLE

The basic recipe for *polenta incatenata* braises together *borlotti* beans, Savoy cabbage, and potatoes, and then adds polenta that "enchains" them. I have collected a few different recipes for this hearty peasant dish. One is a meatless Ligurian version, transcribed by friend and fellow Italo-fanatic Fred Plotkin. Another is a Tuscan version with pancetta from Leonardo Romanelli that appears in the Florence volume of the *Ricette di osterie* series published by Slow Food. Still another Florentine version cooks a prosciutto bone along with the beans and uses pancetta as well. The hearty mixture is topped with extra virgin olive oil and grated cheese, Parmesan in Liguria and pecorino in Tuscany.

1³/4 cups dried borlotti or white beans, picked over, rinsed, and soaked overnight (or see page 240 for quick-soak method)

1 prosciutto bone (optional)

1 head Savoy cabbage, core removed and chopped, or 1 large bunch kale, tough stems discarded and chopped

3 or 4 waxy potatoes such as Yukon Gold or Bintje, about ³/4 pound total weight, peeled and cut into large pieces

3 tablespoons extra virgin olive oil

1/4 pound pancetta, diced

1 yellow onion, chopped

2 cloves garlic, minced

1 small bunch fresh flat-leaf parsley, chopped

Leaves from 2 fresh rosemary sprigs, minced

2 cups polenta

Salt and freshly ground black pepper

Grated pecorino cheese

Drain the beans, transfer to a saucepan, add the prosciutto bone (if using), and add water to cover by 3 or 4 inches. Bring to a gentle boil over medium heat, reduce the heat to low, and simmer, uncovered, for 10 minutes. Add the cabbage or kale and potatoes, cover partially, and continue to cook until the potatoes, greens, and beans are barely tender, about 15 minutes longer.

Meanwhile, in a sauté pan, heat the olive oil over medium heat. Add the pancetta, onion, and garlic and sauté until the onion is softened, about 8 minutes. Add the parsley and rosemary and cook for 1 minute longer. Set aside.

Remove the prosciutto bone (if used) and discard. Add the polenta to the bean mixture, mix well, and bring to a simmer. Stir in the pancetta mixture, reduce the heat to low, and continue to cook, stirring from time to time, until the polenta is smooth and no longer tastes grainy, 35 to 40 minutes, adding water as necessary to keep the polenta creamy.

Season to taste with salt and pepper and serve at once. Pass the pecorino at the table.

WINE: *This filling dish needs a lift and a red would do that. Drink a Chianti Classico or Carmignano.*

Carne dei Poveri

As already noted, polenta alone, because it lacks niacin and certain amino acids, is not a perfect food. While the Italians did not learn to treat the grain with slaked lime to release the niacin and amino acids, as the Mexicans and Central Americans did, they did come up with another solution: they added beans, which are rich in niacin. This nutritious combination became the *carne dei poveri,* or "meat of the poor." The cornmeal provided the complex carbohydrate and the beans provided the protein. With the addition of a little olive oil and perhaps some cheese, hunger was sated and the work in the fields could continue.

The combination of polenta and beans appears on tables all over Italy under a variety of regional names and with many variations. Sometimes the mixture is enhanced with greens, sometimes with potatoes, and, occasionally, with a bit of *lardo* (page 211) or pancetta.

Puccia is the name of a mixture of polenta, *borlotti* beans, and Savoy cabbage in the Monferrato region of the Piedmont. In Modena in Emilia-Romagna, polenta and beans are called *calzagàtt.* Elsewhere in the region, *cirihusla, paparuccia,* and *bagia* are the affectionate names for a similar dish, while *pisarèi e fasò* extends the concept to polenta gnocchi with bean sauce. In Umbria, the mix is called *impastoiata,* and in Calabria, *frascatuli e ciceri* combines chickpeas and polenta and occasionally broccoli.

Polenta Ring with Cheese Fondue and Truffles

This recipe is served at the Antico Ristorante del Furlo in Acqualagna in the Marches. At the restaurant, the chef makes the *fonduta* with *formaggio di fossa,* a traditional cave-aged cheese. Fontina or Gruyère cheese is a successful substitute. If you cannot get black truffles, add some truffle oil to the *fonduta* just before serving. In the absence of a ring mold, use a buttered one-quart soufflé dish or other round baking dish.

SERVES 10
AS A RICH FIRST COURSE

1 1/2 cups polenta

Salt

3 cups boiling water

FOR THE *FONDUTA*

1/2 pound Fontina cheese, shredded

1/2 cup heavy cream

1/2 cup milk

1 tablespoon all-purpose flour

Freshly ground white pepper

2 egg yolks

2 tablespoons unsalted butter

1 black truffle, cut into thin shavings

Preheat the oven to 300°F. Generously oil an 8-inch ring mold.

In a bowl, whisk together the polenta, 1 1/2 teaspoons salt, and boiling water until well combined and free of lumps. Pour into the prepared mold and bake until set, about 40 minutes.

About 15 minutes before the polenta is ready, make the *fonduta:* In the top pan of a double boiler, whisk together the cheese, cream, milk, flour, and a pinch of white pepper. Place over the lower pan of barely simmering water and heat, stirring constantly, until the cheese melts. Then whisk in the egg yolks and butter until the butter melts and the yolks are fully combined. Hold over hot water until ready to serve.

To serve, remove the polenta from the oven and let rest for 10 minutes. Invert a platter on top of the mold, invert the platter and mold together, and lift off the mold. Spoon the *fonduta* into the center of the ring. Alternatively, slice the polenta and spoon the *fonduta* over each serving. Sprinkle with the truffle shavings and serve at once.

WINE: *To stay in the region, pour Rosso Piceno from Laila, Ercole Velenosi, or Tenuta Cocci Grifoni; or Rosso Conero from Umani Ronchi, Moroder, or Le Terrazze. You can also look north for a Nebbiolo-based red from the Piedmont.*

Rice

Food historians have never agreed on how rice came to be cultivated in Italy. Some say the Cistercian monks carried rice to Italy as spoils from the Crusades. Others believe that rice was introduced, directly or indirectly, by the Saracens or Moors of North Africa. They planted the first rice in Spain, and Spain at one time ruled Sicily.

Today, rice is grown in only one area of the country, the Po River delta. In the early days, its cultivation was brutal work. Harvesters worked long days, and were plagued by malaria from the mosquito-infested stagnant waters and by pellagra from a poor diet. (Two well-regarded Italian films, *Bitter Rice* and *The Tree of Wooden Clogs,* dramatize the grim lives of the rice pickers.) In time, production was modernized, and now Italy is Europe's largest rice producer. The centers for cultivation are in the Piedmont, around Vercelli and Novara, in eastern Lombardy, and in parts of the Veneto.

Italians grow short-grain rice. The three best-known varieties are Arborio, the medium-sized grain of the three and the most widely available; Carnaroli, the largest grain and the one with the most beautiful texture; and Vialone Nano, the smallest grain and the one that cooks up the softest. They are all commonly used for making risotto, a dish that calls for adding broth to the kernels gradually over a period of about 25 minutes. But traditional risottos do not fit my definition of slow and savory—they are too fast and too labor-intensive—so I have not included any classic risottos here. Instead, there are three baked rice dishes and one cooked on the stove top that calls for making a stock and then using it to cook rice in the manner of a risotto.

SERVES 6

This hearty dish, which takes its name from *sbirri,* a longtime pejorative for police, reportedly fueled the officers sufficiently to keep them awake on their watch. Nowadays in the Veneto, the term *sbirraglia* is synonymous with rice cooked with chicken. This recipe is from Padua, where the dish is made two different ways. In one version, the chicken is cut up and boiled to make a stock and to cook the meat. (If you opt to make the chicken stock with the pieces of chicken, ask the poultry butcher for some extra necks and backs to make the stock richer.) In the second version, which is used here, the chicken pieces are sautéed along with the veal, and stock is added as it is for a risotto. The result is a substantial dish that is too heavy for a *primo* but perfect for a *secondo.*

1 chicken, about 3 pounds, with giblets

FOR THE STOCK
Chicken neck, wings, back, gizzard, and heart

1 carrot, peeled and chopped

1 yellow onion, chopped

1 celery stalk, chopped

3 1/2 quarts water, or half each water and chicken stock

6 tablespoons unsalted butter

2 tablespoons olive oil

1 carrot, peeled and chopped

1 yellow onion, chopped

1 celery stalk, chopped

cont'd

Rinse the neck, gizzard, and heart and set aside for making the stock. Rinse the chicken, then cut it up. Set aside the back and wings for making the stock. Bone the breasts, thighs, and drumsticks and cut the meat, with the skin intact, into 2-inch pieces. Trim the liver and cut into small pieces. Set the chicken meat and liver aside for adding to the rice mixture.

To make the chicken stock, in a large saucepan, combine the chicken neck, wings, back, gizzard, and heart; carrot; onion; celery; and water or water and stock and place over medium-high heat. Bring to a gentle boil, skim off any scum that forms on the surface, reduce the heat to low, cover partially, and simmer for at least 1 hour or longer. Pour the stock through a fine-mesh sieve placed over a clean saucepan; you should have 9 to 10 cups.

Place the pan over low heat so that the stock is at a bare simmer. In a large sauté pan, melt 2 tablespoons of the butter with the olive oil over medium heat. Add the carrot, onion, celery, and the reserved chicken liver and sauté until the vegetables are golden, about 15 minutes. Add the veal and the reserved chicken meat and sauté slowly, turning often, until golden, about 15 minutes. Add the wine and let it bubble up and be absorbed. Reduce the heat to low, cover, and cook until the chicken is half-cooked, 10 to 15 minutes.

cont'd

SERVES 10 TO 12

This dish seems like it has nearly everything in it. The name comes from the French *surtout,* meaning "above all." Not surprisingly, it is a recipe the imported French-trained *monzù,* or chefs, served to Neapolitan royalty in the eighteenth century. This is your chance to share in their delicious excess. Indeed, some cooks make even more elaborate versions of this rice casserole, or *bomba,* by cooking the peas in butter with prosciutto, adding sausage along with the meatballs, or using a rich cream sauce to bind the filling.

FOR THE RICE

Salt

3 cups Arborio rice

1/2 cup Meat Sauce from Naples (page 49)

3/4 cup grated Parmesan cheese

3 eggs, lightly beaten

FOR THE MEATBALLS

6 ounces ground beef

1/2 cup dried bread crumbs

1 egg

2 tablespoons grated Parmesan cheese

Salt and freshly ground black pepper

1/4 cup olive oil

1 ounce dried porcini mushrooms

2 tablespoons olive oil

cont'd

To cook the rice, bring a large saucepan three-fourths full of water to a boil. Add 1 tablespoon salt and the rice and boil until al dente, 12 to 15 minutes. Drain the rice and transfer to a bowl. Stir in the sauce, cheese, and then the eggs. Set aside.

To make the meatballs, in a bowl, combine the beef, bread crumbs, egg, and Parmesan and mix well. Season with salt and pepper. In a large sauté pan, heat the olive oil over high heat. Fry up a tiny nugget of the mixture, taste it, and then adjust the seasoning. Form the mixture into about 20 small meatballs, each about the size of an unshelled hazelnut (about 1/2 inch in diameter). Add the meatballs to the pan and fry on all sides until golden and cooked through, 10 to 15 minutes. Set aside.

While the meatballs are cooking, begin to soak the porcini mushrooms in hot water to cover for 30 minutes. Drain, reserving the soaking liquid, and chop finely. Pour the liquid through a fine-mesh sieve lined with cheesecloth. Set the mushrooms and liquid aside.

To make the rest of the filling, in a sauté pan, heat the olive oil over medium heat. Add the onion and sauté until soft and golden, about 15 minutes. Raise the heat to high, add the chopped porcini and the chicken livers, and cook rapidly for 3 minutes to color the livers. Stir in 1/4 cup of the sauce and the porcini soaking liquid and simmer for 5 minutes to blend the flavors. Transfer to a bowl.

Preheat the oven to 400°F. Butter a 9-inch springform pan and lightly coat the bottom and sides with a few spoonfuls of the bread crumbs.

cont'd

1 yellow onion, chopped

6 chicken livers, well trimmed and cut into small pieces

2 to 3 cups Meat Sauce from Naples (page 49)

About 1 cup dried bread crumbs

1/4 pound prosciutto, chopped

2 cups shelled fresh English peas, blanched for 1 minute and drained, or thawed, frozen peas

2 hard-boiled eggs, peeled and diced

6 ounces mozzarella cheese, diced

4 tablespoons unsalted butter, cut into small pieces

Grated Parmesan cheese for serving

Set aside one-third of the cooked rice. Using the remaining rice, pat a layer about 1 inch thick onto the bottom and sides of the prepared pan. Layer the prosciutto on the rice on the bottom of the pan. Layer on top in the following order: the peas, the hard-boiled eggs, the chicken liver mixture, the meatballs, and the mozzarella. Top with the reserved rice in an even layer. Sprinkle lightly with the remaining bread crumbs and dot with the butter.

Bake the rice until golden, about 1 hour and 20 minutes. Transfer to a rack and let rest for 10 to 15 minutes.

Reheat the remaining sauce in a small saucepan over low heat. Run a knife along the inside of the pan sides to loosen the rice, then unclamp and remove the pan sides. Slide the casserole onto a serving plate, cut into wedges, and serve accompanied with the warm sauce. Pass the Parmesan at the table.

WINE: *We need a big red wine here. An Aglianico red from Campania such as Taurasi Riserva, a Super Tuscan, or a Cabernet Sauvignon will stand up to the richness.*

A note on making rice casseroles or *bombas:*

If you are in any way nervous about making such an involved dish and then worry about having it collapse when you unmold it, you can get around this by layering it in a lasagna pan or some other rectangular baking dish. Butter the pan or baking dish, add a layer of rice, then the filling and then top with the remaining rice. Bake as directed, until golden, let rest for 10 minutes, and then cut into squares. No unmolding is needed.

Also some cooks still cook the rice as if making a risotto, then add the eggs and cheese. I don't think this is necessary but if you want to do it that way, or if you have made lots of extra plain risotto and have leftovers, you can use it in the *bomba*.

Baked Rice from Liguria

Risotto is a wonderful dish, but it requires steady attention. That is why I love this baked rice dish from Liguria. You cook the meat, and then cook the rice directly in the meat broth in the style of a pilaf. Finally, you combine the two, transfer them to a dish, and bake the mixture as if it were a timbale, but without the usual complex layering.

SERVES 4 TO 6

7 tablespoons unsalted butter

1 yellow onion, chopped

1 pound ground veal or beef

7 cups meat stock

Salt and freshly ground black pepper

2 1/2 cups Italian short-grain rice

1/4 cup grated grana padano *cheese*

Preheat the oven to 350°F. Liberally butter or oil a 3-quart baking dish or gratin dish.

In a large sauté pan, melt 4 tablespoons of the butter over high heat. Add the onion and meat and cook, breaking up the meat with a fork and adding 1/2 to 1 cup stock as needed to prevent scorching, until browned and tender, about 10 minutes. Season to taste with salt and pepper, remove from the heat, and set aside.

Pour the remaining stock into a saucepan and bring to gentle boil over medium heat. Add the rice, reduce the heat to low, cover, and cook until rice is al dente, 10 to 15 minutes.

Fold the cooked meat and the cheese into the rice, distributing them evenly. Turn the mixture into the prepared dish. Cut the remaining 3 tablespoons butter into small pieces and use to dot the top.

Bake the rice until a golden crust forms, about 30 minutes. Transfer to a rack and let cool for 5 minutes, then serve.

WINE: *A light red would be good here, such as Dolcetto or a Nebbiolo-based wine from the Piedmont.*

FISH AND SHELLFISH

Whenever I stroll through the seafood stalls at the Rialto market in Venice, I am nearly overwhelmed by the abundance and variety of fish and shellfish. Most of us are lucky if we can find a fishmonger who delivers on freshness and quality, more so on variety. If you do not already have a reliable fishmonger, seek one out. He or she will offer the best available once you are recognized as a savvy shopper.

While not all varieties of Italian fish and shellfish are found away from Italy, many of them are. *Spigola* is sea bass, *pesce spada* is swordfish, *tonno* is tuna, *coda di rospo* is monkfish (also known as anglerfish), and *storione* is sturgeon. For the other fish dishes I have found substitutes. Texture is a crucial element, and I have tried to match toothsomeness as well as taste. For *palombo,* a type of small shark, the meat of other shark varieties is a good substitute. Halibut, turbot, or snapper will work for *pesce San Pietro,* known in English as Saint Peter's fish or John Dory; porgy or snapper can stand in for *orata,* or sea bream; and sea bass is a good alternative to *ombrina,* a small, flavorful fish of the Mediterranean. Shrimp, mussels, clams, and squid are at most markets, even if cuttlefish and octopus are not. If you do find them, simply cook them until tender and add them to fish soups and stews. Salt cod, or *baccalà,* is sold at many markets and Italian grocery stores, as well as at shops that carry Portuguese and Spanish foods.

Most fish and shellfish are at their best when prepared as soon as they are purchased, as they deteriorate with storage. Usually they are cooked quickly to preserve their delicate character, but some recipes call for longer cooking to achieve a desired texture or for a dish to reach its full flavor. For example, thick steaks cut from large, meaty fish such as swordfish are sometimes braised slowly in sauce and then cut into portions like a meat roast. Olive oil poaching, which calls for covering the fish with olive oil and cooking it at a very low temperature until the fish has absorbed most of the oil, produces moist, flavorful fish that keeps for a week. This is not a new technique. It appears in *Gastronomia sperimentale,* a Venetian cookbook by Antonio Papodopoli published in 1886. Papodopoli calls for putting a thick piece of tuna in a pan not much larger than the fish itself, adding some chopped tomatoes and enough olive oil to cover the fish, and then cooking it very slowly for a couple of hours. Some shellfish, such as squid, octopus, and cuttlefish, are slowly braised to tenderize their flesh and infuse it with deeper flavor.

In this chapter, I have also included some regional fish stews in which the base is simmered for a long time, and then fish and shellfish are cooked quickly in the full-flavored liquid. If the base is brothy, the dish might be called *zuppa di pesce,* or "fish soup," or perhaps *brodetto,* or "stew." These are usually served ladled over toasted bread. If the base is thick, the stew may be given a special name such as *ciuppin* (page 39), *cacciucco,* or *burrida.* Such soups or stews are often prepared by combining a simple fish stock with aromatic vegetables and white wine. They might be *in bianco,* that is, without tomato, or they might be enriched with tomatoes or tomato paste. What is essential is that the soup base simmers for a long time so that it develops a full, rich flavor.

What follows is a selection of fish and shellfish dishes that are ideal for meals when deep flavor takes precedence over expediency.

Coda di rospo con patate
Monkfish with Potatoes

SERVES 6

Monkfish, also called anglerfish, is particularly popular in the regions along the Adriatic coast, the Veneto, the Marches, and the Abruzzo. The rosemary, garlic, and chile pepper are a giveaway that the Abruzzo is the source of this particular recipe. Italians like to cook monkfish on the bone, but many markets elsewhere carry only fillets. Some versions of this recipe suggest wrapping the fish in a layer of pancetta. Thick pieces of sea bass may be used in place of monkfish.

4 russet potatoes, peeled, parboiled (page 121), and sliced ¼ inch thick

Salt and freshly ground black pepper

6 tablespoons extra virgin olive oil

2 pounds monkfish fillet, skinned

4 cloves garlic, minced

4 fresh rosemary sprigs

Pinch of chile pepper flakes (optional)

Fresh lemon juice (optional)

Lemon wedges for serving

Preheat the oven to 350°F. Oil a baking dish large enough to hold the fish.

Arrange a layer of sliced potatoes on the bottom of the prepared dish. Sprinkle with salt and pepper and drizzle with about 3 tablespoons of the olive oil. Top with the monkfish, garlic, rosemary sprigs, and the chile pepper flakes (if using). Add a squeeze of lemon juice if you like. Pour on the remaining 3 tablespoons olive oil, sprinkle with salt and pepper, and cover the pan with aluminum foil.

Roast the fish for about 40 minutes. Uncover the dish and continue to roast until the potatoes are tender and the fish is opaque when a knife tip is inserted in the center, 15 to 20 minutes longer. Serve with lemon wedges.

WINE: *Select a white from the Adriatic coast. From the Abruzzo, try Trebbiano d'Abruzzo from Valentini or Nicodemi. From the Marches, look for Verdicchio dei Castelli di Jesi or Verdicchio di Matelica from Santarelli, Umani Ronchi, Colle Stefano, or Vallerusa Bonci. The assertive seasoning of this dish means that a red wine such as Corvina would complement it as well.*

Tonno al ragù

Braised Tuna with Tomato, Garlic, and Mint

SERVES 6

Braised tuna steak is a specialty of the island of Favignana, a few miles off the coast of Trapani. Favignana is the home of the *mattanza,* or seasonal tuna slaughter, during which fishermen surround a school of fish with anchored nets, stab at them with harpoons until the water turns red with blood, and then haul in their catch. The waters are now overfished and the traditional practice has been reduced to one day a year, making it only ceremonial, rather than a means of gathering food. :: Many Sicilian cooks soak tuna in cold salted water for about 10 minutes to draw out its blood and thus lighten its color. This dish would be wonderful with Baked Eggplant from Sardinia (page 246) or a stew like *ciambotta* (page 260). Again, any leftover tuna would be excellent tossed with pasta.

1 thick piece tuna fillet, 2 to 2 1/2 pounds

3 cloves garlic, cut into thin slivers

Leaves from 6 fresh mint sprigs, plus 2 tablespoons chopped

1/2 cup extra virgin olive oil

1 yellow onion, chopped

1 can (6 ounces) tomato paste and 3 cups water, or 3 cups Rich Tomato Sauce (page 69), Tomato Sauce (page 69), or canned tomato sauce

1 cup dry white wine

1 cinnamon stick

Pinch of chile pepper flakes (optional)

Salt and freshly ground black pepper

If you have soaked the fish in cold salted water (see recipe introduction), pat it dry. Using a small, sharp knife, make small slits all over the tuna and insert the garlic slivers and mint leaves into the slits. Chop any leftover mint leaves and use as needed for the 2 tablespoons.

In a large sauté pan, heat the olive oil over medium heat. Add the onion and sauté until softened, about 8 minutes. Add the tuna and sauté, turning once, to color both sides, about 5 minutes on each side. Use 2 spatulas to turn the fish so that it does not break apart. Dissolve the tomato paste in 1 cup of the water, pour it over the fish, and then add the rest of the water, or add the tomato sauce. Add the wine, the cinnamon stick, the chile pepper flakes (if using), and a few grinds of black pepper. Bring to a simmer, cover, reduce the heat to low, and cook until the fish is tender but not dry, 40 to 60 minutes. Taste and adjust the seasoning with salt.

Using the 2 spatulas, carefully transfer the fish to a warmed platter. It is difficult to slice the fish neatly; it is easier to break the fish into large pieces with a fork. Spoon some of the pan sauce over each serving, and sprinkle with the chopped mint.

cont'd

WINE: *Choose a Sicilian white wine, such as a blend of Inzolia and Catarratto grapes, or a Chardonnay. Look for one from Planeta, Spadafora, Duca di Salaparuta, Villa dell'Acate, or Donnafugata. Because tuna is so meaty and the sauce is tomato based, a red wine will work, too. Try a medium-weight Merlot or Corvina.*

VARIATION: To cook this dish in a slow cooker, brown the fish as directed, then put it in the slow cooker with all the remaining ingredients and cook on low for 3 1/2 to 4 hours. If the pan juices are too thin when the fish is done, reduce them on the stove top.

Two Islands on Tuna

In Syracuse, a lovely seaside town rich in history in southeastern Sicily, local cooks make incisions all over a large, thick piece of tuna fillet and then slip a sliver of garlic, a whole clove, and a coriander seed into each slit. The fish is then simmered with about 4 cups chopped tomatoes for about half an hour, at which point 1/2 cup white wine vinegar and 1 tablespoon dried oregano are added to the sauce. The fish is then braised until tender, another 20 minutes or so.

Cooks in the Sardinian town of Carloforte marinate tuna for a few hours in a mixture of chopped *lardo* (page 211), minced fresh parsley, minced onion, salt, pepper, olive oil, and a touch of vinegar, turning it often in the mixture to keep it moist. They then bake the tuna in the marinade in a 300°F oven for nearly an hour.

Baked Sturgeon with Pancetta and Marsala

SERVES 6

Years ago, the Po River teemed with sturgeon. It was their spawning ground. Overfishing has done its damage, but sturgeon, a dense and fine-fleshed fish, is still greatly prized in Emilia-Romagna, especially in the mosaic-rich city of Ravenna. In this recipe, the fillet is typically studded with strips of *lardo* (page 211). Pancetta is a good alternative to the *lardo,* as it adds a nice hit of salt and some meaty flavor to the already-meaty fish. If you cannot find sturgeon at your market, you can use swordfish. Serve the fish with sautéed spinach, which is harmonious with the sweetness of the Marsala in the sauce.

1 or 2 thick pieces sturgeon fillet, 2 1/2 pounds total weight

2 ounces pancetta, sliced 1/4 inch thick and slices cut into 1/4-inch-wide strips

1/2 cup extra virgin olive oil

1/4 cup fresh lemon juice

Salt and freshly ground pepper

2 bay leaves

1/2 cup dry white wine

4 tablespoons unsalted butter

1/2 cup dry Marsala or other dry sweet wine

Preheat the oven to 300°F. Oil a baking dish large enough to hold the fish.

Using a small, sharp knife, make small slits all over the fish at 1-inch intervals and insert a pancetta strip into each slit, poking it down with your finger.

In a small bowl, whisk together the olive oil and lemon juice. Place the fish in the prepared dish, pour the olive oil mixture over it, and sprinkle with salt and pepper. Add the bay leaves to the dish and then the white wine. (At this point, you can cover the dish, slip it into the refrigerator, and leave the fish to marinate for a few hours, or you can cook it right away.)

Bake the fish, basting from time to time with the pan juices, until it is opaque when a knife tip is inserted in the center, 35 to 45 minutes. The timing will depend on the thickness of the fillet.

Using 2 wide spatulas, carefully transfer the fish to a warmed platter. Pour the pan juices into a saucepan and reduce over high heat to 1/2 cup. Add the butter and Marsala, swirl over low heat for a few minutes, and spoon over the fish. Serve at once.

WINE: *You can go either white or red here. Try a white Albana di Romagna from Tre Monti. Because the sturgeon is meaty and full flavored, you can also drink a Sangiovese from Emilia-Romagna or a Barbera d'Asti from Piedmont. A Pinot Noir from California's central coast, from Sonoma, or from Oregon would also complement the fish.*

Roast Fish with Vegetables from Mantua

Mantua is a charming town in Lombardy known for its superb Ducal Palace and paintings by Mantegna. While the Lombards are not big fish eaters, they do enjoy sea bass and freshwater fish such as pike, carp, and perch. I prepared this recipe both with sea bass and cod, and the dish was lovely and delicate. Salmon is a bit more assertive in flavor, but would work well, too.

SERVES 6

1/4 teaspoon saffron threads, crushed

1/4 cup hot water

2 1/2 pounds sea bass, cod, or salmon, in thick steaks or fillets

1 lemon, sliced paper-thin and each slice quartered

2 yellow onions, sliced

1 pound russet potatoes, peeled and sliced 1/8 inch thick or peeled, parboiled (page 121), and sliced 1/4 inch thick

2 zucchini, sliced 1/4 inch thick

1/2 pound fresh mushrooms, wiped clean and sliced 1/4 inch thick

Salt and freshly ground pepper

1/2 cup extra virgin olive oil, or as needed

Preheat the oven to 350°F. Oil a baking dish just large enough to hold the fish in a single layer.

In a small bowl, combine the saffron and hot water and set aside to steep for 15 minutes.

Place the fish in the prepared dish. Tuck the lemon pieces and onion, potato, zucchini, and mushroom slices in and around the fish pieces. Sprinkle with about 1 tablespoon salt and some pepper and drizzle with the 1/2 cup olive oil, adding more if needed to coat all of the ingredients liberally. Add the saffron infusion and then add water to a depth of about 1/4 inch. Cover the dish with aluminum foil.

Roast the fish and vegetables for about 45 minutes. Uncover and continue to roast until the fish is opaque when a knife tip is inserted in the center, 15 to 20 minutes longer. Serve at once.

WINE: *Pour a Soave or Sauvignon Blanc from the Veneto. For a more festive occasion, try a sparkling wine from Lombardy, such as a Franciacorta from Bellavista, Cavalleri, or Ca' del Bosco.*

Fish and Potatoes

While doing research for this book, I came across many recipes for fish baked in the oven with potatoes. I presumed they would work easily, but I found otherwise. In most cases, the fish was ready long before the potatoes. I persevered. Thinking that maybe it was the potatoes, I tried Yukon Golds, new potatoes, little red potatoes, and, finally, russets, or baking potatoes. No luck. Maybe, I thought, my slices are too thick, so I reduced them from $1/3$ inch to $1/4$ inch and then to $1/8$ inch. They still were not tender when the fish was ready. I also tried covering the dish for part of the time it was in the oven, and then uncovering it to let the fish and potatoes take on some color. Finally, I added a bit of liquid to the dish to give the potatoes something to drink.

Here is my advice on successfully baking fish and potatoes together. First, go with russets. They are more porous than new potatoes, so they absorb more juices and olive oil, which mean they become tender more quickly and thus better integrated into the dish. Second, if you want to be sure that the potatoes will soften along with the fish, be they waxy new potatoes or russets, parboil, or half-cook, them first, then slice.

Impanada di pesce spada
Swordfish Pie

SERVES 8 TO 10

This is a most unusual recipe. It reflects the rich tastes of the Sicilian aristocracy of the end of the nineteenth century, an era when the *monzù,* or imported French chef, began to add French touches to Sicilian dishes, instead of cooking only traditional French food. Rather than enclose the fish in simple bread dough, the crust is a more refined *pasta frolla,* slightly sweet and enriched with citrus zest, and the swordfish and zucchini are enhanced with raisins, pine nuts, olives, capers, tomatoes, and celery. Even if I did not tell you the recipe was Sicilian, these signature flavors would give away its origin. In his interesting book, *Cucina Paradiso,* about Sicilian cuisine and its Arabic roots, author Clifford Wright offers an even more complex version of this recipe called *pasticcio di San Giuseppe.* It replaces the relatively simple zucchini with fennel, cauliflower, asparagus, and artichokes, which are blanched, deep-fried, and then layered with the fish.

FOR THE PASTRY

4 cups all-purpose flour

2 tablespoons sugar

1/2 teaspoon salt

2/3 cup lard and 4 tablespoons unsalted butter, or 3/4 cup unsalted butter

Grated zest of 1 lemon or orange

2 eggs, 1 whole and 1 separated

1/2 cup dry white wine or water, or as needed

To make the pastry, stir together the flour, sugar, and salt in a bowl. Cut the lard and butter or all butter into 1-inch pieces and scatter over the flour mixture. Using a pastry blender, cut in the fat until the mixture resembles cornmeal. Add the citrus zest, the whole egg, and the egg yolk (reserve the white). Gradually add the 1/2 cup wine or water while stirring and tossing with a fork until the dough is evenly moistened and comes together in a mass. If the dough is too dry, add more liquid, a spoonful at a time. Gather the dough together into a ball and divide it into 2 portions, one slightly larger than the other. Flatten each portion into a disk. Wrap separately in plastic wrap and refrigerate for 1 hour.

To make the filling, in a large sauté pan, heat 1/4 cup of the olive oil over medium heat. Working in batches if necessary, add the zucchini or eggplant slices and sauté, turning as needed, until pale gold, 5 to 6 minutes. Transfer the vegetables to a plate and set aside.

Return the pan to low heat and add the remaining 1/2 cup olive oil. When the oil is hot, add the onion and sauté until softened, about 10 minutes. Add the celery, olives, capers, pine nuts, and raisins and cook for 3 minutes. Add the tomatoes and simmer for 5 minutes to blend the flavors. Add the swordfish and simmer until it is opaque when a knife tip is inserted in the center of a piece, about 10 minutes. Remove from the heat, fold in the bread crumbs (they will keep the filling from being too wet), and let cool completely.

FOR THE FILLING

3/4 cup olive oil

4 medium zucchini or Japanese eggplants, sliced 1/4 inch thick

1 yellow onion, minced

1 cup sliced celery

1/2 cup pitted green olives, sliced

1/3 cup salt-packed capers, rinsed

1/2 cup pine nuts, toasted

1/3 cup golden raisins

1 1/2 cups peeled, seeded, and chopped tomatoes (fresh or canned)

2 pounds swordfish steaks, skinned, boned, and cut into 1-inch dice

1/2 cup dried bread crumbs

Preheat the oven to 350°F. Butter a 10-inch pie dish or round baking dish.

Place the larger dough disk between 2 sheets of baker's parchment and roll out the dough into a round about 13 inches in diameter and 1/8 inch thick. Fit it into the prepared dish. Spoon half of the swordfish mixture into the lined dish, top with the zucchini or eggplant, and then top with the remaining swordfish mixture. Roll out the second disk in the same way into a round about 11 inches in diameter. Lay it carefully over the top of the dish, and trim the edges of the top and bottom crusts even. Pinch the edges together, turn them under, and press against rim to seal. Cut 3 or 4 vents in the top crust. (At this point, you can refrigerate the pie for up to 1 day before baking.)

In a small bowl, whisk the reserved egg white until foamy. Brush it over the top crust.

Bake the pie until the crust is set and golden, about 1 hour. Transfer to a rack and let rest for at least 10 minutes before serving. Serve hot or warm, cut into wedges.

WINE: *Choose a Sicilian white from Corvo, or pour a Sardinian Vermentino or Vernaccia di Oristano. If you are interested in pairing a red wine with the swordfish, try Cerasuolo di Vittoria, a light Sicilian red from Cos. A youthful red such as Merlot or Corvina also would work, as would that diplomat of wines, Pinot Noir.*

VARIATION: If you do not want to go to the effort of making a pie, but you do want a Sicilian-style swordfish dish, here's the deconstructed version, known as *pesce spada alla ghiotta*. Oil a baking dish and place 4 thick swordfish steaks side by side in the dish. Omit the zucchini or eggplant. In a sauté pan, heat 1/4 cup olive oil over medium heat and sauté the onion as directed for the pie. Then add and cook the celery, olives, capers, pine nuts, raisins, and tomatoes as directed. Spoon this mixture over the swordfish, cover with aluminum foil, and bake in 350°F oven for 30 minutes. Serve with baked eggplant (page 246) or sautéed zucchini.

Totano is a species of so-called flying squid found in the waters off Liguria and Tuscany. Squid are a natural vehicle for stuffing, so many regional recipes call for preparing them that way. Sicilian fillings typically include bread crumbs, raisins, pine nuts, and anchovies. In Venice, at the Osteria Vivaldi, the chef cooks radicchio with a bit of balsamic vinegar (page 250), stuffs it into squid, drizzles them with olive oil, and then bakes them until tender. I thought this Genoese recipe had a particularly flavorful filling, typical of Liguria with the signature dried porcini. Serve the squid with plenty of crusty bread to sop up the juices.

SERVES 4

12 medium-sized squid, about 1 pound total weight, cleaned with bodies left whole and tentacles reserved (about 1/2 pound after cleaning)

FOR THE FILLING

1/2 ounce dried porcini mushrooms

2 ounces mortadella, chopped

3 tablespoons chopped fresh flat-leaf parsley, or half each parsley and marjoram

1 clove garlic, minced

2/3 cup grated Parmesan cheese

1 egg

1 thick slice coarse country bread, crusts removed, soaked in milk, and squeezed almost dry

Salt and freshly ground black pepper

Ready the squid as directed and set aside.

To make the filling, soak the porcini mushrooms in hot water to cover for 30 minutes. Drain, reserving the soaking liquid, and chop finely. Pour the liquid through a fine-mesh sieve lined with cheesecloth and set aside.

In a bowl, combine the mortadella, chopped porcini, parsley or parsley and marjoram, and garlic and mix well. Add the cheese, egg, and bread, season with salt and pepper, and mix well. (Alternatively, pulse the ingredients together in a food processor; the mixture will be finer and travel through the pastry-bag tip more smoothly.)

Spoon the mixture into a pastry bag fitted with a large, plain tip or a zippered plastic bag with one corner cut off, and fill the squid bodies with the mixture. Skewer the tops closed with toothpicks.

In a sauté pan large enough to hold all of the squid in a single layer, heat the 1/4 cup olive oil over medium heat. Add the onion and celery and sauté until softened, about 8 minutes. Add the tentacles and sauté for 2 minutes longer. Add the stuffed squid, 1/2 cup of the reserved porcini soaking liquid, and the 3/4 cup wine. Reduce the heat to low, cover, and simmer, adding a little more wine if the pan begins to dry out, until the squid are tender, about 40 minutes.

Spoon the squid and pan juices into warmed shallow bowls. Drizzle with olive oil and accompany with lemon wedges.

1/4 cup extra virgin olive oil, plus more for serving

1 yellow onion, chopped

1 celery stalk, chopped

3/4 cup dry white wine, or as needed

Lemon wedges for serving

WINE: *Enoteca Bisson and Colle dei Bardellini are reputable producers of Ligurian Vermentino, but they may be hard to find. You can instead veer off to Tuscany for Antinori's Guado al Tasso Bolgheri Vermentino or a Grattamacco Bianco from Colle Massari.*

VARIATIONS: If you do not eat meat, omit the mortadella and increase the bread by one slice. You can also add 4 tomatoes, peeled, seeded, and chopped, to the braising liquids.

For spinach lovers, take 1 pound of fresh spinach and wash it well. In a large sauté pan, over high heat, wilt the spinach using just the water still clinging to the leaves. Drain, squeeze dry, and chop fine. If using frozen chopped spinach, thaw, drain, and squeeze dry. Heat 3 tablespoons olive oil in a sauté pan over medium heat. Add the chopped spinach, 3 cloves of minced garlic, 1 tablespoon chopped fresh rosemary, and the tentacles (chopped) and sauté until the squid is cooked, about 3 to 5 minutes. Add 1/2 cup dry white wine and let it bubble up and be absorbed, about 5 minutes longer. Transfer the mixture to a bowl. When the mixture is cool, fold in 1 cup ricotta cheese, 1 egg, 1/3 cup grated Pecorino cheese, nutmeg, and 2 tablespoons chopped parsley. Season the mixture to taste with salt and pepper. Stuff into the squid and cook as above.

Spicy Squid with Greens and Tomatoes

SERVES 4

The origin of the term *inzimino* is vague. Some scholars think it is derived from *zamin,* an Arabic word for a fatty or rich sauce. In contemporary Tuscan and Ligurian kitchens, *inzimino* refers to fish or shellfish cooked with greens in a savory and spicy broth. Beet greens or Swiss chard is most commonly used, but you could use spinach instead. Just be aware that its milder flavor might be lost with the addition of the chile peppers. Ligurian cooks might stir in some toasted pine nuts. Some recipes suggest mixing in cooked chickpeas to make the dish more substantial, but usually it is accompanied with thick slices of grilled or toasted bread, making the legumes unnecessary.

Salt

2 pounds beet greens or Swiss chard, tough stems discarded

1/4 cup extra virgin olive oil

1 yellow onion, chopped

1 celery stalk, chopped

4 cloves garlic, chopped

1 fresh chile pepper, minced, or 1 teaspoon chile pepper flakes

1 1/2 pounds squid, cleaned, bodies cut into rings, and tentacles left whole (about 3/4 pound after cleaning)

1 1/2 cups peeled, seeded, and chopped tomatoes, or 2 tablespoons tomato paste diluted in 1/2 cup water

1/2 cup dry white or red wine

Salt and freshly ground black pepper

2 cups cooked chickpeas (optional; page 240)

2 tablespoons toasted pine nuts (optional)

Bring a large saucepan three-fourths full of water to a boil. Salt lightly, add the greens, and boil until softened, about 5 minutes. Drain well, refresh with cold water to set the color, and drain again. Chop coarsely and set aside.

In a large sauté pan, heat the olive oil over medium heat. Add the onion and celery and sauté until softened, about 8 minutes. Add the garlic and fresh chile or chile pepper flakes and cook for a few minutes longer. Add the squid, tomatoes or diluted tomato paste, and wine and sprinkle with salt and black pepper. Stir well, bring to a brisk simmer, reduce the heat to very low, cover, and simmer until the squid are tender, about 40 minutes. If the liquid begins to cook away, add a little water.

Add the reserved greens and the chickpeas or pine nuts (if using) and cook for another 10 minutes to heat through and blend the flavors. Serve at once.

WINE: *If you used white wine in the cooking, go with Vernaccia or Vermentino, or Terre di Tufi from Teruzzi e Puthod. This is a big-flavored dish, so red wine is an option, especially if you used it in the recipe. Try a Rosso di Salento or a Chianti.*

Although Jews are forbidden to cook meat with milk or other dairy products, recipes that call for simmering salt cod in milk are most likely of Jewish origin. The milk tames any excessive saltiness that the cod may retain. This dish can be accompanied, in the Venetian manner, with hot slices of baked or grilled polenta, or plain boiled potatoes.

SERVES 4

1 1/2 pounds salt cod fillets

3 tablespoons olive oil, or as needed

2 yellow onions, chopped

3 cloves garlic, finely minced

About 1 cup all-purpose flour

1 cup dry white wine

3 to 4 cups milk

Freshly grated nutmeg

1 or 2 pinches ground cinnamon

3 tablespoons unsalted butter, cut into slivers

1/2 cup grated Parmesan or grana padano cheese

1/4 cup chopped fresh flat-leaf parsley

Place the salt cod in a large bowl, add water to cover, and refrigerate for at least 24 hours, changing the water 3 times. Drain the salt cod and break it into 2-inch pieces, discarding any errant bones and skin.

In a large, deep flameproof sauté pan, heat the 3 tablespoons olive oil over medium heat. Add the onions and garlic and sauté until translucent and tender, about 10 minutes.

Meanwhile, spread the flour on a plate. Dust the salt cod pieces with the flour, shaking off the excess.

When the onions are tender, add the salt cod and continue to sauté until the onions are golden, about 5 minutes longer. Add more oil if necessary to prevent scorching. Add the wine and simmer until it has evaporated, 5 to 8 minutes. Add milk to cover, a little nutmeg, and the cinnamon, reduce the heat to low, and continue to simmer, uncovered, until the cod is tender, about 30 minutes longer.

Preheat the broiler, or preheat the oven to 400°F.

Remove the pan from the heat, stir in the butter, cheese, and parsley, and mix well. Slip the pan under the broiler and broil until glazed on top, just a few minutes, or place in the oven for 10 minutes until glazed. Serve very hot.

WINE: *A rich Soave from Pieropan, Gini, Anselmi, or Inama will stand up to the salt cod nicely.*

VARIATION: To make *baccalà alla vicentina,* a famous salt cod dish from Vicenza, omit the cinnamon, nutmeg, and cheese and add 4 olive oil–packed anchovy fillets, chopped (or 2 salt-packed anchovies, filleted, rinsed, and chopped), and a few tablespoons rinsed capers with the cod.

SERVES 8

In Genoa, the term *burrida* refers to a stew in which the fish is cooked in pieces, rather than whole. While a flavorful *brodo di pesce,* or fish broth (see note for Fish Soup from Liguria, page 39), would be nice to have on hand, you can make this dish with water, as the fish will have time to give off a good deal of flavor. The classic Genoese *burrida* usually includes monkfish, octopus, and squid or cuttlefish. You can add other kinds of firm fish to the mix, however. But tomatoes are essential, as are garlic and onions. Sometimes dried porcini or a few ground toasted pine nuts are added. *Burrida* is served with garlic-rubbed slices of toasted or fried bread.

3 pounds assorted seafood such as fillets of monkfish, cod, grouper, and shark and cleaned octopus (optional) and squid, cut into 2-inch pieces

Extra virgin olive oil for rubbing on fish, plus 1/3 cup

Salt

2 yellow onions, chopped

3 cloves garlic, minced

1 carrot, peeled and chopped

1 celery stalk, chopped

1/4 cup chopped fresh flat-leaf parsley

1/4 cup fresh basil leaves, finely shredded

2 pounds tomatoes, peeled, seeded, and chopped, or 1 can (28 ounces) plum tomatoes with juice, seeded and chopped

1 1/2 cups dry white wine

2 cups water or fish stock

Freshly ground black pepper

8 thick slices coarse country bread, toasted or fried in olive oil and rubbed with garlic

An hour or two before you are ready to cook, rub the seafood with a little olive oil and sprinkle it with salt. You may also add a bit of the minced garlic to the rub. Refrigerate until needed.

In a large Dutch oven, heat the 1/3 cup olive oil over medium heat. Add the onions and sauté until softened, about 8 minutes. Add the garlic, carrot, celery, parsley, and basil, reduce the heat to low, and cook for about 5 minutes longer. Add the tomatoes, 3/4 cup of the wine, 1 cup of the water or stock, the octopus (if using), and the squid. Cover and simmer over low heat for 30 minutes.

Layer the remaining fish on top of the squid and the octopus (if used), and sprinkle with salt and pepper. Add the remaining 3/4 cup wine and 1 cup water or stock. Cover and simmer for 30 minutes longer. At this point, the fish should be opaque at the center when tested with the tip of a knife. Season with salt and pepper.

Put a bread slice in each warmed shallow bowl. Using a slotted spoon, divide the seafood evenly among the bowls. Ladle the broth over the top and serve at once.

WINE: *It is Vermentino all the way. From Liguria, choose Bisson or Colle dei Bardellini. From Tuscany, select Tenuta Guado al Tasso or Grattamacco Bianco. From Sardinia, look for Conti, Argiolas, or Cantina di Gallura.*

Cacciucco alla livornese
Spicy Fish and Shellfish Stew from Livorno

SERVES 8

In Tuscan dialect, *cacciucco* means "confusion." Some say the word is derived from the Turkish *kucuk,* meaning "small." Others say it comes from the Arabic word *shakshoukli,* which is used to describe a mixture in a cauldron. Actually, none of this is too far-fetched, as the port of Livorno engaged in active trade with North Africa and the Middle East in the past and was once home to a sizable community of exiled North African Jews. This fish stew is unusual in that red, rather than white, wine is used for the base. It traditionally includes five kinds of assorted fish and shellfish, one for every *c* in *cacciucco.* A rich *brodo di pesce* (see note for Fish Soup from Liguria, page 39) will enhance the flavors. Add the fish or shellfish and cook as needed for proper consistency and doneness.

1 1/2 to 2 pounds assorted firm white fish fillets, cut into 2-inch pieces

Extra virgin olive oil for rubbing on fish, plus 1/4 cup

Fresh lemon juice

Salt

2 yellow onions, chopped

8 to 10 cloves garlic, chopped

1 teaspoon chile pepper flakes, or to taste

2 pounds tomatoes, peeled, seeded, and chopped, or 1 can (28 ounces) plum tomatoes with juice, seeded and chopped

2 cups dry red wine

4 cups fish stock

1 pound large shrimp, peeled and deveined

An hour or two before you are ready to cook, rub the fish with a little olive oil and lemon juice and sprinkle it with salt. Refrigerate until needed.

In a large soup pot or Dutch oven, heat the 1/4 cup olive oil over medium heat. Add the onions and sauté until softened, about 8 minutes. Add the garlic and chile pepper flakes and cook for 1 minute. Add the tomatoes, wine, and stock and bring to a gentle boil. Reduce the heat to low and simmer, uncovered, for 40 minutes to concentrate the flavors.

Add the fish and cook for 5 minutes. Add the shrimp, scallops, clams, and mussels, cover, and simmer until the clams and mussels open, about 5 minutes longer. Taste the base and season with salt and black pepper. Add more chile pepper flakes if you like, and a bit more lemon juice if you think it needs some acidity.

Put a bread slice in each warmed shallow bowl. Using a slotted spoon, divide the seafood evenly among the bowls, discarding any clams or mussels that failed to open. Ladle the broth over the top and garnish with the parsley and basil. Serve at once.

16 sea scallops, muscle removed

24 clams, well scrubbed

24 mussels, well scrubbed and debearded

Freshly ground black pepper

8 thick slices coarse country bread, toasted or fried in olive oil and rubbed with garlic

1/4 cup chopped fresh flat-leaf parsley

1/4 cup finely shredded fresh basil

WINE: *This is a white or red situation. If you want white, Vermentino will work. I would probably go with red, possibly the one used in cooking the stew. Dolcetto, Pinot Nero, and Cabernet Franc are options.*

NOTE: If you would like to include squid in this stew, add them either during the last few minutes the stew cooks, or cook them in the base for 25 to 30 minutes while it simmers. In other words, you must either cook them a long time to tenderize them, or you must cook them very briefly. Cook them any length of time in between and they will be tough.

Saffron Fish Soup

SERVES 6 TO 8

Brodetto is possibly the oldest Mediterranean fish soup. Needless to say, its makeup varies widely from town to town and, like most fish soups, it is dependent on the day's catch. Fish that may be included are red and gray mullet, squid, sole, scorpionfish, monkfish, and dogfish. Smaller fish are usually cooked whole, with their heads intact. Sometimes, as in versions from the Veneto and Friuli, there are no tomatoes, but there may be, in addition to the white wine, a good splash of vinegar. In the Marches, saffron is added, while cooks in the Abruzzo favor a touch of their beloved chile pepper. This **brodetto** from the town of Porto Recanati in the Marches can be prepared with water or fish stock.

2 pounds thick fish steaks, cut into 2- or 3-inch pieces, or 2 pounds small whole fish, cleaned

Extra virgin olive oil for rubbing on fish, plus 3 tablespoons

Fresh lemon juice

Salt

1 teaspoon saffron threads, crushed

2 tablespoons hot water

1 yellow onion, chopped

1 pound squid or cuttlefish, cleaned, bodies cut into rings, and tentacles halved if large (about 1/2 pound after cleaning)

4 cups fish stock or water

1 pound tomatoes, peeled, seeded, and chopped (optional)

1 cup dry white wine

Freshly ground black pepper

An hour or two before you are ready to cook, rub the fish with a little olive oil and lemon juice and sprinkle it with salt. Refrigerate until needed.

In a small bowl, combine the saffron and hot water and set aside to steep for 15 minutes.

In a Dutch oven, heat the 3 tablespoons olive oil over medium heat. Add onion and sauté until softened, about 8 minutes. Add the squid or cuttlefish and toss in the oil for a few minutes to coat. Add the saffron infusion, stock or water, tomatoes (if using), wine, and a little salt and black pepper. Reduce the heat to low and simmer, uncovered, for 30 minutes.

Add the fish and poach over low heat until it is opaque when a knife tip is inserted in the thickest part, about 15 minutes. Add the shrimp during the last 10 minutes the fish are cooking. When the seafood is done, add the vinegar to taste and the chile pepper flakes, if using.

Put a bread slice in each warmed shallow bowl. Using a slotted spoon, divide the seafood evenly among the bowls. Ladle the broth over the top and garnish with parsley or fennel, if desired. Serve at once.

1 pound very large shrimp, peeled and deveined

A splash or more of white wine vinegar

Pinch of chile pepper flakes (optional)

6 to 8 slices coarse country bread, toasted or grilled

Chopped fresh flat-leaf parsley or fennel fronds for garnish (optional)

WINE: *Verdicchio or Sauvignon Blanc is your best bet here.*

VARIATIONS: The Marches and the Abruzzo are kissing cousins, so their recipes for *brodetto* are similar. In the Abruzzese towns of Vasto, Ortona, and Pescara, however, a few large, sweet red bell peppers called *fufullone* are chopped and added to the fish stew. You may also add 1 fennel bulb, trimmed and chopped, with the onion.

Zuppa di pesce al forno
Oven-Roasted Fish Stew

This is a great one-pot Sicilian recipe that involves very little work. Instead of simmering fish in a fragrant broth on the stove top, the dish is cooked in the oven. It's also a good candidate for the slow cooker. To make the dish a little fancier, garnish each serving with a dollop of *salsa rossa* (page 182).

SERVES 6

2 1/2 pounds thick fish steaks or fillets such as cod, halibut, shark, monkfish, or snapper, cut into 3-inch pieces

Extra virgin olive oil for rubbing on fish and for drizzling, plus 1/4 cup

Fresh lemon juice

Salt and freshly ground black pepper

2 yellow onions, sliced

4 celery stalks, sliced

4 cloves garlic, minced

3 tablespoons chopped fresh flat-leaf parsley

1 tablespoon dried oregano

4 tomatoes, peeled, seeded, and chopped

1 cup dry white wine

2 to 3 cups fish stock or water

6 slices coarse country bread, toasted or grilled

Chopped fresh flat-leaf parsley or finely shredded fresh basil leaves

An hour or two before you are ready to cook, rub the fish with a little olive oil and lemon juice and sprinkle it with salt. Refrigerate until needed.

Preheat the oven to 350°F.

Sprinkle the fish pieces with a bit more salt and some pepper. Arrange in a single layer in a baking dish or Dutch oven.

In a large sauté pan, heat the 1/4 cup olive oil over medium heat. Add the onions and celery and sauté until softened, about 5 minutes. Add the garlic, parsley, and oregano, sprinkle the vegetables with salt and pepper, and sauté for 2 minutes longer. Stir in the tomatoes and wine, remove from the heat, and pour over the fish. Add enough fish stock or water just to cover the fish and a generous drizzle of olive oil. Cover the dish or pan.

Bake the fish until until it is opaque when a knife tip is inserted in the center, about 40 minutes. Taste and adjust with salt and pepper.

Put a bread slice in each warmed shallow bowl. Using a slotted spoon, divide the fish evenly among the bowls, then ladle the broth over the top. Garnish with parsley or basil and serve at once.

WINE: *You can always drink a glass or two of the cooking wine. Try a Sicilian white from Spadafora, Planeta, Regaleali, or Corvo. Or, pour a light red like Cerasuolo di Vittoria.*

VARIATION: To cook this dish in a slow cooker, assemble it as you would for a baking dish and then cook on low for 3 to 4 hours; the timing depends on the thickness of the fish.

POULTRY AND RABBIT

Today, chicken is widely eaten in Italy, but this was not always the case. In the past, chickens were raised for their eggs and appeared only rarely on the dinner table. Birds were slaughtered when they had grown old, or when a special chicken dish was needed to celebrate a holiday or other important occasion.

In making my selection of poultry recipes for this chapter, I looked primarily to poached or roasted whole chickens, which generally take longer to cook than birds that have been cut up. Most Italian chicken recipes specifically call for a *pollo ruspante,* that is, a bird that has spent time scratching around in an open space. In other words, Italians prefer free-range chickens, rather than the relatively tasteless, mass-produced, cage-confined birds common in many places.

Capon, with its dense and velvety meat, is greatly prized for special occasions in Italy, especially in Emilia-Romagna, Lombardy, Tuscany, and the Veneto. It is a male chicken that is castrated when it is sixty to seventy days old and then is slaughtered at seven months. Capons, which usually weigh six to eight pounds, are frequently poached, as they produce a highly flavorful broth, but they also can be roasted. The best capons have a creamy layer of fat under the skin that prevents the meat from becoming dry. Traditionally, Italian turkeys were not much larger than capons, typically weighing in at eight to ten pounds, but they boasted a particularly full flavor. Nowadays, some producers are raising large birds with big breasts, with hens weighing up to fifteen pounds and toms up to twenty-five pounds. Most Italian recipes, however, are for the smaller fowl.

Duck is popular throughout Italy, but particularly in the Veneto and Tuscany. It is sometimes roasted at a high temperature, perhaps 450°F, for an hour, but you can slow the oven down to 350°F and the timing to an hour and a half or two hours, and the more leisurely cooking will result in a bird with meltingly tender meat.

Pigeons, also known as squabs, are greatly prized in Umbria and the Veneto. Although many contemporary cooks serve up rare birds cooked at high temperatures, a squab's rich, dark meat lends itself to slow cooking. Quail are considered fine table fare in the Piedmont, the Marches, and the Veneto, where they are braised or grilled and often paired with rice or polenta.

Finally, this chapter includes a recipe for rabbit. Italians eat wild hare as well as rabbit, but because hare is difficult to find, I have used only rabbit here. Not every butcher shop carries rabbit either, however, and you may discover that you need to special order it.

Anatra in dolce e forte
Duck in a Sweet and Strong Sauce

SERVES 4

Dolce e forte literally translates as "sweet and strong." Here, strong means intense and spiced, but full flavored rather than spicy hot. The pine nuts and raisins are echoes of Arabic-inspired cookery, brought to Spain by the Moors. The chocolate came from the New World to Spain, then eventually from Spain to Sicily during the Spanish reign of the island. But, as with the tomato, it took a few centuries for chocolate to be used in cooking. The history of this dish is as complex as its flavors. Wild boar is prepared in the same way, sometimes with the addition of prunes.

1 duck, about 5 pounds, neck, wing tips, and excess fat removed, then quartered

Salt and freshly ground black pepper

2 tablespoons extra virgin olive oil

1 yellow onion, chopped

1 celery stalk, chopped

1 carrot, peeled and chopped

1/2 cup dry white wine

3/4 cup poultry or meat stock

1/4 cup pine nuts, toasted

1/4 cup raisins, plumped in hot water and drained

2 tablespoons grated bitter chocolate

1/2 cup red wine vinegar

About 1/4 cup balsamic vinegar

About 1 tablespoon sugar

Rinse the duck quarters and pat dry. Sprinkle with salt and pepper.

In a Dutch oven, heat the olive oil over medium heat. Add the onion, celery, and carrot and sauté until softened, about 8 minutes. Using a slotted spoon, transfer the vegetables to a plate and set aside.

Return the pan to medium-high heat and add the duck quarters to the fat remaining in it. Brown on all sides, about 10 minutes. Return the vegetables to the pan, add the wine, and cook for a few minutes until the liquid is reduced by half. Add the stock, reduce the heat to low, cover, and simmer until the duck is tender, 1 to 1 1/2 hours.

Remove the duck from the pan and set aside. Using a large spoon, skim off the excess fat from the pan juices. Add pine nuts, raisins, chocolate, and red wine vinegar to the pan juices and simmer over low heat for 5 minutes to blend the flavors. Taste and adjust the seasoning, adding the balsamic vinegar and the sugar in small increments until you achieve a good sweet-and-sour balance.

Return the duck to the pan and heat through. Serve at once.

WINE: *Look for wine based on the Nero d'Avola grape from Sicily, such as Cerasuolo di Vittoria from Cos, or a Frappato from Valle dell'Acate. You also cannot go wrong with a Rhône wine or a Rhône-style red or Zinfandel from California.*

Anatra con le lenticchie
Duck with Green Lentils

SERVES 4

Traditionally served on *Festa dei Santi*—All Saints' Day—duck with lentils is a specialty of the Lombard town of Pavia. The duck is cut up, browned in a pan with a *battuto* of chopped aromatic vegetables, and braised with white wine, much in the manner of the Venetian *sugo d'anatra* on page 56, and the lentils are served on the side. In Milan, the lentils are enriched with the addition of chopped sausage. Neapolitan cooks also combine duck with lentils, but they bone the duck and braise the meat along with the lentils. For greater ease of preparation, and versatility of serving options, I prefer to roast the duck slowly, cut it into serving pieces, and either serve it alongside the lentils, or rewarm it in the braised lentils. When reheating the duck in the lentils, the meat can be left on the bone, or it can be removed in the Neapolitan style.

FOR THE DUCK

1 duck, about 5 pounds, neck and wing tips removed, all excess fat removed, and fat rendered if desired

2 cloves garlic, minced

2 tablespoons grated lemon zest

Salt and freshly ground black pepper

1 fresh thyme sprig

Dry white wine for basting

Preheat the oven to 350°F.

Rinse the duck and pat dry. In a mortar using a pestle, pound together the garlic, lemon zest, and a little salt and pepper to make a paste. Rub the paste in the cavity and over the outside of the duck. Place the thyme sprig in the cavity. Using a fork, prick the duck all over so that the fat will drain away as it roasts. Place the duck, breast side up, on a rack in a roasting pan.

Roast the duck, basting occasionally with a little wine, until very tender when tested with a fork, 2 to 2 1/2 hours. Remove from the oven, let cool, and then cut into serving pieces. If you like, you can remove the meat from the bones for adding to the lentils in the Neapolitan style (see recipe introduction). Keep warm.

While the duck is roasting, cook the lentils: In a heavy saucepan, combine the lentils and water and bring to a boil over high heat. Reduce the heat to low, add 1 teaspoon salt, cover, and simmer until the lentils are tender but firm to the bite, about 30 minutes. Start testing for doneness after about 20 minutes. Soft lentils are fine for soup, but you want them to have a little bite when they are served this way. Remove from the heat and set aside.

FOR THE LENTILS

2 cups small green lentils, preferably Italian (page 25), picked over and rinsed

4¹/2 cups water

Salt

4 tablespoons unsalted butter, rendered duck fat, or olive oil

2 yellow onions, finely chopped

2 carrots, peeled and finely chopped

1 celery stalk, finely chopped

¹/4 pound pancetta, cut into ¹/4-inch dice

3 cloves garlic, minced

3 tablespoons chopped fresh flat-leaf parsley

1 tablespoon chopped fresh thyme

³/4 cup chicken stock

Freshly ground black pepper

In a large sauté pan, melt the butter or fat or heat the olive oil over low heat. Add the onions, carrots, celery, and pancetta and cook, stirring occasionally, until the vegetables have softened and the pancetta has started to color, 8 to 10 minutes. Add the garlic, parsley, and thyme and cook for 2 minutes longer.

If you want to serve the bone-in duck pieces or the pieces of duck meat mixed with the lentils, add them to the vegetables in the sauté pan along with the lentils and the stock and simmer for about 10 minutes to heat through. Season with salt and pepper.

Spoon the mixture of duck and lentils into a warmed serving dish, or spoon the lentils into a serving dish and arrange the duck pieces on a separate plate. Serve at once.

WINE: *You need a robust red here. From the region, try a Barbera from Vietti, San Fereolo, Giacomo Bologna, or Bartolo Mascarello. A Barbaresco, Barolo, Sangiovese, or a Cabernet blend like Tignanello or I Griffi would also pair well.*

NOTE: Roast duck can be reheated and recrisped. Cut it into halves or quarters, place the pieces skin side down in an ovenproof skillet (preferably cast iron), and slip into a 450° to 500°F oven for about 10 minutes. When you hear sizzling, it is ready.

Festa del Redentore

To celebrate the end of the plague of 1577, the Venetian Senate commissioned the building of the truly monumental Chiesa del Redentore on the Giudecca, which took a decade and a half to finish. Each year, a festival is held at the church on the third Sunday of July to remember the passing of the plague. The dish traditionally served on this day is *anitra col pien,* roast duck stuffed with a mixture of sausage, bread crumbs, *grana padano,* eggs, milk, rosemary, sage, and nutmeg.

SERVES 6

Although the title implies that this is a soup, do not be fooled. It is essentially a pigeon and bread pudding and is one of the stars of the Treviso kitchen. The earliest written record of the recipe appeared in 1886, when Venice was united with the rest of Italy, but the dish actually dates back to the Renaissance. Giuseppe Maffioli, in his book *La cucina veneziana*, suggests that the name may be related to a Sardinian dish called *quata* that is made with larks. The dialect name comes from the Italian *covare*, "to brood" or "to hatch." This *sopa* "broods" for at least three hours in the oven, until it is ready to hatch. As it is a specialty of the town of Treviso, home of radicchio, a radicchio salad after such a rich dish would not be out of place. :: *Sopa coada* is rustic in appearance and sophisticated in taste. While it does not make an elegant presentation, it impresses the diner with its deep flavors and rich texture. Traditionally, layers of country bread are topped with boned, braised pigeon, aromatic vegetables, and Parmesan cheese in a deep gratin dish, although today home cooks often substitute chickens for the more costly game birds. The mixture is then bathed with a rich stock and baked in the oven for many hours. The dish emerges golden, the stock fully absorbed, and the bread soft and custardy. Yes, this dish takes some work to make, but once it is assembled, it can be held in the refrigerator for a day, minus the stock topping. When you are ready to bake, ladle on the hot stock, sprinkle the top with Parmesan, and slip the dish in the oven.

3 pigeons (squabs), each about 1 pound, with livers

6 tablespoons unsalted butter, plus more for frying bread

2 tablespoons olive oil

1 large yellow onion, finely chopped

2 celery stalks, finely chopped

2 large carrots, peeled and finely chopped

1 cup dry white wine

8 cups chicken stock, or as needed

Salt and freshly ground black pepper

Pinch of ground cinnamon

Rinse the birds and pat dry. Cut into quarters and set aside. Reserve the livers.

In a wide saucepan, melt the 6 tablespoons butter with the olive oil over medium heat. Add the onion, celery, and carrots and sauté until well softened, about 10 minutes. Add the pigeon quarters and sauté, turning occasionally, until golden, 10 to 15 minutes. Pour in the wine and cook until it evaporates, 8 to 10 minutes. Then add the 8 cups chicken stock, a little salt and pepper, and a pinch of cinnamon. Reduce the heat to low, cover, and simmer until the pigeons are tender, about 30 minutes. Add the livers and simmer for 5 minutes longer.

Remove from the heat. Remove the pigeon pieces and the livers from the pan and, when cool enough to handle, carefully pull the meat from the bones. Cut any large pieces into bite-sized chunks. Cut the livers into small pieces. Set the meat and livers aside. Taste the stock that remains in the pan. If it is not as rich as you

1 1/2 pounds coarse country bread, sliced 1/2 inch thick and crusts removed

1/4 pound Parmesan cheese, preferably Parmigiano-Reggiano, grated

would like, strain it through a sieve, reserving the vegetables. Pour the stock into a saucepan, add the bones just stripped of meat, and boil over high heat until the flavor intensifies. Remove from the heat and measure the stock. You should have about 6 cups; add additional chicken stock as needed to reach that amount.

Meanwhile, melt 2 or 3 tablespoons butter in a large sauté pan over medium heat. Working in batches, add the bread slices and fry on both sides until pale gold, 3 to 5 minutes total, adding more butter as needed. Alternatively, toast the bread slices and spread them lightly with butter while they are still warm.

Preheat the oven to 300°F.

Line a gratin dish or other baking dish 3 to 4 inches deep and about 12 inches long with one-third of the bread. Sprinkle with one-fourth of the Parmesan, then top with half of the pigeon meat and livers and half of the aromatic vegetables. Lay half of the remaining bread over the vegetables, sprinkle with half of the remaining cheese, and then top with the remaining pigeon and aromatic vegetables. Lay the remaining bread on top and pour in the stock to cover. Sprinkle with the remaining Parmesan. Cover tightly with aluminum foil.

Bake the gratin for 3 hours, adding stock as needed. To judge if more stock is needed, push down on the bread with the back of a wooden spoon; if the mixture seems dry, add more stock.

To serve, cut into wedges or scoop out portions with a large spoon. Place in warmed soup bowls and top with a little hot stock and grated Parmesan.

WINE: *A special-occasion dish deserves a special-occasion wine. Now's the time for Maculan's Fratta, a Super Tuscan, or a rich Cabernet Sauvignon.*

Quaglie con salvia e uva
Quail with Sage and Grapes on a Bed of Polenta

SERVES 4

September is quail season in the Veneto, and it is also harvesttime in the vineyards, making this dish using quail, grapes, and sage a natural autumn dinner. As the Italians would say, *si sposa,* "it marries." You can also make it with poussins or Cornish hens, increasing the cooking time to about an hour and serving one per person. I have even seen versions of this recipe made with a small turkey. Serve the quail reclining on a bed *(sul letto)* of polenta. You can season the polenta with a bit of chopped sage to echo the sauce, or mix it with mashed or diced cooked butternut squash.

8 boneless quail

Salt and freshly ground black pepper

32 fresh sage leaves, plus 2 tablespoons chopped

3 cups seedless grapes, any color

2 tablespoons unsalted butter

2 tablespoons olive oil

2 cups chicken stock, reduced to 1 cup over high heat

2 cups polenta, cooked (page 89)

Rinse the quail and pat dry. Sprinkle inside and out with salt and pepper. Using your fingertips, carefully loosen the skin on each quail breast and slip 1 whole sage leaf under the skin on each side of the breast. Tuck 2 whole leaves inside each quail cavity.

In a blender or food processor, purée 2 cups of the grapes until smooth. Cut the remaining 1 cup grapes in half. Set aside the puréed grapes and halved grapes.

Preheat the oven to 350°F. Select a roasting pan just large enough to hold the birds.

In a large sauté pan, melt the butter with the olive oil over medium-high heat. Working in batches, brown the birds on all sides, turning often. Each batch should take about 15 minutes. Transfer the birds to the roasting pan. Set the sauté pan aside.

Roast the quail until their juices run clear when a thigh is pierced with a knife, 30 to 40 minutes (see note).

While the birds are roasting, add the reduced stock and grape purée to the sauté pan, place over high heat, and cook until reduced by half, about 10 minutes. Add the chopped sage and simmer to blend the flavors, about 5 minutes longer.

cont'd

When the quail are ready, remove from the oven and leave whole or cut in half lengthwise with poultry shears. Add the halved grapes to the sauce and warm gently. Spoon the polenta onto warmed individual plates and top with the quail. Spoon the sauce over and around the quail. Serve immediately.

WINE: *You can go white or red. For a white, go with a complex Soave from Inama or Pieropan, or a big Chardonnay. For a red, try a Pinot Nero from nearby Alto Adige, either from Alois Lageder or Cantina Terlano, or a Valpolicella.*

———————

NOTE: Most Italian recipes suggest cooking quail longer that the time given here, but I find that the boneless quail I buy cook rather quickly. Begin checking for doneness after 25 minutes.

Quaglie con piselli
Pancetta-Wrapped Quail with Spring Peas

SERVES 4

This quail recipe from the Campania is an ideal spring dish, as new peas are just starting to appear at the market. In a similar recipe from the Marches, the pancetta wrap is dropped, but strips of prosciutto are added to the braising pan along with the peas. If you like their slightly gamier flavor, pigeons (squabs) may be prepared the same way. Allow one per person and adjust the braising time to 1¼ hours. Serve the quail and peas with chive mashed potatoes or polenta, or on a bed of risotto.

8 boneless quail

Salt and freshly ground black pepper

2 cloves garlic, slivered

8 small fresh rosemary sprigs

8 slices pancetta

4 tablespoons olive oil or unsalted butter

1 yellow onion, chopped

1½ cups dry white wine, or half each wine and poultry stock

2 cups shelled fresh English peas or thawed, frozen peas

Rinse the quail and pat dry. Sprinkle inside and out with salt and pepper. Slip an equal amount of the garlic slivers and 1 rosemary sprig into the cavity of each bird. Wrap each bird in a slice of pancetta and secure in place with kitchen string.

In a large sauté pan, heat the olive oil or melt the butter over medium heat. Add the onion and sauté until softened, about 8 minutes. Add the birds and cook, turning them often, until the birds and the onion are golden brown, about 20 minutes. Add the wine or wine and stock, reduce the heat to low, cover, and simmer until the quail are very tender, 25 to 30 minutes longer.

Transfer the quail to a heated platter and keep warm. Add the peas to the sauce in the pan, place over medium heat, and cook briefly until heated through. Taste and adjust the seasoning. Spoon the sauce over the quail and serve at once.

WINE: *The best choice is the local Aglianico. The Taurasi DOC should be the easiest red wine from Campania to find. Look for Caggiano, Villa Matilde, or Terredora.*

Poached Capon with Walnut and Bread Stuffing

SERVES 6

Italians appreciate the moist texture of poached foods. The flavors are usually mild, but they are commonly spiced up at the table with wonderful condiments such as *salsa verde* (page 182) and *mostarda di frutta* (page 180). The walnut stuffing for this Lombardian poached bird is quite rich and flavorful, so you may want to serve only vegetables, and not a starch, along-side. Cooks in the Trentino, to the northeast of Lombardy, also make a popular walnut stuffing for poultry. :: Capon is a flavorful and densely textured bird. Because of the compactness of its flesh, it may seem dry to some palates. It is also an expensive bird, usually must be special ordered, and some cooks may find it diffcult to lift the plump bird from its poaching broth. If you feel this will be the case, I suggest that you cook a large roaster of about 6 pounds, or two smaller chickens of about 4 pounds each; the former will cook in about 1 1/2 hours, and the latter in about 1 hour. They will have a softer texture and be easier to handle.

1 capon, about 8 pounds

Fresh lemon juice

Salt

2 cups walnuts, toasted and coarsely chopped

1 1/2 cups fresh bread crumbs

1/2 cup grated Parmesan cheese

4 tablespoons unsalted butter, melted

1/2 cup heavy cream, or as needed

3 egg yolks

Freshly ground black pepper

1 or 2 pinches of freshly grated nutmeg

Pinch of ground cinnamon

1 large yellow onion, chopped

Rinse the capon and pat dry with paper towels. Rub lemon juice and salt in the cavity and over the outside of the bird.

In a mortar using a pestle, crush the nuts (or pulse in a food processor). Transfer to a bowl and stir in the bread crumbs, cheese, butter, 1/2 cup cream, and egg yolks. Season with a little salt and pepper and the nutmeg and cinnamon. If the stuffing seems too stiff, add a little more cream.

Spoon the nut mixture into the neck and body cavities of the capon and sew the cavities closed with kitchen string. If you like, wrap the bird in a large piece of cheesecloth. It will be easier to remove it from the pot when it is cooked—you will be able to grab the tails of the knot—and it will help keep the stuffing in place.

Bring a large kettle of water to a boil. Place the bird in a large Dutch oven or soup pot and pour in the boiling water to cover. Place over medium heat, add the onion, carrots, celery, and herb sachet, and bring to a gentle boil. Skim off any scum that forms on the surface. Reduce the heat to low, cover, and simmer until the juices run clear when you pierce a thigh joint with a skewer or an instant-read thermometer inserted into a thigh away from bone registers 165° to 170°F, about 2 hours.

2 carrots, peeled and chopped

2 celery stalks, chopped

4 or 5 fresh flat-leaf parsley sprigs, 1 bay leaf, and 1 fresh thyme sprig, tied in a cheesecloth sachet

Mostarda di frutta

Carefully lift the bird from the broth and place it on a platter. (You may strain the broth through a fine-mesh sieve, boil it until it is reduced by half, and then reserve it for using in soups or other dishes.) If you have used cheesecloth, remove and discard it. Cut the strings on the cavities, and scoop the stuffing into a bowl. Carve the bird and serve along with spoonfuls of the stuffing. Pass *mostarda di frutta* at the table.

WINE: *Red or white will work here, but a local wine may be difficult to find. Look to northern Lombardy to the Valtellina for a Nebbiolo from Negri. Or, cross over into the Piedmont for a Dolcetto from Albona, Villa Sparina, or San Fereolo. For a white, try Gavi di Gavi from Villa Sparina or a Lugano DOC white from Zenato.*

VARIATIONS: If the heart and liver are included with the capon, you can chop them, sauté them in a little butter until lightly browned, season with salt and freshly ground black pepper, and then add them to stuffing. Or, you can add 1/4 pound pancetta, chopped, to the stuffing.

If you prefer to roast the capon, stuff as directed and rub the outside of the bird with softened unsalted butter and freshly ground black pepper in addition to the lemon juice and salt. Omit all the ingredients that go into the broth. Place the capon, breast side up, on a rack in a roasting pan and roast in a 400°F oven until the juices run clear when you pierce a thigh joint with a skewer or an instant-read thermometer inserted into a thigh away from bone registers 165° to 170°F, about 2 hours. If desired, baste with cream during the last 30 minutes of roasting. If you use a large roasting chicken or 2 smaller chickens, reduce the cooking time to 1 1/4 hours and 1 hour, respectively.

Roast Turkey Glazed with Pomegranate and Orange

SERVES 6 TO 8

This is a Renaissance-inspired recipe from the Veneto, known in the local dialect as *paeta al malgarano*. If you are not in the mood to roast a turkey, you might try the pomegranate sauce with duck, as its rich meat and skin are wonderful with this tart-sweet mixture. Cornish hens, poussins, or even a large roasting chicken would work as well. Garnish the plate with a sprinkling of ruby red pomegranate seeds if they are in season, and serve with saffron-tinged risotto and sautéed spinach, for the joy of color, or Braised Radicchio with Balsamic Vinegar (double recipe; page 250) or Slow-Roasted Onions with Aged Balsamic Vinegar (page 263).

1 turkey, 8 to 10 pounds

Juice of 4 pomegranates (about 1 cup), reduced to ¹/₂ cup over high heat, or ¹/₂ cup pomegranate molasses (see note)

1 cup fresh regular orange or blood orange juice

¹/₂ cup honey, or to taste

2 cups chicken stock, reduced to 1 cup over high heat

2 tablespoons grated orange zest

Salt and freshly ground black pepper

1 cup pomegranate seeds (optional)

Preheat the oven to 350°F.

Rinse the turkey and pat dry. Place on a rack in a roasting pan.

In a small bowl, combine the reduced pomegranate juice or pomegranate molasses, orange juice, and ¹/₂ cup honey. Taste and adjust with more honey if more sweetness is desired. You should have about 2 cups. Measure out 1 cup and set aside for finishing the sauce. Use the remaining cup for basting the bird.

Roast the turkey, basting every 20 minutes with the pomegranate mixture, until the juices run clear when you pierce a thigh joint with a skewer or an instant-read thermometer inserted into a thigh away from bone registers 165°F, about 2¹/₂ hours. Transfer the turkey to a carving board and let rest for 15 minutes before carving.

While the turkey is resting, make the sauce: In a small saucepan, combine the reserved pomegranate mixture, the reduced stock, and orange zest over low heat and simmer for a few minutes. Season to taste with salt and pepper.

Carve the turkey and arrange on a platter. Spoon the sauce over the meat, and garnish with the pomegranate seeds, if desired. Serve at once.

WINE: *A Merlot or Valpolicella from the Veneto is a superb match for the bird. Look for Valpolicella producers such as Bussola, Allegrini, Corte Sant'Alda, and Tenuta di Sant'Antonio. If you prefer an Amarone, try one from Allegrini, Bussola, or Quintarelli. You might even try a Barbera, a Dolcetto, or a ripe fruity Zinfandel.*

VARIATIONS: You can substitute 2 ducks (5 pounds each), 6 Cornish hens or poussins, or a large roasting chicken (6 to 7 pounds) for the turkey. The ducks and large chicken will roast in about $1^1/_2$ to 2 hours, and the Cornish hens and poussins will be ready in about 1 hour. Baste them all often with the pomegranate-orange mixture, and carve the ducks and chickens into serving pieces. Cut the whole smaller birds in half lengthwise to serve.

NOTE: Pomegranate molasses is available at stores that specialize in Middle Eastern foods. Cortas is an excellent brand.

Chicken with Sweet Peppers, Pancetta, and Marjoram

SERVES 4

Chicken with peppers is popular all over the boot. This recipe could be from the Abruzzo, except for the absence of hot peppers. It could be from Calabria, but it would need hot peppers, raisins, and pine nuts. Apulian cooks make the dish sweet and sour, while *pollo alla romana* adds chopped prosciutto and a pinch of hot pepper to the *battuto*, uses white wine instead of red, and stirs in peeled and sliced roasted peppers at the last minute. In the Piedmont, the locals make this dish with rabbit. So this leaves us with Umbria or Tuscany. While any region would be proud to claim this delicious dish of chicken with sweet peppers, the pancetta-marjoram mixture tilts it in the direction of Umbria.

3 pounds chicken parts, or 1 chicken, cut into serving pieces

Salt and freshly ground black pepper

6 tablespoons olive oil

2 yellow onions, chopped

2 carrots, peeled and chopped

2 celery stalks, chopped

2 tablespoons finely minced garlic

2 ounces pancetta, chopped

2 tablespoons chopped fresh marjoram

4 large yellow or red bell peppers, seeded and cut lengthwise into 1/2-inch-wide strips

4 large tomatoes, peeled, seeded, and cut into 1/2-inch-wide strips, with juice

1 1/2 cups dry red wine

Rinse the chicken and pat dry with paper towels. Sprinkle with salt and pepper.

In a large sauté pan, heat 4 tablespoons of the olive oil over high heat. Add the chicken pieces and brown on all sides, 10 to 15 minutes. Remove from the heat and set aside.

In a large saucepan, heat the remaining 2 tablespoons olive oil over medium heat. Add the onions, carrots, and celery and sauté until golden, about 12 minutes. Add the garlic, pancetta, marjoram, and bell peppers and sauté until well blended, about 5 minutes. Add the chicken, tomatoes and their juice, and wine, raise the heat to high, and bring to a boil. Quickly reduce the heat to low, cover, and simmer until the chicken is tender, 30 to 40 minutes.

Transfer the chicken and its sauce to a warmed platter and serve at once.

WINE. *A medium-bodied red is the best choice. To stay local, try Montepulciano d'Abruzzo or Rosso Conero. From neighboring Molise, try the Sangiovese from Di Majo Norante. Rosso di Montalcino would also stand up to the assertive peppers.*

Pollo allo spiedo
Spit-Roasted Stuffed Chicken

SERVES 4

Even if you don't have a rotisserie, you still can prepare this tasty chicken from the Tuscan town of Arezzo. Just place the chicken on a lightly oiled rack and roast it in the oven. If you can get *lardo,* chop a few ounces and add it to the stuffing. It melts and moistens the bird as it cooks. Roast or panfried potatoes are the perfect accompaniment, and perhaps some green beans.

1 chicken, about 4 pounds

3 ounces prosciutto, plus a few thin slices if spit roasting

2 ounces lardo *(page 211) or pancetta, chopped*

4 cloves garlic

10 large fresh sage leaves

1¹/2 tablespoons fennel seeds, toasted in a dry pan and chopped in a spice grinder

Salt and freshly ground black pepper

Extra virgin olive oil

Rinse the chicken and pat dry with paper towels. The seasoning paste you make can be slipped under the skin of breast, rubbed into the body cavity, or divided between the two. If you want to stuff some or all of it under the breast skin, use your fingertips to loosen the skin, being careful not to tear it.

Place the 3 ounces prosciutto, the *lardo* or pancetta, 3 cloves of the garlic, 8 of the sage leaves, and the chopped fennel seeds on a cutting board and chop together finely to form a paste. Season the paste with 1 teaspoon each salt and pepper. Carefully slip the paste under the breast skin and/or into the cavity. Rub the outside of the chicken with olive oil, season with salt and pepper, cover, and refrigerate for a few hours.

If you are using a rotisserie, prepare a fire in a charcoal or gas grill for spit roasting. If you are using the oven, preheat it to 400°F.

Smash the remaining garlic clove and insert it in the neck cavity of the bird along with the remaining 2 sage leaves.

If you are using a rotisserie, truss the chicken, then wrap it in a few slices of prosciutto and secure them in place with kitchen string. Spit roast the chicken until the juices run clear when you pierce a thigh joint with a skewer or an instant-read thermometer inserted into a thigh away from bone registers 165° to 170°F, about 1 hour.

If you are using the oven, place the chicken, breast side up, on a rack in a roasting pan. Roast until the juices run clear when you pierce a thigh joint with a skewer or an instant-read thermometer inserted into a thigh away from bone registers 165° to 170°F, 1 1/4 to 1 1/2 hours.

Transfer the chicken to a carving board and let rest for 15 minutes, then carve into serving pieces. Arrange on a warmed platter and serve at once.

WINE: *Pour a Chianti Classico from Badia a Coltibuono, Castello di Volpaia, or your own favorite producer.*

VARIATION: Cooks in Umbria prepare *pollo in porchetta,* which is similar to this Tuscan chicken, but alters the seasonings slightly in the stuffing paste. To prepare it, chop together 2 ounces prosciutto, 2 ounces *lardo* or pancetta, 2 cloves garlic, and 2 tablespoons fresh rosemary leaves. Add 1/4 cup chopped fresh fennel fronds or 1 tablespoon fennel seeds, toasted in a dry pan and chopped, and season with 1 teaspoon each salt and freshly ground black pepper. Slip the paste under the breast skin and/or rub it in the cavity and tuck under the skin of the chicken. Rub the outside of the chicken with olive oil, salt, pepper, and a bit more chopped rosemary. Roast in the oven as directed for the Tuscan chicken.

NOTE: You can use the same herb and spice pastes in the main recipe and the variation with pigeon (squab) or duck. Also, if you are feeling a bit lazy, you can assemble the paste in a small food processor.

SERVES 4 TO 6

Sardinian cooks make wonderful stuffed chicken dishes. In Cagliari, the island's largest city, the locals stuff chickens and then simmer them in broth, rather than roast them. The rich broth is then used to poach meatballs for serving alongside the chicken and stuffing, or you can use the broth to cook the meatballs, adding some *fregola* pasta (page 30) as well, if desired, and offer the simple meatball soup before the chicken. The bird is also good served at room temperature on a bed of fresh bay leaves with the cold stuffing alongside. Again, the meatball soup is an excellent *primo*.

1 chicken, about 5 pounds

FOR THE STUFFING

³/4 cup raisins, plumped in hot water and drained

1 cup dried bread crumbs

¹/4 cup chopped walnuts

2 eggs

3 tablespoons unsalted butter, at room temperature

2 teaspoons sugar

¹/2 teaspoon ground cinnamon

¹/2 teaspoon saffron threads, crushed and steeped in 2 tablespoons hot water for 15 minutes

Grated zest of 1 lemon

Rinse the chicken and pat dry with paper towels.

To make the stuffing, in a bowl, combine the raisins, bread crumbs, walnuts, eggs, butter, sugar, cinnamon, saffron infusion, and lemon zest. Mix well.

Spoon the raisin mixture into the neck and body cavities of the chicken and sew the cavities closed with kitchen string. If you like, wrap the bird in a large piece of cheesecloth. It will be easier to remove it from the pot when it is cooked—you will be able to grab the tails of the knot—and it will help keep the stuffing in place.

Put the chicken in a large Dutch oven or soup pot and add the celery, onion, carrot, sun-dried tomatoes, and parsley and mint sprigs. Add water to cover, place over medium heat, and bring to a gentle boil. Skim off any scum that forms on the surface. Reduce the heat to low, cover, and simmer until the juices run clear when you pierce a thigh joint with a skewer or an instant-read thermometer inserted into a thigh away from bone registers 165° to 170°F, about 1 hour.

1 celery stalk, chopped

1 yellow onion, chopped

1 carrot, peeled and chopped

4 to 6 olive oil–packed sun-dried tomatoes

2 fresh flat-leaf parsley sprigs

2 fresh mint sprigs

FOR THE MEATBALLS

2/3 pound ground beef

2 slices coarse country bread, crusts removed, soaked in milk, and squeezed almost dry

1/2 cup mashed cooked potato

1 egg

6 tablespoons grated pecorino cheese

3 tablespoons chopped fresh flat-leaf parsley

Salt and freshly ground black pepper

While the chicken is cooking, make the meatballs: In a bowl, combine the beef, bread, potato, egg, cheese, parsley, and a little salt and pepper and mix well. Scoop out a small amount of the broth from the chicken pot, place in a small saucepan over medium heat, and bring to a simmer. Shape a small nugget of the beef mixture, add to the simmering broth, and poach until cooked through. Taste and adjust the seasoning of the beef mixture. Form the beef mixture into walnut sized balls and set aside.

When the chicken is ready, carefully lift it from the broth and place it on a platter. Return the broth to a simmer, add the meatballs, and poach gently until cooked through, about 15 minutes.

Meanwhile, if you have used cheesecloth, remove it from the chicken and discard. Cut the strings on the cavities, and scoop the stuffing into a bowl. Carve the bird into serving pieces and arrange on a warmed platter. When the meatballs are ready, use a slotted spoon to lift them from the broth and arrange them along side the chicken. Serve at once.

WINE: *For a local wine, pour a Cannonau. A Salice Salentino from Apulia or a California Zinfandel would also be good.*

SERVES 6 TO 8

Coniglio in agrodolce, or sweet-and-sour sauce, is sometimes called *coniglio alla stemperata,* a term used for dishes that include the addition of vinegar at the end of cooking to temper the sauce. In Calabria, such a preparation would be relatively simple, with the rabbit braised in wine and/or wine vinegar. But in the Sicilian city of Syracuse, cooks prepare dishes to satisfy the local sweet tooth, which means that raisins, pine nuts, and a little sugar are added to the pot. This dish is traditionally made with wild hare, but rabbit—or even chicken—works well in place of the game.

2 rabbits, 2 1/2 to 3 pounds each, cut into serving pieces

FOR THE MARINADE

1 large yellow onion, sliced

2 carrots, peeled and chopped

2 celery stalks, chopped

2 bay leaves

4 juniper berries, crushed

3 tablespoons olive oil

1 cup red wine vinegar

1 cup dry red wine, or as needed

Rinse the rabbit pieces and pat dry with paper towels.

To make the marinade, in a nonreactive container, combine the onion, carrots, celery, bay leaves, juniper berries, and olive oil. Add the rabbit pieces and then pour in the vinegar and enough red wine to just cover the rabbit pieces. Cover and marinate at room temperature for 2 hours.

Remove the rabbit pieces from the marinade and pat dry. Sprinkle with salt and pepper. Strain the marinade and reserve.

In a large sauté pan, heat the olive oil over high heat. Working in batches, brown the rabbit pieces quickly on all sides, about 10 minutes for each batch. As each batch is ready, use a slotted spoon to transfer it to a Dutch oven.

Return the sauté pan to medium heat, add the pancetta, and cook until it renders its fat, 3 to 5 minutes. Add the onions and sauté until softened, 8 to 10 minutes. Add the sage (if using) and cook for about 2 minutes.

Add the onions to the rabbit and enough marinade almost to cover. Bring to a boil over medium-high heat, reduce the heat to low, cover, and simmer until the rabbit is just tender, about 45 minutes. Add the olives, capers, raisins, and pine nuts and simmer for 10 minutes longer to blend the flavors.

Salt and freshly ground black pepper

2 tablespoons olive oil

¹⁄₄ pound pancetta, diced

2 yellow onions, sliced

3 or 4 fresh sage leaves (optional)

24 full-flavored green olives, pitted

3 tablespoons capers, rinsed

¹⁄₂ cup golden or dark raisins, plumped in hot water and drained

¹⁄₂ cup pine nuts

Sugar and red wine vinegar as needed to balance sauce

If the sauce is too thin, transfer the rabbit to a platter and keep it warm while you reduce the sauce over high heat until thickened. Taste the sauce and adjust the sweet-and-sour balance with sugar and/or vinegar. Serve the rabbit with the sauce spooned over the top.

WINE: *Try to find a Sicilian red such as a Syrah from Aziende Vinicole Miceli, a rosso from Spadafora or Planeta, or a Nero d'Avola from Cos or Duca di Salaparuta. A Cabernet from Tasca d'Almerita Regaleali or Abbazia Sant'Anastasia would also be a fine choice.*

VARIATIONS: To make *coniglio alla valleogrina*, a specialty of the Leogra Valley in the Veneto, omit the capers, olives, and pancetta. Make sure that the livers come with the rabbits, then chop them along with a sweet sausage and sauté in butter and olive oil along with the onion. Other recipes call for dusting the rabbit pieces with flour before browning them, or for adding a few tablespoons tomato purée to the sauce.

MEATS

The vocabulary surrounding the cooking of meat in Italy is rich in variety. For example, the Italians have a wealth of different terms for roasted and braised meats alone. When meat is braised in one piece it can be called a *brasato* or a *stracotto*. *Arrosto* can mean *arrosto al forno,* basically an oven roast such as roast chicken or roast beef, or a roast cooked on a spit over an open fire, sometimes also called *girarrosto,* or "turning roast." If the meat is cooked in the oven and there is liquid in the pan in the manner of a braise, the dish still can be termed *arrosto*. In fact, *arrosto morto,* the "dead roast," a term used for veal, lamb, pork, or even chicken, calls for searing the meat in oil and then braising it on the stove top. In Emilia-Romagna, the term *arrosto matto,* "crazy roast," implies a gastronomic stunt because the meat is braised without an initial browning in fat such as oil or butter. More often than not it refers to a stout leg of lamb studded with garlic and rosemary and simmered slowly in a covered casserole with white wine, with a bit of tomato paste or chopped tomatoes added near the end of cooking.

Many meat dishes are also named according to how they are shaped. The term *rollata* or *rotolo* signals that the meat is rolled and stuffed, while the term *rollatine* is used for small stuffed rolls, usually of beef or veal. A *braciola* is a chop, but it can also mean a piece of meat that is stuffed and rolled; most sources suggest that it takes its name from *brace,* the spit used for roasting meat, even if the meat is braised rather than cooked on a spit. A *braciolona* is a large meat roll, while *involtini* are small meat rolls. If the meat is cut into pieces, it can be called *stufato* (stew), *stufatino* (little stew), *bocconcini* (little mouthfuls), or *spezzatini* (literally "broken pieces"). Stews are named after cooking vessels, too, such as *tegame, tegamino, pigneti or pignata, caldaio,* and *calderotto.*

In Italy, meat is traditionally served as a second course, after a first course of soup, pasta, or risotto. If the braised meat produces rich and abundant pan juices, these are used as a sauce, or *sugo,* to dress pasta at another meal. (Serving pasta as a side dish along with a stew, roast, or braise is mainly an Italian-American tradition.) Leftover braised meat is often chopped and used as a filling for ravioli and cannelloni.

The classic accompaniment for most stews is the potato, roasted, boiled, or mashed. Sometimes toasted or grilled bread or grilled or baked polenta is served in place of potatoes.

Beef and Veal

In Italy, bovine categories range from youth to age: *vitello, vitellone, manzo, bue, vacca,* and *toro.* The recipe terms you will see most often are *vitello* and *manzo. Bue* is an old-fashioned name for a castrated male animal over four years of age. Most Italian *manzo* comes from an animal three to four years old. Veal is milk-fed with pale pink meat, while baby beef, or *vitellone,* is older, eighteen to twenty-four months of age, and the meat is darker, indicating the animal has eaten grain and grazed on grass. True veal is prized more than beef because of its delicate flavor and pale hue.

For the most part, Italian butchers portion meat differently than many butchers elsewhere, and even the different regions identify the same cuts by different names. Italians do not have chuck, London broil, or top round, for example, but they do have *scamone* (sort of a culotte steak), *noce* (a cut between the short loin and the flank), and *lacerto* (round steak or rump). To accommodate these differences, I have made some decisions as to what cuts of beef will work with Italy's traditional recipes.

Italian beef is of good quality, though generally it is not as well marbled or as tender as beef in the United States. Because of this, I found that some beef recipes I tested cooked more quickly than they do when using Italian-raised beef. They are still slow and savory, however. When making a stew, look for meat with some marbling, such as chuck or brisket. For most of the pot roasts, I have used rump roast or top round.

Bue brasato al Barolo
Beef Braised in Barolo Wine

SERVES 6

Braised beef from the Piedmont uses the famed Barolo wine of the region. While you may use another big red wine, try making this recipe with the regional classic at least once. It's a perfect fit, so drink some with your dinner, too, to get a true sense of Piedmontese *terroir*. Serve the beef with polenta or mashed potatoes.

4 strips pancetta, each 4 inches long and
¹/4 inch wide

1 beef rump roast, about 3 pounds

FOR THE MARINADE
1 bottle Barolo wine

1 yellow onion, chopped

2 celery stalks, chopped

3 fresh thyme sprigs

2 cloves garlic, smashed

1 bay leaf

3 tablespoons unsalted butter or chopped
pancetta fat

¹/3 cup grappa or other brandy

¹/4 cup prepared mustard, or to taste (optional)

¹/4 cup tomato purée (optional)

If you are skilled with a larding needle, thread the pancetta strips through the heart of the roast. If not, cut the pancetta strips into 1-inch pieces. Using a small, sharp knife, make small slits all over the surface of the beef and insert the pancetta pieces into the slits. Either technique will moisten the meat from within while it braises.

To make the marinade, in a shallow, nonreactive bowl just large enough to hold the roast, stir together the wine, onion, celery, thyme, garlic, and bay leaf. Add the roast, turn to coat, cover, and refrigerate for at least 8 hours or for up to 2 days. Remove the meat from the refrigerator about 30 minutes before you begin cooking.

Remove the meat from the marinade and pat dry with paper towels; reserve the marinade. In a Dutch oven or a deep, heavy sauté pan, melt the butter or render the pancetta fat over medium-high heat. Add the roast and brown on all sides, 10 to 15 minutes. Deglaze the pan with the brandy, scraping up the brown bits. Reduce the heat to medium, add the marinade, and bring to a boil. Reduce the heat to low, cover, and simmer until tender, 2¹/2 to 3 hours.

Transfer the meat to a carving board and cover with aluminum foil to keep warm. Pour the contents of the pan through a sieve placed over a clean saucepan. Discard the thyme sprigs and bay leaf, then purée the vegetables in a food mill or a food processor. Add the puréed vegetables to the pan juices, stir well, and simmer over low heat for 10 minutes to blend the flavors. Add the mustard or tomato purée, if desired, but not both. Adjust the seasoning.

Slice the roast and serve hot, with the pan juices spooned over the top.

WINE: *Barolo is the choice here. Go with a traditional producer such as Marcarini or Vietti, or with a modernist such as Clerico or Seghesio.*

Garofolato di manzo alla romana
Clove-Scented Beef from Rome

SERVES 6

Cloves are called *chiodi di garofano*. *Garofano* alone means "carnation," a flower that I—and the Italians, too, I suspect—believe has a spicy scent. The perfume of clove permeates this dish, but it is not cloying or overpowering. Traditionally, the Roman *garofolato* is prepared with a single large piece of meat, such as a rump roast. The meat is served as a separate course and the pan juices are used as a sauce for pasta. Like most braises, *garofolato* can be cooked the day before and reheated. And yes, it is delicious served with mashed potatoes. Any leftover beef can be shredded and used as a filling for cannolloni.

¹/2 cup olive oil, or as needed

1 rump roast or top round roast, about 3 pounds

¹/2 pound pancetta, cut into ¹/2-inch dice

3 large yellow onions, chopped (4 to 5 cups)

6 carrots, peeled and chopped (about 2 cups)

3 celery stalks, chopped (about 1 cup)

2 tablespoons minced garlic

1 teaspoon ground cloves

2 teaspoons chopped thyme

6 tablespoons tomato paste

2 cups dry red wine

2 cups beef stock

6 orange zest strips, each 2 inches long (optional)

Salt and freshly ground black pepper

Place a large, deep skillet over high heat and film the bottom with olive oil. Add the roast and brown on all sides, 10 to 15 minutes. Set aside.

Place a large Dutch oven over medium heat and film the bottom with olive oil. Add the pancetta and let it render some of its fat, 3 to 5 minutes. Add the onions, carrots, and celery and cook, stirring occasionally, until softened, about 10 minutes. Add the garlic, cloves, and thyme and cook for 2 minutes to blend the flavors. Stir in the tomato paste, then add the beef, wine, stock, and the orange zest, if using. Bring to a gentle boil, reduce the heat to low, cover, and simmer until the beef is very tender, 2¹/2 to 3 hours.

Season to taste with salt and pepper, then serve.

WINE: *If you want a big red from Lazio, Falesco's Montiano may be the only choice. Look outside the area for a Rosso di Montalcino, a Morellino di Scansano, or a Tuscan Cabernet blend.*

VARIATIONS: You can add 6 to 8 additional celery stalks (a favorite Roman vegetable), cut into 2-inch lengths and blanched, during the last 30 minutes of cooking. If you are in the mood for stew, you can use boneless brisket or chuck cut into 2-inch cubes in place of the roast. You can also braise the roast or stew in a 325°F oven—it will take the same amount of time as on the stove top—or you can reduce the liquids by half, put everything in a slow cooker, and cook on low for 5¹/2 to 6 hours.

Manzo alla California
Braised Beef Roast with Cream

SERVES 6

No, this is not California cuisine. It is instead an old Milanese recipe, adapted from the book *La cucina degli stomachi debole* (Cooking for delicate stomachs) written in 1862. The dish takes its name from a farming area near the town of Lesmo in Lombardy, north of Milan. The cream is added to tenderize the meat. In some versions of the recipe, the cream is added at the end of cooking, and in others the beef cooks in a mixture of stock and cream. In neighboring towns, milk is used place of cream. Milk will curdle, however, and you will need to emulsify the sauce in a blender before it can be served. With cream, the sauce remains smooth and rich. You can also cook this roast in a covered pot in a 300°F oven for 2 1/2 hours.

4 strips pancetta, each 4 inches long and 1/4 inch wide

1 rump roast or top round roast, 2 1/2 to 3 pounds

About 1/2 cup all-purpose flour

Salt and freshly ground black pepper

2 tablespoons unsalted butter

2 tablespoons olive oil

1 yellow onion, quartered and each quarter studded with 2 whole cloves

1/2 cup red wine vinegar

Freshly grated nutmeg

1 1/2 cups beef stock

1 cup heavy cream

If you are skilled with a larding needle, thread the pancetta strips through the heart of the roast. If not, cut the pancetta strips into 1-inch pieces. Using a small, sharp knife, make small slits all over the surface of the meat and insert the pancetta pieces into the slits. Either technique will moisten the meat from within while it braises.

Using kitchen string, tie the roast into a compact shape. Spread the flour on a platter and season it with salt and pepper. Dust the roast on all sides with the seasoned flour, shaking off the excess.

In a Dutch oven or other heavy pot, melt the butter with the oil over medium-high heat. Add the onion and sauté until browned, about 10 minutes. Using a slotted spoon, remove and discard the onion quarters. Add the roast to the onion-scented butter and brown on all sides, 10 to 15 minutes.

Spoon out the excess fat from the pan. Add the vinegar and a generous addition of nutmeg and cook over medium heat until the vinegar evaporates, 5 to 8 minutes. Pour in the stock and 1/2 cup of the cream. Bring to a gentle boil, reduce the heat to very low, cover, and simmer until the beef is tender, 2 1/2 to 3 hours.

Transfer the meat to a carving board and cover with aluminum foil to keep warm. Add the remaining $1/2$ cup cream to the pan and cook over high heat until the sauce is reduced by half, 10 to 15 minutes. Taste and adjust the seasoning.

Slice the roast and serve hot, with the pan juices spooned over the top.

WINE: *Go with a Barbera for earthiness, a Dolcetto for rich, juicy sweetness, or a Merlot as a compromise between the two.*

———————————

VARIATION: Cooks in Trento make *manzo brasato alla vecchia Trento,* which is similar to the Lombardian beef and cream dish. But they chop the onion and cook it and a little rosemary along with the beef and cream, and then strain them out before serving the pan sauce. In Ravenna, the locals prepare *stufato al latte,* beef stew braised in milk and rum, with pearl onions added near the end of cooking.

Brasato di manzo al Rosso Conero
Cocoa-Crusted Beef Braised in Rosso Conero Wine

SERVES 4

This unusual *brasato* is a specialty of Osteria dei Fiori in Macerata in the Marches, the region where Rosso Conero wine is produced. While grated bitter chocolate is often used to deepen *dolce e forte*—"sweet and strong"—dishes, in which it is paired with pine nuts, raisins, and sometimes dried fruit, here it is used in the form of cocoa powder, adding a subtle rich undertone to a red wine sauce. Serve with mashed potatoes and braised cabbage.

1 rump roast or top sirloin roast, about
2 pounds, tied into a compact shape

Salt and freshly ground black pepper

1/4 cup all-purpose flour

1/4 cup unsweetened cocoa powder

3 tablespoons olive oil

3 tablespoons unsalted butter

1 yellow onion, chopped

1 carrot, peeled and chopped

1 celery stalk, chopped

2 tablespoons chopped fresh flat-leaf parsley

2 tablespoons chopped fresh rosemary

2 bay leaves

2 cloves garlic, chopped

1 bottle Rosso Conero or other dry red wine

Sprinkle the meat with salt and pepper. On a large plate, stir together the flour and cocoa. Dust the roast on all sides with the flour-cocoa mixture, shaking off the excess and reserving it.

In a heavy skillet, heat the olive oil over high heat. Add the roast and brown on all sides, 10 to 15 minutes. Set aside.

In a Dutch oven, melt the butter over medium heat. Add the onion, carrot, celery, parsley, rosemary, bay leaves, and garlic and sauté until softened, 8 to 10 minutes. Add the browned meat and the wine and bring to a gentle boil. Reduce the heat to low, cover, and simmer until the meat is tender, about 2 1/2 hours.

Transfer the meat to a carving board and cover with aluminum foil to keep warm. Remove and discard the bay leaves. If the sauce is too thin, reduce over high heat to a satisfactory consistency, adding 2 tablespoons of the reserved flour-cocoa mixture as the sauce reduces.

Slice the roast and serve hot, with the pan juices spooned over the top.

WINE: *Look for a Rosso Conero from Umani Ronchi or Moroder. If you cannot find one, look for its neighbor, a Rosso Piceno from Ercole Velenosi, or shift to Umbria for a Sagrantino di Montefalco. This is also a good time to drink a California Sangiovese.*

VARIATION: To prepare this recipe in a slow cooker, reduce the wine by half and cook on low for about 5 1/2 hours.

Arrosto di manzo alle erbe
Beef Roast with Herbs and Horseradish

SERVES 6

Grating fresh horseradish root over cooked meats is a common culinary practice in Trieste. Although I have most often enjoyed this piquant accent as a topping for cooked pork, here's a recipe for a beef roast that gets the pungent garnish. A sharp grater such as a Microplane (based on the carpenter's rasp) will speed up the grating process and spare you excess tears.

1 rump roast or top round roast, about 2 1/2 pounds

Salt and freshly ground black pepper, 1/2 teaspoon ground cloves, and 1/2 teaspoon ground cumin for marinating (optional)

2 tablespoons unsalted butter

2 tablespoons chopped pancetta fat or lard, or 1/4 cup finely chopped pancetta

1 yellow onion, chopped

1 carrot, peeled and chopped

1 celery stalk, chopped

1/2 teaspoon ground cloves

2 teaspoons ground cumin

1 tablespoon chopped fresh marjoram

2 cups beef stock or water

1/2 cup tomato purée

Freshly grated horseradish

If you have the time and foresight, rub the meat with a little salt and pepper and the cloves and cumin, cover, and marinate overnight in the refrigerator or at room temperature for 2 hours.

Preheat an oven to 350°F.

In a Dutch oven, melt the butter with the pancetta fat, lard, or chopped pancetta over high heat. Add the roast and quickly brown on all sides, about 10 minutes. Transfer to a large plate and set aside.

Return the pan to medium heat, add the onion, carrot, and celery to the fat remaining in the pan, and sauté until softened, 8 to 10 minutes. Add the cloves, cumin, and marjoram and cook for 3 minutes longer to blend the flavors.

Return the beef to the pan, add the stock or water and tomato purée, and bring to a gentle boil over medium heat. Cover, place in the oven, and cook until the meat is tender, 2 to 2 1/2 hours.

Transfer the meat to a carving board and cover with aluminum foil to keep warm. Strain the pan juices through a sieve. If they are too thin, reduce them over high heat until thickened and rich. Taste and adjust the seasoning.

Slice the roast and spoon the pan juices over the slices. Top with lots of freshly grated horseradish.

WINE: *Pour a Cabernet Sauvignon from Friuli or a Rhône blend.*

VARIATIONS: If you cannot find fresh horseradish, you can add 2 tablespoons prepared horseradish with the tomato purée, although the dish will not be as good.

Gulyas alla triestina
Beef Stew with Sweet and Hot Paprika from Trieste

SERVES 6

Trieste is next door to Slovenia and Croatia and near the Austro-Hungarian border, good reasons why this stew is reminiscent of a fine Hungarian goulash. The big seasoning decision for me is whether to use Hungarian paprika, or, for a smoky overtone, the Spanish *pimentón de La Vera*. I have made this both ways, and I lean toward the *pimentón*, but you may decide you prefer the more authentic paprika. Similar recipes from the Trentino add cumin or caraway to the sauce and grated lemon zest. While traditionally served with boiled potatoes, I like to serve the *gulyas* with homemade *pappardelle*.

3 pounds boneless beef chuck or brisket, cut into 2-inch cubes

1 tablespoon sweet paprika or pimentón dulce, *salt, and* 1/4 *cup olive oil for marinating (optional)*

About 1/2 *cup olive oil*

1/2 *pound pancetta, sliced* 1/4 *inch thick and slices cut into* 1/4*-inch-wide strips*

3 large yellow onions, chopped (4 to 5 cups)

2 tablespoons sweet paprika or pimentón dulce, *or to taste*

1/4 *to* 1/2 *teaspoon cayenne pepper or* pimentón picante, *or to taste*

2 teaspoons ground cumin

2 tablespoons minced garlic

1 cup dry red wine

2 cups seeded, chopped canned plum tomatoes with juice

1 each fresh rosemary and marjoram sprig and 1 bay leaf, tied in a cheesecloth sachet

Grated zest of 1 lemon

Salt and freshly ground black pepper

If you have the time and foresight, rub the meat with the paprika, about 2 teaspoons salt, and the olive oil, cover, and marinate overnight in the refrigerator or at room temperature for 2 hours.

Place a large sauté pan over medium heat and film the bottom with a little of the 1/2 cup of olive oil. Add the pancetta and let it render its fat until it is half-cooked, about 7 minutes. Using a slotted spoon, transfer the pancetta to a plate.

Raise the heat to high and, working in batches, brown the beef cubes on all sides in the fat remaining in the pan, adding olive oil as needed. Each batch should take 8 to 10 minutes. As each batch is ready, transfer it a Dutch oven. Reduce the heat to medium, add the onions, and sauté, adding more oil as needed, until softened, about 8 minutes. Stir in the paprika, cayenne, cumin, and garlic and cook for 5 minutes longer to blend the flavors.

Add the seasoned onions to the beef along with the pancetta, wine, tomatoes and their juice, herb sachet, and lemon zest, place over medium heat, and stir well to combine. Bring to a gentle boil, reduce the heat to low, cover, and simmer until the beef is tender. This may take as long as 3 hours.

Discard the herb sachet. Season the stew to taste with salt and black pepper and more paprika or cayenne, if desired, then serve.

WINE: *From Friuli, try a Merlot or Refosco from Dorigo, Scarbolo, or Venica & Venica. If they are impossible to find, switch to a California Syrah or a California Rhône blend.*

Farsu magru
Sicilian Stuffed Beef Roll with Tomatoes and Red Wine

SERVES 6 TO 8

I prepare *farsu magru,* also known as *farsumauru,* just to get the *sugo* for pasta. Literally the name means "false lean," perhaps because you are making something rich out of particularly lean ingredients. In other words, a little meat goes a long way. Outside of Sicily, this dish is usually considered a *braciolone,* that is, a big meat roll. You can serve the sliced meat with any starch you like, but be sure to save a good amount of the sauce for the next day's rigatoni. The sauce will also keep in the refrigerator for a few days and may even be frozen. Sicilians also serve the sliced meat roll at room temperature accompanied with a fennel salad.

3 pounds top sirloin steak or round steak, in one piece

³/4 pound ground beef

6 eggs, 2 raw, 4 hard-boiled, peeled but left whole

2 tablespoons chopped fresh flat-leaf parsley

2 slices coarse country bread, crusts removed and crumbled

2 tablespoons grated Parmesan cheese

Salt and freshly ground black pepper

¹/4 pound mortadella, thinly sliced

¹/4 pound prosciutto, thinly sliced but not paper-thin

¹/4 pound provolone cheese, cut into strips ¹/2 inch square and 3 inches long

First butterfly the steak: Using a long, sharp knife, cut it nearly in half horizontally, stopping within about ¹/2 inch of the opposite side. Open it up to lie relatively flat, like a book. Place it between 2 sheets of plastic wrap and, using a meat pounder, pound as thin as possible without tearing the meat.

In a bowl, combine the ground beef, raw eggs, parsley, bread, Parmesan cheese, and a little salt and pepper. Using your hands, mix well, then pat the mixture in a uniform layer over the meat. Top evenly with the mortadella and then the prosciutto. Trim off the round ends of each hard-boiled egg, then arrange the eggs in a line down the center of the filling. Place the provolone cheese strips on either side of the eggs, distributing them evenly. Working from a long side, carefully roll up the steak, then tie with kitchen string at regular intervals along the length of the roll to secure it.

In a heavy skillet or sauté pan, heat 3 tablespoons of the olive oil over high heat. Add the meat roll and brown on all sides, 10 to 15 minutes. Transfer to a Dutch oven.

Drain off the burned oil from the skillet, add 2 or 3 tablespoons fresh oil, and place over medium heat. Add the onions and sauté until softened, about 8 minutes. Add the garlic and stir for 1 minute longer. Add the onions to the Dutch oven along with the wine and tomato purée, mixing well. Place over medium heat and bring to a gentle boil. Reduce the heat to low, cover, and simmer until the meat is tender, 2 to 2¹/2 hours.

5 to 6 tablespoons olive oil

2 large yellow onions, chopped

1 tablespoon minced garlic

2 cups dry red wine

4 cups tomato purée

Transfer the meat to a carving board, reserving the pan sauce in the pot, and let rest for 10 to 15 minutes. Snip the strings on the meat and cut into slices about 1/4 inch thick. Arrange the slices on a warmed platter. Meanwhile, reheat the sauce to serving temperature and season with salt and pepper. Spoon the sauce over the meat, then serve.

WINE: *Your house table red will be fine here, but if you want to stay in Sicily, look for a red from Planeta, Cos, Regaleali, Morgante, or Abbazia Sant'Anastasia.*

VARIATIONS: Some recipes call for baby beef or veal, which will cook in about 1 1/2 hours. Others use *caciocavallo* cheese in place of the provolone and add a few strips of green onion to the stuffing. And still others call for roasting the meat in a 350°F oven for about 3 hours and basting it with white wine.

In a large, deep sauté pan with a tight-fitting lid, heat the remaining 3 tablespoons olive oil over high heat. Add the rolls and sear on all sides, 8 to 10 minutes. Pour in 1½ cups stock and the tomatoes (if using) and bring to a gentle boil. Reduce the heat to low, cover, and cook slowly, turning occasionally, until the meat is tender, about 40 minutes if using veal and up to 1½ hours if using beef. Check the liquid level from time to time and add more stock if the mixture seems dry.

Transfer the rolls to a warmed platter and remove the toothpicks or snip the strings. Cover to keep warm. Raise the heat and reduce the pan juices until slightly thickened. If you have not added the tomatoes, stir in the butter or cream. Spoon the pan juices over the meat rolls and serve at once.

WINE: *Chianti Classico is a good compromise wine here. Or, if you have used tomatoes, go with a southern red, such as a Salice Salentino from Apulia or an Aglianico from Campania. If you have added butter or cream, select a rich white, such as a Chardonnay or a blend like Vintage Tunina from Jermann or Terre Alte from Livio Felluga.*

Carne alla pizzaiola
Beef with Pizza Sauce

SERVES 6

I have always prepared this dish by making a zippy *pizzaiola* sauce, quickly sautéing beef or pork *scaloppine,* and then turning the sautéed meat around in the sauce. So I was surprised to come upon a recipe in Jeanne Carola Francesconi's encyclopedic *La cucina napoletana* in which she talks about "reclaiming" this dish. She lists two methods of preparation. One is as I remember It, with the *pizzaiola* sauce prepared separately and the meat sautéed and then reheated in the sauce. The second method is slow and savory: thick slices of top sirloin steak are topped with tomato, oregano, and garlic, and then simmered in a littler wine and olive oil until the tomatoes break down to form a sauce and the meat becomes tender. Serve the tender meat with mashed potatoes and "Sitting Down" Broccoflower (page 261).

2 1/2 pounds well-marbled top sirloin or chuck steak, cut into slices 1 inch thick

1 can (28 ounces) plum tomatoes, drained and halved or quartered

2 tablespoons dried oregano

4 to 6 cloves garlic, minced

Salt and freshly ground black pepper

Pinch of chile pepper flakes (optional)

1/2 cup dry white wine

1/2 cup extra virgin olive oil

Arrange the beef slices in a single layer in a large sauté pan, making sure they lie flat (or use 2 pans, if necessary). Top each slice with some tomato pieces, a sprinkle of oregano, some garlic, a sprinkle of salt and black pepper, and the chile pepper flakes, if using. Add the wine and olive oil to the pan, cover, place over low heat, bring to a simmer, and cook until the meat is tender and the sauce reduced, about 1½ hours.

Transfer the meat slices to a warmed platter. If the sauce seems too thin, reduce it a bit over high heat. Spoon the sauce over the meat, then serve.

WINE: *The obvious wine choice is an Aglianico from Campania. Some labels will say Taurasi, rather than the name of the grape. Among the most reliable producers are Mastroberardino, Feudi San Gregorio, Villa Matilde, Antonio Caggiano, and Maffini.*

VARIATION: Substitute 6 pounds beef short ribs for the steak and increase the cooking time to about 2 hours.

Bollito misto alla piemontese
Mixed Boiled Meats from the Piedmont

SERVES 8 TO 10

Bollito misto, a generous mixture of gently poached meats, is a cornerstone of Piedmontese cuisine. Seven cuts of meat are traditional: brisket of beef, *cotechino* (a large fresh pork sausage), beef tongue, a hen, pork shoulder, veal shoulder, and a calf's head. I have omitted the last three here, but you will still find yourself happily sated. The accompanying sauces elevate the homey-sounding *bollito* into an exceptional dish. These might include homemade *salsa di rafano* (horseradish sauce), *salsa verde* (green sauce, known as *bagnet verd* in the local dialect), and *salsa rossa* (red sauce, known as *bagnet ross* in the local dialect), plus *cognà* (a conserve of fruits and grape must) and *mostarda di frutta* (cooked fruits in a strong mustard sauce), both of which can be found in specialty-food shops. Of course, you do not have to serve all of these sauces (although most of them keep well and can be used to accompany other dishes), but try to have some of them on hand, as they make the dish special. You can also set out a variety of mustards. :: You can make a poaching broth with water, vegetables, bay leaves, and a few cloves, or you can use part beef and/or poultry stock with water. The latter will give you a much richer product at the end and some great stock for another use. Vegetables are not usually served with the meats, but you can poach some in the broth and serve them on the side. :: This is not a dish to be undertaken lightly. While it is not complicated to prepare, it does take time, and many of the parts have to be poached separately. It also makes quite a bit of food, so plan a dinner party for eight or ten of your best carnivorous friends, open a few fine bottles of Barbaresco or Barolo, and enjoy a festive evening you will never forget. If you do not finish all of the *bollito,* you will have great leftovers for one or more wonderful meals.

---

3 quarts beef stock, poultry stock, or water, or a combination

2 bay leaves

A few whole cloves

1 beef brisket, about 3 pounds

1 chicken, 5 pounds; 4 whole chicken breasts, 1 pound each; or 5 pounds assorted chicken parts

1 beef tongue

2 pounds cotechino *sausage, or 6 garlic sausages, about 2 pounds total weight*

In a large Dutch oven, combine the stock and/or water, bay leaves, and cloves and bring to a boil over high heat. Add the brisket and the chicken, bring the liquid back to a simmer, reduce the heat to low, cover, and cook until tender. The chicken parts will cook in about 45 minutes and the whole chicken in 1½ to 2 hours. The brisket will take 2½ to 3 hours. The liquid should bubble only very slowly throughout the cooking. Remove the chicken and brisket from the broth when each is ready and set aside. Strain the broth through a fine-mesh sieve and reserve. If you like, reduce the broth over high heat to concentrate its flavor.

Meanwhile, in a separate pan, combine the beef tongue with water to cover, and in yet another pan, the *cotechino* or garlic sausages with water to cover. Bring them to a boil, reduce the heat,

16 leeks, including tender green tops (optional)

8 large carrots, peeled and cut into 12 pieces total, each about 4 inches long and 1/2 inch wide (optional)

16 to 24 small new potatoes (optional)

Coarse sea salt

Green Sauce (page 182), Red Sauce (page 182), and Horseradish Sauce (page 183) and mostarda di frutta *and* cognà

and cook until tender. The tongue and *cotechino* will be ready in about 2 hours, and the garlic sausages in about 30 minutes. Remove from the water and set aside. Discard the water. When the tongue is cool enough to handle, trim away any fat or gristle from around the base, remove the small bones, and peel off the skin.

If you decide to serve vegetables, poach the leeks in the broth and, when they are done, remove them from the broth and set aside. Repeat with the carrots and then the potatoes. Test for doneness with the point of a knife; the leeks should take about 20 minutes, the carrots 10 to 15 minutes, and the potatoes about 20 minutes. (The best test, of course, is to bite into the vegetables.) The meats and vegetables can be kept warm on a covered heated platter, bathed in some of the broth.

To serve, bring the broth to a simmer in a wide saucepan and gently rewarm the meats and the vegetables (if using) in the broth. Remove each piece of meat or poultry, slice as much brisket, chicken, sausage, and tongue per person as needed and distribute on warmed dinner plates. If you have prepared the vegetables, arrange a few of them alongside the meats. Spoon a little of the broth over all or pass it in a sauceboat. Save the rest of the broth for another use. Pass a small bowl of coarse sea salt, and one or more of the sauces.

WINE: *Barbaresco or Barolo would be ideal. Look for a Barbaresco from Moccagatta, Bruno Giacosa, Bruno Rocca, or Bricco Rocche. For Barolo, seek out wines from Aldo Conterno, Elio Altare, Vietti, or Bruno Giacosa.*

1 cup chopped fresh flat-leaf parsley

¹/₄ cup salt-packed capers, rinsed and chopped

2 tablespoons finely chopped olive oil–packed anchovy fillets (4 or 5)

¹/₄ cup dried bread crumbs

4 cloves garlic, minced

¹/₄ cup red wine vinegar

¹/₄ cup finely minced yellow onion (optional)

1 cup extra virgin olive oil

Salt and freshly ground black pepper

Salsa verde :: *Green Sauce*

In a bowl, stir together the parsley, capers, anchovies, bread crumbs, garlic, vinegar, and the onion, if using. Whisk in the olive oil and season to taste with salt and pepper.

---

2 teaspoons chile pepper flakes

¹/₃ cup extra virgin olive oil

2 cups peeled, seeded, and finely chopped plum tomatoes (fresh or canned)

¹/₂ cup tomato purée

¹/₄ cup red wine vinegar

Sugar, if needed

Salt and freshly ground black pepper

Salsa rossa :: *Red Sauce*

In a small saucepan, heat the chile pepper flakes in the olive oil over medium heat for a few minutes. Turn off the heat and let stand for a few minutes longer so that the chile infuses the oil. Add the tomatoes, tomato purée, vinegar, and a little sugar for balance if the sauce seems too tart, place over low heat, and simmer until thickened, about 20 minutes. Season to taste with salt and black pepper.

FOR THE COOKED SAUCE

3 tablespoons unsalted butter

1/2 cup dried bread crumbs

1/4 cup freshly grated horseradish

1 tablespoon white wine vinegar, or to taste

1 cup meat stock

1 to 2 tablespoons sugar

FOR THE CREAMY SAUCE

1/3 cup freshly grated horseradish

2 to 3 tablespoons white vinegar

1 cup sour cream

Salt and freshly ground black pepper

Sugar

Salsa di rafano :: *Horseradish Sauce, Cooked or Creamy*

To make the cooked sauce, in a small saucepan, melt the butter over low heat and stir in the bread crumbs. Add the horseradish, vinegar, stock, and 1 tablespoon sugar and simmer gently until thickened, about 10 minutes. Taste and add more sugar if the sauce is too tart.

To make the creamy sauce, in a bowl, stir together the horseradish, 2 tablespoons vinegar, and sour cream. Season with salt, pepper, more vinegar, and with a little sugar if the sauce is too tart.

A Night of Piedmont Classics

One night during a Slow Food conference in Turin, after a day spent tasting many different foods, I and a few others actually imagined that we might still be hungry and agreed to go out to dinner with Roberto Donna, a well-known chef in Washington, D.C., who was born in the Piedmont. He drove us to one of his favorite restaurants, Canone d'Oro, which is near his mother's home. Not surprisingly, we were treated as "friends of the house" and were served many delicious courses. Until that moment, I had almost forgotten that Piedmont is the region of endless antipasti and *primi*. Then, just when we thought we were about to be offered dessert, out came the cart with the *bollito misto*. I do not know how we did it, but somehow we found room for more food. It was fabulous.

Ossobuco alla milanese
Braised Veal Shanks from Milan

SERVES 6

Ossobuco, a classic braise of meaty veal shanks, is all about texture, richness, and marrow, the prize to be scooped out from the hollow of the bones with a special spoon. (*Ossobuco* means "bone with a hole.") Veal has a mild taste, so any flavor intensity comes from the *gremolata,* a traditional mixture of lemon zest, garlic, parsley, and sometimes anchovy that adds a lively note to an essentially mild and comforting dish. If you use diced tomatoes, the sauce will be lighter and brothier. If you use tomato sauce, the pan juices will be richer and will cling to the meat. The classic accompaniment for *ossobuco* is *risotto alla milanese,* or saffron-scented rice, making this a rather filling dish. If peas are in season, you may add them to the rice for a note of color.

1 1/2 cups all-purpose flour

Salt and freshly ground black pepper

6 veal shanks, about 1 1/2 pounds each, sawed crosswise into 2 pieces, or 6 large bottom parts of the shank, each weighing about 1 pound

1/2 cup olive oil, or as needed

1/2 cup unsalted butter

2 large or 3 medium yellow onions

4 large carrots, peeled and chopped

4 celery stalks, chopped

2 cups dry white wine

2 cups beef stock

2 cups peeled, seeded, and chopped plum tomatoes (fresh or canned), Rich Tomato Sauce (page 69), Tomato Sauce (page 69), or canned tomato sauce

cont'd

Spread the flour on a plate and season with salt and pepper. Dust the veal shanks with the seasoned flour, shaking off the excess.

In a large, heavy skillet, heat 1/4 cup of the olive oil over high heat. Add half of the shanks and brown on all sides (do not crowd them in the pan or they will steam rather than brown), 10 to 15 minutes. Transfer to a plate. Repeat with the remaining shanks and 1/4 cup olive oil, using more oil if needed.

In a large Dutch oven, melt the butter over medium heat. Add the onions, carrots, and celery and sauté until pale gold, about 12 minutes. Place the veal shanks, marrow side up, on top of the vegetables and pour in the wine, stock, and tomatoes or tomato sauce. Bring to a gentle boil, reduce the heat to low, cover, and simmer until the veal is very tender, 1 1/2 to 2 hours; the timing will depend on the size of the shanks. The meat should be fork tender and almost falling off the bones. Reduce pan juices if necessary and season with salt and pepper.

cont'd

FOR THE *GREMOLATA*

1 tablespoon minced garlic

2 tablespoons grated lemon zest

6 tablespoons chopped fresh flat-leaf parsley

To make the *gremolata,* in a small bowl, stir together the garlic, lemon zest, and parsley, then sprinkle it evenly over the shanks. Cook for 5 minutes longer to give the *gremolata* time to infuse the dish with its lovely perfume, then serve.

WINE: *This dish calls for a big red wine. Drink Barolo or Barbaresco.*

———————

VARIATIONS: In the town of Reggio Emilia, *ossobuco alla reggiana* is made in a similar way. Proceed as directed, but use dry Marsala in place of the white wine; substitute 6 tablespoons tomato paste diluted in $1/2$ cup water for the tomatoes or tomato sauce; and add $1 1/2$ pounds fresh mushrooms, wiped clean, sliced, and sautéed in olive oil until tender, during the last half hour of cooking. The carrots and celery are optional.

If you find veal too mild, and prefer fuller-flavored beef short ribs, you can prepare the dish as they do in Milan with only minor variations. Brown 6 beef short ribs, 1 pound each, in olive oil, then cook the vegetables as directed. Return the short ribs to the pan and add stock and tomatoes or tomato sauce and red wine in place of the white wine. Cover and simmer until the ribs are tender, about 2 to $2 1/2$ hours. You may add *gremolata* made with part orange zest and part lemon zest during the last 5 minutes, or instead top the ribs with freshly grated horseradish at the table, as cooks do in Friuli.

Stracotto di vitello al latte e senape
Veal Braised with Mustard Cream

SERVES 6 TO 8

In the Piedmont and Emilia-Romagna, cooks regularly braise meat in milk, which gives the meat a particularly tender texture. However, when the dish is ready, the resulting sauce appears curdled, a homely appearance that is quickly remedied by whirling the sauce in a blender or food processor. To avoid the curdling altogether, you can use half-and-half or heavy cream, as cream is less likely to curdle. A pork loin can be braised the same way (see Pork Loin Cooked in Milk with Hazelnuts, page 221).

1 boneless leg of veal, rolled and tied into a compact shape

4 fresh sage leaves

2 cloves garlic, cut into slivers

5 tablespoons olive oil

Salt

1 yellow onion, chopped

1 carrot, peeled and chopped

1 celery stalk, chopped

1 tablespoon chopped fresh rosemary

2 cups milk, or as needed

Meat stock if needed

2 tablespoons prepared mustard, or to taste

Using a small, sharp knife, make small slits all over the meat and insert the sage leaves and garlic slivers into the slits.

In a Dutch oven, heat 4 tablespoons of the olive oil over medium-high heat. Add the meat and brown on all sides, sprinkling it with salt as you turn it, 10 to 15 minutes. Transfer to a large plate.

Return the pan to medium heat and add the remaining 1 tablespoon olive oil. Add the onion, carrot, celery, and rosemary and sauté until softened, 8 to 10 minutes. Return the veal to the pan and enough milk to reach halfway up the sides of the veal. Bring to a gentle boil, reduce the heat to low, cover, and simmer until the veal is tender, about 1 1/2 hours. If the pan juices seem to be cooking away, add some stock.

Transfer the veal to a carving board, cover with aluminum foil to keep warm, and let rest for about 10 minutes before cutting. Pour the contents of the pan into a blender and process until smooth. Mix in the mustard and season with salt and pepper. Reheat to serving temperature.

Snip the strings on the meat and cut into slices about 1/4 inch thick. Arrange the slices on a warmed platter and serve with the mustard cream sauce.

WINE: *If you want to drink white, try a Riesling or Pinot Grigio from Friuli. If you prefer red, go light with Merlot or a Dolcetto from Pio Cesare, Villa Spanna, or San Fereolo.*

Rollata di vitello alla piemontese
Braised Stuffed Leg of Veal from the Piedmont

SERVES 6

When I was living in Rome, I used to buy a prepared *rollata di vitello* from my butcher, which he called *rollé*. He presented it so beautifully—stuffed with mortadella and prosciutto, tied neatly with a branch of fresh rosemary on the top—that it was quite irresistible. Years later, while researching dishes for a series of Italian regional menus that I served at Square One, I discovered that this *rollé* was not a Roman dish at all, but a specialty of the Piedmont. Its other name is *polpettone alla moncalvese,* which means meat loaf in the style of Moncalvo, even though it bears no resemblance to a meat loaf. The town of Moncalvo, which lies north of Asti in the area known as Monferrato, is known for its wine and its white truffles, and when the latter are in season, they are shaved on the meat roll. I also discovered that the *mortadella* in the *rollata* was a creative touch added by my Roman butcher. Here is the classic recipe.

1 boneless leg of veal, 3 to 4 pounds

2 cloves garlic, finely chopped, plus 1 plump clove, cut into slivers

1 tablespoon fresh rosemary leaves, finely chopped, plus 2 sprigs

Salt and freshly ground black pepper

Freshly grated nutmeg

6 slices prosciutto, thinly sliced but not paper-thin

6 to 7 tablespoons unsalted butter

1 tablespoon olive oil

2 yellow onions, cut into ¼-inch cubes (about 3 cups)

3 small carrots, peeled and cut into ¼-inch cubes (about 1 cup)

3 celery stalks, cut into ¼-inch cubes (about 1 cup)

1½ to 2 cups dry white wine

1½ to 2 cups chicken or veal stock

First butterfly the veal leg: Using a long, sharp knife, cut it nearly in half horizontally, stopping within about ½ inch of the opposite side (or ask your butcher to butterfly it). Open it up to lie relatively flat, like a book, and trim away any visible gristle and any excess tendons and fat. Place the meat between 2 sheets of plastic wrap and, using a meat pounder, pound it to a uniform thickness of about 1 inch, being careful not to tear it.

In a bowl, stir together the chopped garlic and rosemary and a little salt and pepper and spread the mixture over the meat. Grate a bit of nutmeg over the garlic mixture, then lay the slices of prosciutto on top. Roll up the veal, and tie with kitchen string at 1-inch intervals to secure. Using a sharp knife, make several, regularly spaced small slits all over the veal roll, and insert a sliver of garlic into each slit. Slip the 2 rosemary sprigs under the string binding the roll, and sprinkle the veal evenly with salt and pepper, then season lightly with nutmeg.

In a large Dutch oven, melt 3 tablespoons of the butter with the olive oil over medium-high heat. Add the veal and brown on all sides, 10 to 15 minutes. Transfer to a plate and set aside.

Return the pot to medium heat. Add the onions, carrots, and celery to the fat remaining in the pot and sauté until softened and pale gold, about 12 minutes. Return the veal to the pot. Add equal parts white wine and stock almost to cover the roast. (The amount of wine and stock you will need depends on the dimensions of your braising pan.) Gradually bring to a boil over medium heat. Reduce the heat to low, cover, and simmer until tender when pierced with a knife or an instant-read meat thermometer inserted into the thickest part registers 140°F, 1 1/2 to 2 hours.

Transfer the veal to a carving board, cover with aluminum foil to keep warm, and let rest for about 15 minutes before cutting. Meanwhile, reduce the pan juices over high heat until you have about 1 1/2 cups, then stir in the remaining 3 tablespoons butter to thicken.

Snip the strings on the meat and cut into slices about 1/4 inch thick. Arrange the slices on a warmed platter and spoon the pan juices and braising vegetables over the top, then serve.

WINE: *Drink a medium-bodied red such as Barbera or Nebbiolo d'Alba from the Piedmont, a Merlot from the Veneto or Friuli, or Vino Nobile di Montepulciano. You might also try a full-bodied white.*

NOTE: You can instead braise the stuffed veal leg in a 350°F oven for about the same amount of time.

Coda alla vaccinara
Oxtail Ragout with Celery

SERVES 6

Many great dishes have evolved from using lesser cuts of meat, and *coda alla vaccinara* is a jewel of Roman cooking. It is an example of the cuisine of the *quinto quarto,* the "fifth quarter," the parts of the animal—heart, spleen, liver, tongue, sweetbreads, brains, intestines, tails— never sold to the rich. I first ate this dish at Ristorante Checchino dal 1887 in Testaccio, a neighborhood known for its slaughterhouses and *vaccinari,* the latter Roman dialect for "butchers." Serve this rich stew with puréed or roast potatoes, over polenta, or, if you take the meat off the bone, as a sturdy sauce for *pappardelle,* a favorite of mine. :: Of course, this recipe would not be Italian if there were not at least a few different ways to prepare it. One version boils the meat and a few vegetables in water until the meat is tender, reserves the cooking liquid for soup, and then braises the meat and vegetables with wine and tomatoes. Another recipe simply browns and braises the meat along with the *battuto* of chopped vegetables and prosciutto. The original recipe, as still prepared at Checchino dal 1887, includes pine nuts, raisins, and a bit of grated bitter chocolate, all mixed in near the end of cooking. Not every Roman cook adds these final, old-fashioned *dolce e forte* touches, of course. What is essential to this dish, however, are strips of celery, a favorite Roman vegetable. You can make the stew a day or two ahead of time, but do not add the blanched celery until the day you are going to serve it.

4 pounds oxtails, in 2-inch-thick pieces

1/2 cup olive oil

Salt and freshly ground black pepper

2 yellow onions, chopped

2 carrots, peeled and chopped

1/4 pound fatty prosciutto, diced

2 or 3 cloves garlic, chopped

1/2 pound pancetta, diced (optional)

1 cup dry white wine

1/4 cup tomato paste diluted in 2 cups meat stock, or 2 pounds plum tomatoes, peeled, seeded, and cut into strips, plus meat stock as needed

2 fresh thyme sprigs, 2 bay leaves, and 2 whole cloves, tied in a cheesecloth sachet

Bring a large saucepan three-fourths full of water to a boil. Add the oxtails, blanch for about 5 minutes to remove excess blood, then drain and rinse under running cold water. Drain well and pat dry with paper towels.

In a large sauté pan, heat 1/4 cup of the olive oil over high heat. Working in batches, add the oxtails and brown on all sides, sprinkling them with salt and pepper as you turn them, 10 to 15 minutes for each batch. As each batch is ready, transfer it to a plate.

In a Dutch oven, heat the remaining 1/4 cup olive oil over medium heat. Add the onions, carrots, prosciutto, garlic, and the pancetta (if using) and cook until the vegetables are softened, about 8 minutes. Add the oxtails and cook for a few minutes, mixing well. Raise the heat to high, add the wine, and cook until it is reduced by half, 10 to 15 minutes. Add the diluted tomato paste, or the tomato strips and enough stock just to cover the meat, and the herb sachet. Mix well, reduce the heat to very low, cover, and simmer slowly, turning the meat occasionally, until the meat is almost tender, 2 1/2 to 3 hours.

1 large head celery, about 1 1/2 pounds, cut into 2-inch pieces, blanched, and drained

1/2 cup pine nuts, toasted (optional)

1/2 cup raisins, plumped in hot water and drained (optional)

2 tablespoons grated bitter chocolate (optional)

Pinch of ground cinnamon (optional)

Pinch of freshly grated nutmeg (optional)

Using a large spoon, skim the excess fat from the surface. Add the celery and the pine nuts, raisins, and bitter chocolate (if using) and cook for 30 minutes longer. Some cooks add a little cinnamon and nutmeg as a final touch. Remove and discard the herb sachet.

Scoop the oxtails and pan sauce into warmed individual bowls and serve at once.

WINE: *For now, the best reds of Lazio are from Falesco, either Montiano or the less costly Vitiano. Or, go with a full-bodied red such as Cabernet Sauvignon or a Tuscan blend.*

Cassola d'agnello al latte e limone
Lamb Stew Braised in Milk and Lemon

SERVES 8

This stew from the Sardinian city of Cagliari resembles an ancient Apulian dish called *caldariello,* which also calls for braising lamb in milk, but without the lemon zest. Rather than simmering the stew in a *caldaio,* or "cauldron," however, the Sardinians bake it in a *cassola,* a traditional terra-cotta cooking pot. Both the pot and the stew take their name from the similar Spanish *cazuela,* introduced to the island during the years of Spanish rule. In Sardinia, the stew is baked in a medium-hot oven. If you prefer to braise the dish on the stove top, be sure that the heat is very low and extend the cooking time by about 45 minutes. Serve the stew with braised fennel or carrots.

4 tablespoons olive oil, or as needed

4 pounds boneless lamb shoulder, trimmed of excess fat and cut into 2-inch pieces

Salt and freshly ground black pepper

2 yellow onions, chopped

4 cloves garlic, minced

3 cups milk, or as needed

Grated zest of 2 lemons

1/4 cup chopped fresh flat-leaf parsley

Lemon wedges for serving

Preheat the oven to 350°F.

In a large sauté pan, heat 2 tablespoons of the olive oil over high heat. Working in batches, add the lamb and brown on all sides, adding oil as needed and seasoning with salt and pepper as you turn the meat. Each batch should take 8 to 10 minutes. As each batch is ready, use a slotted spoon to transfer it to an earthenware or other baking dish or pan with a lid.

Return the sauté pan to medium heat and add the remaining 2 tablespoons olive oil. Add the onions and sauté until softened, about 8 minutes. Add the garlic and sauté for 1 or 2 minutes longer. Add the onions and garlic to the lamb, and then pour in enough milk to just cover the meat. Cover the lamb and bake until tender, about 1 1/2 hours.

Remove the lamb from the oven. When you lift the lid, you may fear that you have made a mistake, as the sauce will have curdled. This is normal for all meat dishes cooked in milk, and the solution is easy. Using a slotted spoon, transfer the lamb pieces to a clean, heavy pan. Pour the curdled sauce into a blender and process until smooth, then pour it over the lamb. Stir in the lemon zest and parsley, and heat through gently.

Spoon the stew onto warmed plates and accompany with lemon wedges. Serve immediately.

WINE: *For a local red, look for a Cannonau from Contini, Gabbas, or Argiolas. If you want to venture into Apulia, try a Primitivo from Felline or Sinfarossa, or a blend from Conti Zecca or Taurino. Because of the lemon and milk, a white, such as a Sardinian Vermentino, would work, too.*

A Kosher Past

Some versions of this stew call for beating together a couple of eggs with some lemon juice until frothy, and then whisking in the mixture at the last minute. I find the addition unnecessary, however, as the dish is already quite rich. I suspect that the idea originated in Jewish households where the milk was omitted, but cooks still wanted a way to enrich the dish. Egg and lemon would nicely thicken the sauce while not violating the kosher law that forbade kid (or lamb) from being cooked in its mother's milk.

Spezzatino d'agnello alle olive
Braised Lamb with Citrus-Marinated Olives

In Italy, lamb with olives—black or green—is a common combination. In the Abruzzo and Umbria, black olives are often marinated with garlic, lemon or orange zest, and herbs, with bay, marjoram, rosemary, and oregano the herbs of choice. A bit of lemon juice may be added to the lamb at the end of cooking to cut the richness. Serve with mashed potatoes or polenta.

FOR THE OLIVES

1 cup pitted oil-cured black olives

2 cloves garlic, minced

Grated zest of 1 orange or 1 lemon

2 or 3 bay leaves

3 or 4 tablespoons extra virgin olive oil

4 tablespoons olive oil, or as needed

3 pounds boneless lamb shoulder, trimmed of excess fat and cut into 2-inch pieces

Salt and freshly ground black pepper

3 yellow onions, sliced

Pinch of ground cinnamon

2 cups meat stock, or as needed

1/2 cup dry white wine (optional)

1 tablespoon chopped fresh rosemary, or 2 tablespoons chopped fresh marjoram

Fresh lemon juice (optional)

To prepare the olives, combine them in a small sauté pan with the garlic, citrus zest, bay leaves, and extra virgin olive oil, place over low heat, and warm gently. Remove from the heat, let cool, transfer to a covered container, and marinate at least overnight or for up to 3 days in the refrigerator.

Place a large sauté pan over high heat and film the bottom with about 2 tablespoons of the olive oil. Working in batches, add the lamb and brown on all sides, adding oil as needed and seasoning with salt and pepper as you turn the meat. Each batch should take 8 to 10 minutes. As each batch is ready, use a slotted spoon to transfer it to a Dutch oven or other heavy pot.

Return the sauté pan to medium heat and add the onions to the fat remaining in the pan. Sprinkle them with the cinnamon and sauté until softened, about 8 minutes. Add the onions to the lamb. Pour 1/2 cup of the stock and the wine (if using) into the sauté pan and deglaze the pan over medium-high heat, scraping up all the brown bits, then add to the lamb. Add the rosemary or marjoram and the remaining 1 1/2 cups stock to the lamb, or as needed just to cover the meat. Bring to a gentle boil over medium-high heat, reduce the heat to low, cover, and simmer for 1 1/2 hours. Add the olives, re-cover, and continue to simmer until the meat is tender, about 25 minutes longer.

Taste and adjust the seasoning. Add a little lemon juice if needed to temper the richness, and then serve.

WINE: *Pairing olives and wine can be tricky because of the bitterness of the olives. Look for a big Umbrian red, such as Sagrantino di Montefalco from Caprai or Torgiano Rosso from Lungarotti. From Lazio, try Falesco Vitiano.*

Fricassea d'agnello con carciofi
Lamb Stew with Artichokes, Egg, and Lemon

SERVES 6

Variously called *uova e limone, brodettato,* and *fricassea,* and found throughout Italy, egg-and-lemon-enriched sauces are Easter or Passover specialties that celebrate the lamb and vegetables of springtime. To make them, egg yolks and lemon juice are beaten into a zabaglione like frothiness and stirred into a dish at the end of cooking, off the heat. The eggs thicken the pan juices and the lemon adds a delightful tang that cuts the richness of the meat. Various vegetables can be added to the stew. Artichokes are traditional, as are fennel, favas, asparagus, and peas. This recipe can also be prepared with *capretto* (kid), although you will need to extend the cooking time, as the meat is tougher.

1/4 cup olive oil, plus as needed

1 large yellow onion, chopped

4 tablespoons chopped fresh flat-leaf parsley

3 1/2 pounds boneless lamb shoulder, trimmed of excess fat and cut into 2-inch pieces

Salt and freshly ground black pepper

1 cup dry white wine

Water or meat stock as needed

1 lemon, halved, plus juice of 2 large lemons (about 1/2 cup)

6 small artichokes

3 egg yolks

1 tablespoon chopped fresh marjoram or mint

In a large sauté pan, warm 2 tablespoons of the olive oil over medium heat. Add the onion and 2 tablespoons of the parsley and sauté until softened, about 8 minutes. Using a slotted spoon, transfer the onion mixture to a Dutch oven or other heavy pot.

Return the sauté pan to high heat and film the bottom with about 2 tablespoons olive oil. Working in batches, add the lamb and brown on all sides, adding oil as needed and seasoning with salt and pepper as you turn the meat. Each batch should take 8 to 10 minutes. As each batch is ready, use a slotted spoon to transfer it to the Dutch oven. Place the lamb over medium-high heat, add the wine, and bring to a gentle boil. Reduce the heat to low, cover, and simmer for 35 to 40 minutes, adding water or stock if the stew looks dry.

Meanwhile, prepare the artichokes: Squeeze the juice from the lemon halves into a bowl of cold water. Working with 1 artichoke at a time, remove all of the leaves, then trim away any dark green parts from the base and stem. If the stem seems tough, cut it off flush with the base. Cut the artichoke into quarters lengthwise. Scoop out the prickly choke from each quarter with a spoon, or cut it out with a paring knife. As each artichoke is trimmed, drop the quarters into the lemon water and leave them in the water until ready to cook.

When the lamb has cooked for about 40 minutes, drain the artichokes and add to the pot, re-cover, and continue to cook until the meat and artichokes are tender, 25 to 30 minutes longer. Taste and adjust the seasoning.

In a bowl, whisk together the egg yolks, juice from the two large lemons, the remaining 2 tablespoons parsley, and marjoram or mint until very frothy. Remove the pot holding the lamb from the heat and beat in the egg-lemon mixture, stirring constantly. Re-cover the pan and let stand until the eggs thicken the sauce, about 3 minutes. Serve at once.

WINE: *Because of the eggs and lemon, we need a big red with high acidity. Among the possibilities are a Nero d'Avola from Sicily made by Corvo or Abbazia Sant'Anastasia, an Aglianico from Campania made by Terredora or Feudi di San Gregorio, or a Corvina from the north. The presence of eggs, lemon, and artichokes make white wine an option, too. Consider a Vermentino from Sardinia or a Sauvignon Blanc from Friuli.*

VARIATIONS: You can add fennel bulbs, fava beans, English peas, and/or asparagus in addition to the artichokes. To add fennel bulbs to the stew, trim them, quarter lengthwise, parboil in boiling water for 15 minutes, and drain. To add fava beans (2 to 3 pounds) or English peas (about 1 1/2 pounds) to the stew, shell them. Blanch the favas for 1 to 2 minutes in boiling water, drain, and then slip off the thin skin covering each bean. To add asparagus to the stew, trim off the tough ends, cut into 2-inch lengths, parboil in boiling water for 5 minutes, and drain. Add any one or more of these vegetables to the stew during the last 10 to 15 minutes of cooking. When adding any of these vegetables, you may need to add more stock to keep the stew sufficiently moist. You can also parboil the trimmed artichokes for 15 minutes and add them at the same time. Finally, cardoons (page 247) can added in place of the artichokes: trim well, cut into 2-inch lengths, and cook until tender in boiling water before adding during the last 10 to 15 minutes of cooking.

Agnello al forno alla madonita
Lamb Stew with Mushrooms and Sweet Peppers from the Madonie

SERVES 6

The Madonie is a mountain range in northern Sicily between the towns of Cefalù and Enna. This recipe is a bit unusual for the cooks in the region, who usually prefer oregano over rosemary, and who would add peppers or mushrooms, but not both. However, after testing the recipe, I had to include it, typical or not, because it is so tasty. This recipe is also good made with shoulder meat from *capretto* (kid), which is cut into the same-sized pieces but cooked longer. Serve the lamb or the kid with roast or mashed potatoes.

3 pounds boneless lamb shoulder, trimmed of excess fat and cut into 2-inch pieces

4 cloves garlic, smashed, plus 2 cloves, minced

2 tablespoons chopped fresh rosemary or dried oregano

1/4 cup fresh lemon juice, plus more to taste

About 1 cup olive oil

3 yellow onions, thickly sliced

1/2 cup dry white wine

3 red or yellow bell peppers, seeded and cut lengthwise into wide strips

1 1/2 pounds large, fresh brown mushrooms such as porcini or portobello, wiped clean and quartered

Salt and freshly ground black pepper

In a bowl, toss together the lamb, smashed garlic, rosemary or oregano, 1/4 cup lemon juice, and 1/2 cup of the olive oil. Cover and refrigerate for at least a few hours or for as long as overnight.

Preheat the oven to 400°F. Remove the lamb from the marinade and place in a Dutch oven or a baking dish with a lid. Reserve the garlic and bits of herb from the marinade.

In a large sauté pan, heat 2 or 3 tablespoons olive oil over medium heat. Add the onions and sauté until softened, about 10 minutes. Add the onions to the lamb along with the wine and reserved garlic and herb and mix well. Cover tightly and bake for 45 minutes.

While the lamb is cooking, return the sauté pan to medium heat and add 2 tablespoons olive oil. Add the bell pepper strips and sauté until tender, about 8 minutes. Using a slotted spoon, transfer the pepper strips to a plate.

Return the pan to medium heat and add 2 or 3 tablespoons olive oil. Add the mushrooms and sauté until softened, about 5 minutes. Stir in the minced garlic and cook for 1 to 2 minutes longer.

Remove the lamb from the oven and reduce the oven temperature to 325°F. Add the sautéed peppers and mushrooms to the lamb, re-cover, and return to the oven. Continue to cook until the lamb is tender, about 1 hour longer.

Remove the lamb from the oven and season to taste with salt, pepper, and lemon juice. Serve at once.

WINE: *There are many emerging red blends using Syrah, Cabernet Sauvignon, and Merlot in Sicily. Look for regional producers such as Spadafora, Gulfi, Planeta, Abbazia Sant'Anastasia, and Morgante.*

Agnello brucialingua
Lamb to Burn Your Tongue

SERVES 6

One year in the dead of winter, I toured the Abruzzo with a group of travel agents. We stopped for a tasting at a winery, and in the front garden, I noticed a bush thick with small, red lantern-shaped peppers despite the bitter cold. They were *diavolilli* (oddly, a term used for candied almonds elsewhere in the country), sometimes called *diavoletti*, the incendiary chile peppers much beloved by the Abruzzese and used in a local condiment called *olio santo*, "holy oil," that is as hot as the devil. A friend and I picked a few of the peppers for their seeds, which we hoped to plant in her garden in warm Sonoma County, north of San Francisco. I tried to grow them, too, but my cool city climate did not suit them. Fortunately, my friend brought me some of hers for testing this stew. The dish also includes two other signature flavors of the Abruzzo, rosemary and garlic.

About 1 cup all-purpose flour

Salt and freshly ground black pepper

3 pounds boneless lamb shoulder, trimmed of excess fat and cut into 2-inch pieces

Olive oil for browning

4 cloves garlic, minced

2 to 3 teaspoons chile pepper flakes or minced fresh chile pepper

2 tablespoons chopped fresh rosemary

1 cup dry white wine

Spread the flour on a plate and season with salt and black pepper. Dust the lamb with the seasoned flour, shaking off the excess.

Place a large sauté pan over high heat and film the bottom with olive oil. Working in batches, add the lamb and brown on all sides, adding oil as needed. Each batch should take 8 to 10 minutes. As each batch is ready, use a slotted spoon to transfer it to a Dutch oven or other heavy pot.

Add the garlic, chile pepper, and rosemary to the fat remaining in the pot and stir well to coat the ingredients. Add the wine, place over medium heat, and bring to a boil. Reduce the heat to low, cover, and simmer until the meat is quite tender, about 2 hours.

Taste and adjust the seasoning, then serve.

WINE: *A hearty Montepulciano d'Abruzzo from Masciarelli or Illuminati, or from the more expensive Valentini, will handle the spice. So, too, will the reasonably priced Dí Majo Norante from neighboring Molise. Failing those, try a juicy, fruity wine with soft tannins such as Dolcetto di Dogliani from the Piedmont.*

VARIATION: To make *agnello e peperoni*, another popular dish of the Abruzzo, add 5 or 6 canned tomatoes, seeded and chopped, and 2 red bell peppers, seeded and cut lengthwise into strips, with the wine.

Agnello al calderotto
Lamb Stew with Bitter Greens and Sheep's Milk Cheese

SERVES 6 TO 8

An ancient pastoral recipe from Apulia, this stew takes its name from a cooking pot, the *caldaio*. Sometimes the lamb is cooked in sheep's milk and later smothered in greens (see page 194 for a Sardinian version of the milk-braised stew). In this version, the process is reversed: the lamb is first braised with greens, and sheep's milk in the form of pecorino cheese is added at the end of cooking. This dish is typically prepared with curly endive (chicory), but you can mix the endive with other greens as well. Accompany with roast potatoes or grilled bread.

Olive oil for browning, plus 3 to 4 tablespoons

3 pounds boneless lamb shoulder, trimmed of excess fat and cut into 1 1/2-inch pieces

Salt and freshly ground black pepper

2 large yellow onions, chopped

1/2 cup dry white wine

2 tablespoons minced garlic

Pinch of chile pepper flakes (optional)

3 cups peeled, seeded, and chopped plum tomatoes (fresh or canned)

Meat stock, if needed

8 to 12 cups coarsely chopped curly endive (chicory) or a mixture of curly endive, dandelion greens, and fennel fronds (see recipe introduction)

1/4 cup chopped fresh flat-leaf parsley

1 1/2 cups crumbled pecorino cheese

Place a large sauté pan over high heat and film the bottom with olive oil. Working in batches, add the lamb and brown on all sides, adding oil as needed and seasoning with salt and black pepper as you turn the meat. Each batch should take 8 to 10 minutes. As each batch is ready, use a slotted spoon to transfer it to a Dutch oven or other heavy pot.

Return the sauté pan to medium heat and add the 3 to 4 tablespoons olive oil to the pan. Add the onions and sauté until softened, about 8 minutes. Add the onions to the lamb. Pour the wine into the sauté pan and deglaze the pan, scraping up all of the brown bits, then add to the lamb. Add the garlic, chile pepper flakes (if using), and tomatoes and bring to a gentle boil. Reduce the heat to low, cover, and simmer until the meat is tender, about 1 1/2 hours. Check from time to time and add a little stock if there seems to be too little liquid.

While the lamb is cooking, bring a large saucepan three-fourths full of water to a boil. Salt lightly, add the greens, and boil until tender, about 5 minutes. Drain well. Add the greens and the parsley to the lamb during the last 30 minutes of cooking.

Season the pan sauce with salt and black pepper. Spoon the stew into warmed bowls and sprinkle with the cheese. Serve at once.

WINE: *Pour a local Primitivo or Negroamaro from Felline, Sinfarossa, Santa Lucia, or A Mano, or a Zinfandel from California.*

Cosciotto di castrato sulle tegole
Roast Leg of Lamb Cooked on Tiles

SERVES 6 TO 8

While doing research for a Sicilian-themed dinner, I came upon a reference to an old recipe in which a leg of lamb was cooked directly on curved roof tiles in a wood-burning oven. Slices of garlic, rosemary needles, and strips of pancetta rolled in black pepper were stuffed into slits cut into the leg, and the meat was basted with olive oil and lemon juice while it cooked. Alas, I did not have the curved roof tiles or the wood-burning oven, but I tested the dish in a conventional oven and it was delicious.

1 bone-in leg of lamb, about 6 pounds

2 ounces pancetta, cut into strips

Freshly ground black pepper

Needles from 2 fresh rosemary sprigs, plus 2 or 3 teaspoons, chopped

2 or 3 cloves garlic, cut into slivers

Salt

1/2 cup olive oil

1/4 cup fresh lemon juice

FOR SERVING

1 1/2 cups meat stock

2 teaspoons minced garlic

1 teaspoon chopped fresh rosemary

Freshly ground black pepper

Preheat the oven to 400°F. Using a small, sharp knife, make small slits all over the surface of the lamb. Dip the pancetta strips into the pepper, then tuck the strips along with the whole rosemary needles and the garlic slivers into the slits. Rub the outside of the lamb with the chopped rosemary, 2 teaspoons salt, and 1 teaspoon pepper. Place the lamb leg in a roasting pan, on a rack if desired. In a small bowl, stir together the olive oil and lemon juice.

Roast the lamb, basting occasionally with the olive oil mixture, until an instant-read thermometer inserted into the thickest part away from bone registers 120°F, about 1 hour. This timing will yield meat that is quite rare. For meat cooked to medium, the thermometer should register 130° to 135°F and cook for about 10 minutes longer. Remember, the meat will continue to cook when it is removed from the oven.

Meanwhile, prepare a simple sauce for serving: Pour the stock into a small saucepan, place over high heat, and boil until reduced to about 1 cup. Stir in the garlic and rosemary and season with a little pepper.

Remove the lamb from the oven, cover loosely with aluminum foil to keep warm, and let rest for 10 to 15 minutes, then carve, arrange on a warmed platter, and serve with the sauce.

WINE: *Try one of Sicily's emerging red blends using Syrah, Cabernet Sauvignon, or Merlot from Spadafora, Gulfi, Planeta, Abbazia Sant'Anastasia, or Morgante. If you are feeling a bit extravagant, try a Super Tuscan such as Sassicaia, Ornellaia, Saffredi, or Flaccianello. A big Cabernet from California or a Meritage blend is a possibility, too.*

Agnello con finocchi selvatici alla sarda
Lamb, Fennel, and Bread Casserole from Sardinia

SERVES 4

This dish bears a resemblance to a Turkish dish called *talas borek* in which stewed lamb and cheese are layered within a thin pastry crust. The Sardinians make an unusual flat bread called *pane carasau*, or "music paper bread," so named because it is paper-thin like aging sheet music. The bread resembles *lahvosh* in that it can be dried for storage and then moistened and rolled around a filling. It is used to line the bottom of the stew pot, in the manner of a *panada* (bread soup). You can use thin slices of fried bread in place of the flat bread, or you can omit the bread on the bottom, and instead top the dish with a more dramatic filo crust.

Olive oil as needed

2 pounds boneless lamb shoulder, trimmed of excess fat and cut into 1 1/2-inch pieces

Salt and freshly ground black pepper

1 yellow onion, chopped

6 cloves garlic, minced

4 tablespoons chopped fresh flat-leaf parsley

2 teaspoons fennel seeds, toasted in a dry pan and crushed

Pinch of chile pepper flakes (optional)

3 cups meat stock or water, or as needed

3 fennel bulbs, preferably with fronds intact

Sheets of soft lahvosh to cover the bottom of the baking dish, 6 or 7 pita breads, or 4 to 8 thin slices coarse country bread

4 tablespoons unsalted butter for frying if using coarse country bread, plus 2 tablespoons, cut into small pieces

About 1 1/2 cups crumbled ricotta salata or sheep's milk feta cheese

Place a large, deep sauté pan or Dutch oven over high heat and film the bottom with olive oil. Working in batches, add the lamb and brown on all sides, adding oil as needed and seasoning with salt and black pepper as you turn the meat. Each batch should take 8 to 10 minutes. As each batch is ready, use a slotted spoon to transfer it to a plate.

Return the pan to medium heat and add the onion, garlic, parsley, fennel seeds, and chile pepper flakes (if using) to the oil remaining in the pan, adding more oil if needed. Sauté until the onion is softened, about 8 minutes. Add 2 cups of the stock or water, return the lamb to the pan, raise the heat to medium-high, and bring to a boil. Reduce the heat to low, cover, and simmer until the lamb is very tender, about 1 1/2 hours. Taste and adjust seasoning.

While the lamb is cooking, cut off the stalks and fronds from the fennel bulbs if still attached, and reserve the fronds for garnish, if desired. Cut the fennel bulbs in quarters or eighths and cut out the tough core from each piece. Peel off any discolored outer leaves. Bring a saucepan three-fourths full of water to a boil. Salt lightly, add the fennel, reduce the heat to medium, and cook until tender, about 15 minutes. Remove from the heat, drain well, and set aside.

If using *lahvosh* or pita bread, set aside. If using country bread, melt 2 tablespoons of the butter and 1 tablespoon olive oil in a large sauté pan over medium heat. Add half of the bread slices and fry on both sides until golden, 3 to 5 minutes total. Transfer to paper towels to drain. Return the pan to medium heat, add 2 more tablespoons butter and 1 tablespoon oil, and fry the remaining bread in the same way, then drain. Cut each slice into 2- or 3-inch squares.

Preheat the oven to 350°F. Select a large earthenware baking dish, about 10 by 12 by 3 inches (3-quart capacity).

If using *lahvosh* or pita bread, oil the baking dish. Line the bottom of the dish with the *lahvosh* (if the *lahvosh* is very thin, you may use 2 layers) or pita bread, tearing or cutting as necessary to fit. Spoon the lamb stew evenly over the bread and top with the fennel. Drizzle the remaining 1 cup stock or water evenly over the top, adding more as needed to moisten the fennel and bread lightly. Scatter the cheese evenly over the surface, and dot with the 2 tablespoons butter pieces.

If using fried bread, do not oil the baking dish. Arrange the bread in the bottom of the dish, cutting again as necessary to fit, spoon the lamb stew evenly over the bread, and scatter half of the cheese evenly over the top. Arrange the fennel in a layer over the cheese, then drizzle the remaining 1 cup stock or water evenly over the top, adding more as needed to moisten the fennel and bread lightly. Top with the remaining cheese, and dot the surface evenly with the butter pieces.

Bake until the cheese melts and is tinged with gold, about 30 minutes. Remove from the oven. Chop the fennel fronds, if using, and scatter over the top. Serve immediately.

WINE: *Look for a Sardinian red from Argiolas, Contini, or Cantina Sociale di Santadi or, even better, try to find a dry, earthy* rosato *from the island. If you must turn to another region, consider a Dolcetto or a Barbera from the Piedmont.*

VARIATION: To top the dish with a filo crust, omit the bread. Spoon the stew into the lightly oiled baking dish and top evenly with the fennel. Pour in the stock, and then scatter the cheese evenly over the surface. Omit the butter pieces. Lay a filo sheet over the filled dish and brush it with melted butter. Repeat, topping with 5 more sheets and brushing each one with butter. Tuck the overhanging filo edges into the sides of the dish. Bake until golden, 25 to 30 minutes.

Panada d'agnello e maiale
Lamb and Pork Pie from Sardinia

SERVES 8

This rich and savory pie may be formed into individual portions, in the *impanada* style, or into a single large pie. The traditional dough is rolled very thin, almost like filo, so rather than suggesting that you struggle with making this strudel-type dough, I have suggested buttered filo as an easy and successful alternative.

Olive oil for browning

1 pound boneless lamb shoulder, trimmed of excess fat and cut into 1/2-inch pieces

1/2 pound boneless pork shoulder, trimmed of excess fat and cut into 1/2-inch pieces

Salt and freshly ground black pepper

1/2 cup meat stock

6 olive oil–packed sun-dried tomatoes, cut into strips or chopped (about 1/2 cup)

2 tablespoons minced garlic

2 tablespoons chopped fresh flat-leaf parsley

8 to 12 filo sheets

1/2 cup unsalted butter, melted

Place a large sauté pan over high heat and film the bottom with olive oil. Working in batches, add the lamb and pork and brown on all sides, adding oil as needed and seasoning with salt and pepper as you turn the meat. Each batch should take 8 to 10 minutes. As each batch is ready, use a slotted spoon to transfer it to a plate.

When all the meat has been browned, return it to the pan over medium-high heat. Add the stock, bring to a gentle boil, reduce the heat to low, and simmer, uncovered, until the meat absorbs all the liquid, 15 to 20 minutes. Using a slotted spoon, transfer the meat to a bowl. Add the sun-dried tomatoes, garlic, and parsley to the meat and toss together to mix. Set aside.

Preheat the oven to 350°F.

To make individual pastries, line a rimmed baking sheet with baker's parchment. Lay the stack of 8 filo sheets on a work surface and cut in half lengthwise. Cover them with a damp towel to keep them from drying out. Remove 1 half sheet from the stack, lay it on the work surface, and brush with melted butter. Top with another half sheet and brush it with butter. Place one-eighth of the filling in the center of the stack and then fold in all 4 sides, overlapping them, to create a rectangular packet. Alternatively, place the filling near the edge of a narrow end of the stack. Fold on the diagonal to form a triangular shape, then bring the bottom of the triangle up against the straight edge. Repeat the folding until you reach the top of the stack, creating a triangle. Place the pastry seam side down on the prepared baking sheet. Repeat with the remaining filling and filo to make 8 packets in all. Brush the tops with butter.

cont'd

To make a large pie, butter a large baking sheet or a pizza pan. Lay the stack of 12 filo sheets on a work surface. Cover with a damp towel to keep them from drying out. Remove 1 sheet from the stack, lay it on the work surface, and brush with melted butter. Top with 5 more sheets, brushing each sheet with butter. Lay the buttered stack of sheets on the prepared pan. Spoon the filling into the center, flatten it a bit, and fold the edges of the filo stack over the filling, forming an informal circle. Cover with 6 more filo sheets, brushing each sheet with melted butter. Tuck the edges of the pastry under to create a free-form round. Brush the top with butter.

Bake the pastries or large pie until golden, allowing 25 minutes for the pastries and 45 minutes for the large pie. Remove from the oven and serve immediately. If you have made the large pie, cut it into wedges.

WINE: *Be adventurous here and try a Sardinian Cannonau from Argiolas, Mancini, or Sella & Mosca or a* rosato *from Sella & Mosca. If you cannot find these, look for a Nebbiolo from the Piedmont.*

VARIATIONS: Add 1 1/2 cups cooked cut-up artichoke hearts, peas, and/or favas to the meat filling with the sun-dried tomatoes. You can also add 2 tablespoons finely chopped fresh rosemary or 1/4 cup finely chopped fresh mint with the parsley.

Pork

When it comes to pork, or *maiale,* it is said that the Italians eat everything but the oink. The loin, chops, shoulder, and ribs are roasted and braised. Sometimes the legs are cured for making various hams, such as prosciutto and *culatello;* the belly is used for pancetta; and the cheeks become *guanciale* (another type of bacon). Other parts, including the head, are transformed into *insaccati* (sausages and salamis). Even the fat comes in two forms: *strutto* and *lardo. Strutto,* sometimes called *sugna,* is rendered pork fat, or lard, and is used in cooking and baking. *Lardo* is the creamy pork fat directly under the skin, cured with herbs, and served in thin slices on bread, or chopped and used in a *battuto* or *soffritto* or for larding meats and fish. The blood is used in sausage, and even the skin, called *cotenna* or *cotica,* is used to flavor stews and soups.

Suckling pigs are popular in Umbria, Tuscany, and Lazio. Sometimes they are called *porcellino,* or "little pig." In culinary terms, they are *porchetto* (or *porcetto*) or *porchetta,* depending on how they are prepared. *Porchetto* is a roast baby pig, prepared either in an oven or on a spit. *Porchetta* is a pig richly seasoned with aromatics, such as rosemary, wild fennel, garlic, and black pepper, and then usually spit roasted. When you see a recipe name that includes the term *in porchetta,* it means that the food has been seasoned with the same seasonings used for *porchetta.* In Italy, this flavorfully cooked pig is sold by the slice at open markets.

A *cinghiale* is a wild boar, and in the past these animals freely roamed the Italian countryside in great numbers. Nowadays, however, they are farm raised in a combination of free-range and confined areas in Tuscany, Lazio, Calabria, Lombardy, Emilia-Romagna, and the Piedmont. Four kinds of *cinghiale* are sold at butcher shops. The youngest, at three to six months of age, is called *cinghialetto.* It is quite tender and mild in flavor and is ideal for grilling and roasting. *Cinghiale giovane,* at six to twelve months of age, is also tender but is stronger in flavor and sometimes calls for a light marinade. *Cinghiale* of one to two years of age has a pronounced gamy flavor and requires longer marinating. Finally, the oldsters, which are up to six years old, are highly gamy and call for a strong and lengthy marinade and a robust sauce, such as *agrodolce* or *dolce e forte.* At the average market, however, you will find mostly the mildly gamy *cinghiale giovane.* Specialty butchers can usually order farm-raised wild boar for you, or you can substitute pork in the recipe here. In general, this domestic boar needs no more than overnight marination to infuse it with additional flavor.

Most of the pork recipes in this book use the major cuts: *costine,* or "ribs"; *lombo,* or "loin"; *spalla,* or "shoulder"; and *costarelle,* or "chops." The loin is ideal for roasting, and may also be braised. For stews, I suggest country-style ribs or pork shoulder or butt. I did find a few recipes using the shank, or *stinco di maiale,* and *cosciotto,* or pork leg, but they are not easily found at the average market. Where *strutto* and *lardo* have been called for, I recommend *lardo,* if you can find it; lard, if you will use it; or pancetta fat. If none of the three is possible, use unsalted butter or olive oil.

Finally, I want to put in a strong recommendation for the stews in this chapter. They are among the most flavorful and delicious in the book.

Spezzatino di maiale all'abruzzese
Pork Stew with Sweet and Hot Peppers from the Abruzzo

SERVES 6

The Abruzzese love hot peppers and delight in drizzling *olio santo* over dishes they believe need a little gastronomic kick. In this rich pork stew, red bell peppers add sweetness and balance the heat of the *diavolicchi,* or "little devils." Some versions of this recipe use chopped rosemary instead of fennel seed. Serve this ideal cold-weather dish over soft polenta.

About 1/2 cup olive oil

2 1/2 pounds boneless pork shoulder, cut into 1 1/2-inch pieces

Salt and freshly ground black pepper

1 large yellow onion, finely chopped

5 cloves garlic, minced

1 tablespoon fennel seeds, toasted in a dry pan and crushed

1 fresh chile pepper, chopped, or 1/2 teaspoon chile pepper flakes, or to taste

1 cup dry red wine

1 can (28 ounces) plum tomatoes with juice, crushed

2 large red bell peppers, seeded and cut into large dice

Red wine vinegar (optional)

Olio santo (see note; optional)

In a large sauté pan or Dutch oven, heat 1/4 cup of the olive oil over medium-high heat. Working in batches, brown the pork on all sides, adding the remaining oil as needed and seasoning with salt and black pepper as you turn the meat. Each batch should take 8 to 10 minutes. As each batch is ready, use a slotted spoon to transfer it to a plate.

Return the pan to medium heat, add the onion to the fat remaining in the pan, and sauté until very soft, about 10 minutes. Add the garlic, fennel seeds, and chile pepper and cook for 3 minutes longer. Add the wine and tomatoes and their juice and simmer for a few minutes to blend the flavors. Return the pork to the pan, add the bell peppers, raise the heat to medium-high, and bring to a gentle boil. Reduce the heat to low, cover, and simmer until the pork is meltingly tender, 1 to 1 1/2 hours.

Taste the stew and adjust the seasoning. You may want to add a few spoonfuls of vinegar for balance. If you want a spicier dish, sprinkle in a few drops of *olio santo.* Serve at once.

WINE: *Old, reliable Montepulciano d'Abruzzo will work here, as will a Sangiovese from Molise or a Rosso Conero from the Marches.*

***

NOTE: To make *olio santo,* warm 1 cup extra virgin olive oil over medium heat. Add 1 tablespoon chile pepper flakes and heat to about 180°F. Remove from the heat and set aside to steep for 1 to 2 days. Strain through a fine-mesh sieve and store in a tightly capped bottle in a cool place.

Prosciutto, *Lardo, Guanciale,* and Pancetta

This quartet of cured meats represents some of the most prized products of the beloved pig. Simply put, Italians cooks would be bereft without them. The most famous of the four is prosciutto, with the most renowned example *prosciutto di Parma.* Made from the hind thigh of the pig, prosciutto is a salt-cured, air-dried ham, and a government stamp on its rounded side attests to its being produced according to strict government regulations. Other stellar examples that are exported include the darker and sweeter *prosciutto di San Daniele* from Friuli, and *prosciutto di Carpegna* from a town on the border of Tuscany and the Marches.

Lardo, creamy pork fat cured with salt and herbs, is a treat that you are most likely to sample first in Italy. It is usually sliced paper-thin and served on top of warm bread. It is also used for larding and may be chopped and used in a *soffritto* or a *battuto* for a stew or soup. Among the most well-regarded products are those from Colonnata in Tuscany, where it is cured

in marble boxes; from Langhirano in Emilia-Romagna; and from the Aosta Valley, home of *lardo di Arnad.* Some companies outside of Italy have started to produce this delicacy, including Niman Ranch in California.

Guanciale, pig's cheek cured with salt and pepper, is often used in Roman cooking for such dishes as *spaghetti alla gricia* (with garlic, onion, and *guanciale*) or *spaghetti alla carbonara.* I know only that California's Niman Ranch makes this product, but others outside of Italy probably do as well. In a pinch, pancetta can be substituted.

Finally, *pancetta arrotolata* is pork belly that is rolled, seasoned with pepper and cloves, salt cured, and then enclosed in a thin casing. It is a popular filling for *panini,* is served on antipasto platters, and is used in cooking. Unlike *guanciale* and *lardo,* pancetta is made by a number of producers outside of Italy.

Arista di maiale alla fiorentina
Roast Pork Loin as Cooked in Florence

SERVES 6

The term *arista* is traditionally associated with roast pork loin. There is more than one legend explaining its origin, but the most popular one takes place in Florence: In 1430 (others say 1450), the Medici family held a conference in the city during which a dinner of roast pork was served to visiting dignitaries. The meat was so delicious that the Greek representative (some sources say it was a Byzantine patriarch) exclaimed *"Àrista!"* which means "excellent." Others, of course, say that the name was around even before this famed dinner. Whichever is the case, the name has stuck. The classic accompaniments are roast potatoes and braised greens—Swiss chard, dandelion greens, broccoli rabe—the last a good balance to the richness of the meat. The seasoning for this Florentine pork is similar to that for *porchetta* (roast pig).

1 bone-in pork loin roast, 4 to 5 pounds

4 to 6 cloves garlic, 2 cloves cut into slivers and 2 to 4 cloves chopped

2 tablespoons fresh rosemary needles, about one-fourth left whole and the balance chopped

1 tablespoon minced fresh sage

Grated zest of 1 lemon

1/2 teaspoon ground cloves

Salt and freshly ground black pepper

3 tablespoons fresh lemon juice

Preheat the oven to 350°F.

Using a small, sharp knife, make small slits between the bones of the roast and a few on the top of the roast as well. Insert the garlic slivers and whole rosemary needles into the slits. In a mortar using a pestle, pound together the chopped garlic and rosemary, the sage, lemon zest, cloves, a little salt and pepper, and lemon juice until a paste forms. Rub the paste all over the surface of the roast. (For a more intense flavor, do this step the night before you plan to cook the roast, and refrigerate the roast overnight.) Place the roast in a roasting pan.

Roast the pork until an instant-read meat thermometer inserted into the thickest part away from bone registers 145°F, about 1 hour. Remove from the oven and let rest for 15 minutes before carving.

Cut the roast into chops and serve at once.

WINE: *Brunello di Montalcino and Rosso di Montalcino are good candidates, as are Chianti Classico, Dolcetto, and Pinot Nero. Do not overlook the possibility of a white wine. Try a Riesling from Friuli, or a Spatlese Riesling from Germany or Washington State.*

NOTE: For a slower variation, roast the pork in a 225°F oven for 4 hours.

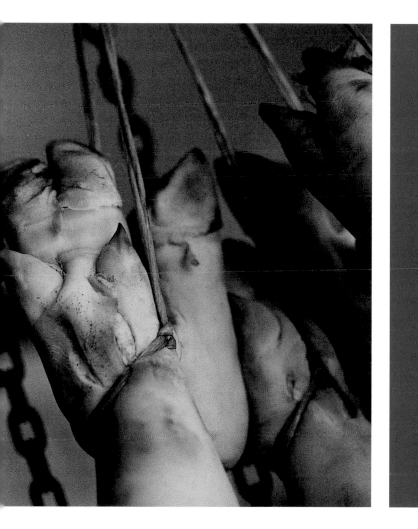

How to Make *Porchetta* without a Whole Pig

You can season a pork roast in the classic manner
used for a whole roast pig. Make a paste of 10 cloves
garlic, chopped; 2 tablespoons fennel seeds, toasted
in a dry pan and crushed; 3 tablespoons chopped
fresh rosemary; 1/4 cup chopped fresh fennel fronds;
2 tablespoons salt; 1 tablespoon coarsely ground or
cracked black pepper; and a generous pinch of
ground cloves. Moisten the paste with a little olive
oil. Butterfly a boneless 3- to 3 1/2-pound pork loin
roast: Using a long, sharp knife, cut the pork nearly
in half horizontally, stopping within about 1/2 inch of
the opposite side. Open it up to lie relatively flat, like
a book. Place between 2 sheets of plastic wrap and,
using a meat pounder, pound it a bit to flatten it
evenly, and then rub it with half of the paste. Roll up
the pork and tie securely with kitchen string. Rub
the remaining paste evenly over the outside of the
pork, then cover and marinate in the refrigerator for
at least overnight or for up to 2 days. Roast in a
350°F oven for about 1 1/2 hours, or in a 225°F oven
for about 4 hours. It is ready when an instant-read
meat thermometer inserted into the thickest part
registers 145°F.

Braciole alla calabrese
Rolled Pork Shoulder from Calabria

SERVES 4

As with Sicilian *farsu magru* (page 174), in which the rolled stuffed meat is braised in tomatoes and wine, two separate courses are produced here: a rich meat-infused sauce for *maccheroni* for the *primo* and braised meat for the *secondo*. Sometimes called *braciola alla brugia* (named for the Brugi, an ancient people who lived in the area where the dish is now eaten), this specialty of the Calabrian town of Cosenza may also be prepared with veal. The traditional accompaniment is diced sautéed eggplant, but "Sitting Down" Broccoflower (page 261) is an excellent stand-in. In neighboring Basilicata, a similar meat roll is made, but nutmeg replaces the cinnamon, the wine is white, and the sauce is served over pasta or wheat berries.

1 piece boneless pork shoulder or pork loin, 2 1/2 pounds

8 cloves garlic, minced (about 1/4 cup)

6 black peppercorns

2 tablespoons chopped fresh flat-leaf parsley sprigs

5 pancetta slices, about 5 ounces total weight

1/2 cup diced pecorino cheese

1 teaspoon ground cinnamon, plus more to taste

1/4 cup lard or olive oil

Salt and freshly ground black pepper

1 1/2 cups dry red wine

1/2 cup water, or as needed

1 can (28 ounces) plum tomatoes, chopped, with juice, or 1 can (28 ounces) ground or crushed tomatoes packed in purée

1/2 teaspoon chile pepper flakes

A few fresh basil leaves (optional)

Pinch of sugar (optional)

Place the pork between 2 sheets of plastic wrap and, using a meat pounder, pound it until it is a relatively flat, even piece no more than about 3/4 inch thick. If the pork is quite thick to start, butterfly it first: Using a long, sharp knife, cut the pork nearly in half horizontally, stopping within about 1/2 inch of the opposite side. Open it up to lie relatively flat, like a book, then place between sheets of plastic wrap and pound as described.

In a mortar using a pestle, pound together three-fourths of the garlic, the peppercorns, and the parsley to form a paste. (Alternatively, use a mini food processor to make the paste.) Rub the paste on top of the pork, lay the pancetta slices in a single layer over the paste, sprinkle with the cheese, and then dust with the 1 teaspoon cinnamon. Roll up, forming a compact cylinder, and tie securely with kitchen string.

In a Dutch oven, heat the lard or olive oil over medium-high heat. Add the pork and brown on all sides, seasoning with salt and black pepper as you turn the meat. The browning should take 8 to 10 minutes. If the oil has turned dark, pour it out of the pan. Add the wine, 1/2 cup water, the tomatoes, the chile pepper flakes, the remaining garlic, and the basil, if using. Bring to a gentle boil, reduce the heat to low, cover, and simmer, adding water if needed and turning occasionally, until the meat is very tender, 1 1/2 hours.

Transfer the meat to a carving board, cover with aluminum foil to keep warm, and let rest for at least 10 minutes before carving.

Taste the pan sauce and adjust the seasoning with salt, black pepper, cinnamon, and a pinch of sugar for balance. Reheat the sauce. (If you are serving pasta as a first course, toss it with the sauce, reserving a little of the sauce for serving with the meat.) To serve the meat roll, snip the strings, cut into thick slices, and arrange the slices on a warmed platter. Spoon a little of the sauce over the top, then serve.

WINE: *Calabrian wines are difficult to find outside of Italy. You can instead drink a Sicilian red, such as a Nero d'Avola from Corvo, Cos, Abbazia Sant'Anastasia, or Gulfi, or an Apulian Salice Salentino.*

Spezzatino di maiale e castagne
Pork Stew with Chestnuts

SERVES 6

This Piedmontese recipe was originally prepared with wild boar, a rare commodity at most markets. I always use pork shoulder for this dish, however, and the results are sensational. If you want to try the more exotic version, ask your butcher to order some boar for you. True wild boar, rather than farm raised, would need to be marinated in the wine and vegetables for a few days to tame the gamy taste before it could be cooked. But if you are using pork or even farm-raised boar, you can marinate it overnight to infuse it with flavor if you like, or you can skip the marination step. The chestnuts make a superb addition. Peeling them is tedious work, of course, but the effort is worth it in this case, as the nuts add immeasurable sweetness and richness to the stew. If fresh chestnuts are not in the market, use dried chestnuts or vacuum-packed cooked chestnuts. Serve the stew with polenta.

1 1/2 pounds fresh chestnuts, 3/4 pound dried chestnuts, or 1/2 pound vacuum-packed cooked chestnuts

Salt

1 lemon zest strip, 1 tablespoon sugar, 3 whole cloves, and 1 cinnamon stick, about 3 inches long, if using dried chestnuts

5 to 6 tablespoons olive oil

1 yellow onion, finely chopped

2 carrots, peeled and finely chopped

1 celery heart, finely chopped

6 to 8 fresh sage leaves, finely chopped

2 pounds boneless pork shoulder, cut into 2-inch pieces

Freshly ground black pepper

6 juniper berries, smashed; 4 or 5 whole cloves; and 1 cinnamon stick, 3 inches long, tied in a cheesecloth sachet

3 cups Barbera or other dry red wine

If using fresh chestnuts, cut an X on the flat side of each chestnut. Place the chestnuts in a saucepan, add water to cover, bring to a boil, salt lightly, and boil for 5 to 10 minutes. Remove from the heat. Lift the chestnuts from the water one at a time and peel, starting at the X and removing both the hard outer shell and the bitter inner skin (they are easiest to peel while still hot). Set the peeled chestnuts aside. If using dried chestnuts, soak them in hot water to cover for 3 hours, changing the water as necessary to maintain a good temperature, then drain, place in a saucepan, and add the lemon zest strip, sugar, cloves, cinnamon stick, and ample water to cover. Place over medium heat, bring to a simmer, and cook until tender, about 1 hour; the timing will depend on the age of the nuts. Drain, discard the seasonings, and set aside. If using vacuum-packed chestnuts, set aside.

In a large sauté pan, heat 2 tablespoons of the olive oil over medium heat. Add the onion, carrots, celery, and sage and sauté until pale gold, about 12 minutes. Using a slotted spoon, transfer the vegetables to a Dutch oven.

cont'd

Return the sauté pan to high heat and add 2 to 3 table-spoons of the olive oil. Working in batches, brown the pork on all sides, adding oil as needed and seasoning with salt and pepper as you turn the meat. Each batch should take 8 to 10 minutes. As each batch is ready, use a slotted spoon to transfer it to the Dutch oven.

When all of the pork has been browned, add the spice sachet and wine to the Dutch oven. Place over medium heat and bring to a gentle boil. Reduce the heat to low, cover, and simmer until the meat is tender, about 1 1/2 hours, adding the chestnuts during the last 20 minutes.

Remove and discard the spice sachet. If there is too much liquid in the pot, use a slotted spoon to transfer the pork and chest-nuts to a bowl. Return the pan to high heat and boil the pan juices until they are reduced to a good consistency. Return the pork and chestnuts to the pan, reheat gently, then serve.

WINE: *The Piedmont's Barbera d'Alba or Barbera di Monferrato will match the earthiness and the perfume of this dish. If you are in the mood to splurge, look for the local Barbaresco from Gaja, Renato Ratti, or Cantina del Pino.*

———————————

VARIATION: Add 1/2 cup grappa- or Cognac-plumped prunes with the chestnuts.

Costine di maiale e salamelle
Braised Pork Ribs and Sausage with Tomatoes and Red Wine

SERVES 8

Versions of this rustic, soulful recipe appear all over Italy. The amount of tomatoes in the dish varies. As you go farther south, more tomato and red wine are used in the sauce. Up north, less tomato is used and white wine prevails. Some cooks add a tiny bit of vinegar, while others might add a pinch of cinnamon. In Lombardy, where the dish is variously spelled *cassoeula*, *cazzoeula,* and *casoeûla,* among other ways, a generous measure of cabbage is braised along with the ribs and sausage, and pig's ears, pig's feet, and pig skin are included. I recommend using so-called country-style ribs (more meat) for this filling braise, but you can use back ribs as well. If you are friends with your local Italian delicatessen owner, ask him or her to save you the outer pieces of prosciutto fat that are usually trimmed away and discarded. The fat will enrich this dish. Serve with soft polenta and spicy braised greens.

1/4 pound prosciutto fat (see recipe introduction) or pancetta, chopped

1 yellow onion, chopped

1 carrot, peeled and chopped

1 celery stalk, chopped

4 cloves garlic, chopped

2 tablespoons chopped fresh marjoram

2 tablespoons olive oil

12 small or 6 large hot pork sausages

1 1/2 pounds pork ribs, cut into 2-inch pieces

1 cup dry white or red wine

1 cup water

1 can (28 ounces) ground or crushed tomatoes packed in purée

Salt and freshly ground black pepper

Grated pecorino cheese for serving

Combine the prosciutto fat or pancetta, onion, carrot, celery, garlic, and marjoram on a chopping board and chop together to form a medium-fine *battuto*. In a large sauté pan or Dutch oven, heat the olive oil over medium heat. Add the *battuto* and sauté until softened and pale gold, about 12 minutes.

Prick the sausages with a fork in a few places, then add the sausages and ribs to the pan. When they have taken on a bit of color, after 10 minutes or so, add the wine. When it has evaporated, add the water, reduce the heat to low, cover, and simmer for 30 minutes longer. Add the tomatoes, season with salt and pepper, re-cover, and cook over low heat until the pork is falling-off-the-bone tender and the sauce is thick, about 1 1/2 hours longer.

Using a large spoon, spoon off and discard the excess fat. Serve the dish sprinkled with pecorino cheese.

WINE: *Go south to Apulia for Primitivo di Manduria from Felline or a Primitivo di Salento from Conti Zecca. A California Zinfandel from Rafanelli, Ridge, Renwood, or Biale would also do nicely.*

Bocconcini di cinghiale con polenta di farro
Wild Boar Stew with Farro *Polenta*

SERVES 4

For a long time, I was curious about *farro* cultivation and processing, so on a visit to the Abruzzo, I was delighted to have the opportunity to meet Amadeo Fiore, who owns a *farro* company, Gioie di Fattoria, in Torano Nuovo. Along with whole-grain *farro,* he produces a quick-cooking ground *farro* for polenta, called *puls,* and a coarsely ground *farro* called *farricello,* which resembles cracked wheat. He served a delicious wild boar stew spooned over *farro* polenta. If you cannot find ground *farro* at the market, you can serve the stew with cornmeal polenta or *polenta di taragna* (page 90), or you can try grinding whole-grain *farro* in a spice mill or blender and then cook it as you would polenta (page 89). And if you cannot find wild boar, use pork shoulder.

2 tablespoons olive oil, plus more for browning

1 yellow onion, chopped

3 carrots, peeled and chopped

2 celery stalks, chopped

2 pounds boneless wild or farm-raised boar, cut into 1 1/2-inch pieces

Salt and freshly ground black pepper

2 cups dry red wine

2 tablespoons Dijon mustard

About 2 cups meat stock

In a Dutch oven, heat the 2 tablespoons olive oil over medium heat. Add the onion, carrots, and celery and sauté until softened, about 8 minutes. Remove the pot from the heat.

Place a large sauté pan over high heat and film the bottom with olive oil. Working in batches, add the boar and brown on all sides, adding oil as needed and seasoning with salt and pepper as you turn the meat. Each batch should take 8 to 10 minutes. As each batch is ready, use a slotted spoon to transfer it to the Dutch oven.

When all of the meat is in the Dutch oven, return the pot to medium heat. Add the wine, cover, and cook for 15 minutes. Stir in the mustard, reduce the heat to low, re-cover, and cook, adding the stock as needed to keep the stew moist and juicy, until the meat is very tender, about 1 1/2 to 2 hours.

Taste and adjust the seasoning, then serve.

WINE: *Montepulciano d'Abruzzo is the logical local choice, but Rosso Conero or Rosso Piceno from the neighboring Marches would also satisfy.*

NOTE: To make this a sauce instead of a stew, either cut the meat into 1/2-inch pieces in the manner of *bruscitt* (page 59) before cooking it, or chop the meat coarsely after cooking and reheat it in the pan juices.

Arrosto di maiale al latte e nocciole
Pork Loin Cooked in Milk with Hazelnuts

SERVES 6 TO 8

Braising meat in milk is a regional specialty of the Piedmont, Lombardy, and Emilia-Romagna, although I have found recipes for this delicate dish as far south as Sardinia. Slow cooking in milk results in meat that is incredibly tender and moist, but the pan sauce curdles over heat and you will need to emulsify it in a blender before serving. In this recipe from the Piedmont, the sauce is thickened with toasted ground hazelnuts. If you prefer a bit of crunch, you can chop the nuts instead.

2 tablespoons unsalted butter

2 tablespoons olive oil, or as needed

1 boneless pork loin roast, 3 to 4 pounds, rolled and tied into a compact shape

Salt and freshly ground black pepper

2 yellow onions, sliced

8 fresh sage leaves

4 cups milk

1/2 cup hazelnuts, toasted and ground or chopped

Freshly grated nutmeg (optional)

Juice of 1/2 lemon (optional)

Preheat the oven to 350°F.

In a Dutch oven or other heavy ovenproof pot, melt the butter with the 2 tablespoons olive oil over high heat. Add the pork, fat side down first, and brown on all sides, seasoning with salt and pepper as you turn the meat. It should take 8 to 10 minutes. Transfer the pork to a plate. If the cooking fat has turned dark, discard it.

Return the pot to medium heat and add about 2 tablespoons olive oil if the fat has been discarded. Add the onions and sage and sauté until the onions are softened, about 8 minutes. Return the pork to the pot and pour in the milk. Cover, place in the oven, and cook, turning 3 or 4 times, until very tender when pierced with a fork, about 2 hours. Remove from the oven, transfer the meat to a cutting board, and cover with aluminum foil to keep warm.

Using a large spoon, skim off the excess fat from the pan juices and discard. The sauce will look curdled. Pour it into a blender or food processor and process until smooth. Return the sauce to the pot and add the hazelnuts. Season with salt and pepper and add a little nutmeg or lemon juice if needed for balance. Reheat to serving temperature.

Snip the strings on the meat. Cut into slices and arrange on a warmed platter. Spoon the sauce over the top and serve.

WINE: *If you want to play up the cream and nuts, go white with Sauvignon Blanc, Pinot Grigio, Verdicchio, or Greco di Tufo. If you want to drink a red, go light with Dolcetto, Pinot Nero, or a Barbera with some acidity.*

Rifritto di maiale e mele
Pork Stew with Apples

SERVES 4

At Ristorante Le Berri in Valle Castellano in the Abruzzo, pork and apples are cooked together in a stew. It is traditionally prepared with Renette apples, which are rust-gold on the outside, similar to Golden Delicious. I have also made the dish with Gala apples, and they were wonderful. After cooking the recipe a few times as written, I made some changes because the meat was too dry. I now cook the pork covered at all times. I also mince the chile pepper so that the heat infuses the meat and the sauce. The orange slices give the dish a festive tropical look, but they are not required. They are a restaurant touch that adds color to the plate.

Olive oil for browning

1¹/₂ to 2 pounds fatty boneless pork shoulder, cut into 2-inch pieces

Salt and freshly ground black pepper

10 cloves garlic, chopped

1 fresh chile pepper, minced

3 fresh rosemary sprigs

1 cup dry white wine

4 apples, halved, peeled, cored, and sliced

2 oranges (optional)

Place a large sauté pan over high heat and film the bottom with olive oil. Working in batches, add the pork and brown on all sides, adding oil as needed and seasoning with salt and black pepper as you turn the meat. Each batch should take 8 to 10 minutes. As each batch is ready, use a slotted spoon to transfer it to a plate.

Return all the pork to the pan, place over medium heat, and add the garlic, chile pepper, rosemary, and wine. Mix well, bring to a gentle boil, reduce the heat to low, cover, and simmer for about 50 minutes.

Uncover and skim off the excess fat with a large spoon. Add the apples and a few ladlefuls of water, re-cover, and continue to cook over low heat until the pork is tender, about 30 minutes longer. Check from time to time and add water if the liquid has reduced too much.

Meanwhile, if using the oranges, cut a thick slice off the top and bottom of 1 orange, exposing the flesh. Stand the orange upright and, following the contour of the fruit, cut downward to remove the peel and pith in thick slices. Slice the orange crosswise, set the slices aside, and repeat with the second orange.

cont'd

Remove and discard the rosemary sprigs from the pot. Add the orange slices and simmer for 3 minutes to heat through. Taste and adjust the seasoning, then serve.

WINE: *If you want red, try Rosso Piceno Superiore from Ercole Velenosi or Tenuta Cocci Grifoni, or Rosso Conero from Moroder or Umani Ronchi. Pinot Nero or Dolcetto would be harmonious as well. But the fruit means that you can also go with a complex white from Friuli, such as Sauvignon de la Tour from Villa Russiz, Tocai Friulano from Mario Schiopetto, or Vintage Tunina, a blend from Jermann.*

NOTE: In Trieste, a similar dish is made with pork chops. If you want to use pork chops to make this dish, first brine the chops as directed on page 227. Then, remove them from the brine, pat dry, and brown as directed. Proceed as directed, but reduce the cooking time to 35 to 45 minutes.

Bombas alla sarda
Meatballs from Sardinia

SERVES 4

One day, my grandchildren requested spaghetti and meatballs for dinner because they had tried the dish at a local pasta chain restaurant. After I gave my son "the look" for taking them there, I decided that I would make spaghetti and meatballs the classic way, with my favorite Apulian *polpette* (meatballs). I carefully browned the meatballs and heated them in the sauce. My granddaughter, ever the diplomat, said "Grandma, I don't want to hurt your feelings, but I like the other meatballs better. These are too crunchy. I like them when they are soft." I knew then that she would have preferred them Sardinian style. Sardinian cooks braise their *polpette,* also known as *bombas,* directly in the tomato sauce for a more tender texture. Serve these meatballs with mashed potatoes, or, if you are cooking for children, with spaghetti. For those who like their meatballs with crunch, brown them quickly in olive oil and then heat them in the sauce. By the way, the next time I made Sardinian-style meatballs for the diplomat, and she said she now liked meatballs both ways, soft and crunchy.

FOR THE MEATBALLS

1 pound ground pork

1/4 cup dried bread crumbs, or 1/2 cup fresh bread crumbs

2 eggs

6 tablespoons grated pecorino cheese

2 cloves garlic, minced

1/4 cup chopped fresh flat-leaf parsley

Salt and freshly ground black pepper

FOR THE SAUCE

2 to 3 tablespoons olive oil

1 yellow onion, chopped

1 pound tomatoes, peeled, seeded, and chopped, or 2 cups canned tomatoes, seeded and chopped

1/2 cup water

Salt and freshly ground black pepper

To make the meatballs, in a bowl, combine the pork, bread crumbs, eggs, cheese, garlic, parsley, and a little salt and pepper and mix together until smooth. Fry a small nugget of the mixture, taste, and adjust the seasoning. Form the mixture into balls about 1 inch in diameter.

To make the sauce, in a sauté pan, heat the olive oil over medium heat. Add the onion and sauté until softened, about 8 minutes. Add the tomatoes and water, mix well, and then add the meatballs. Bring to a gentle boil, reduce the heat to low, and simmer, uncovered, until the meatballs are cooked through and tender, about 45 minutes.

Season the sauce with salt and pepper, then serve the meatballs and sauce.

WINE: *Pour a Sardinian Cannonau. If you want something a bit lighter, drink a Rosso Conero from the Marches or a Nebbiolo d'Alba from the Piedmont.*

Costarelle in porchetta con patate e finocchio
Pork Chops with Potatoes and Fennel

SERVES 6

When you see the term *in porchetta*, you automatically expect the magic trio of fennel, garlic, and rosemary. The last is missing in this recipe from the Agriturismo La Cittidella dei Sibillini in the Marches town of Montemonaco, but the dish is still deliciously fragrant. While the original recipe calls for wild fennel fronds, they may be hard to find. You either will need to buy several fennel bulbs with their fronds intact, or you can ask the produce person at your market to save the fennel fronds that are usually discarded when bulbs are trimmed before putting them out for sale. Failing those two options, the variation provides yet another solution.

6 bone-in pork chops, each 1 to 1 1/2 inches thick, brined for 2 hours (see note)

Salt and freshly ground black pepper

1 pound fennel fronds, coarsely chopped

2 yellow onions, chopped

2 carrots, peeled and chopped

2 celery stalks, chopped

6 cloves garlic, chopped

1/4 cup extra virgin olive oil, or as needed

1 cup dry white wine

2 cups Rich Tomato Sauce (page 69), Tomato Sauce (page 69), or canned tomato sauce

2 pounds new potatoes, cut into thick wedges if large or in half if small

Meat stock or water to cover

Fennel seeds, toasted in a dry pan and ground, or fennel pollen, if needed

Season the pork chops with salt and pepper and set aside. Combine half of the fennel fronds, the onions, carrots, celery, and garlic on a chopping board and chop together to form a medium-fine *battuto*.

In a Dutch oven or heavy skillet, heat the olive oil over medium heat. Add the chopped vegetables and sauté until softened, about 8 minutes. Using a slotted spoon, transfer to a bowl. Return the pan to high heat. Working in batches if necessary, add the chops and sear on each side for a few minutes until golden, adding oil as needed. As each batch is ready, transfer it to a plate.

Return the chops and the vegetables to the pan, add the wine, and cook over medium heat until the wine reduces but does not evaporate entirely. Add the tomato sauce, the remaining fennel fronds, the potatoes, and enough stock or water just to cover all of the ingredients. Bring to a gentle boil, reduce the heat to low, cover, and simmer until the meat and potatoes are tender and the sauce has thickened, about 1 hour or a bit longer. Check from time to time and add water if the liquid has reduced too much.

Taste the sauce. If you think it needs a stronger fennel flavor, add ground toasted fennel seeds or fennel pollen to taste. Season with salt and pepper, then serve.

VARIATION: If you cannot find fennel fronds, you can use ground toasted fennel seeds or fennel pollen (extracted from the dried flowers of wild fennel), a popular Tuscan seasoning, in their place. Add 2 tablespoons fennel seeds, toasted in a dry pan and ground, or 2 teaspoons fennel pollen with the stock or water. To heighten the overall fennel profile of the meal, serve braised fennel bulbs on the side.

NOTE: Today, pork chops are often so lean that they become dry in cooking. To keep them moist and juicy, take the time to put them in a brine for a spell. To create a simple brine, dissolve 2 tablespoons each sugar and kosher salt in $1/2$ cup hot water. Place the chops in a shallow dish, add the cooled sugar-salt mixture, and then add cold water just to cover the chops. Marinate at room temperature for 1 or 2 hours, or in the refrigerator for up to 4 hours. Drain well and pat dry before proceeding with the recipe.

Rambasicci
Stuffed Cabbage from Trieste

SERVES 6

Nowadays, I find it almost impossible to find Savoy cabbage at my market, but these little cabbage packets from Trieste are so tasty that you will have success even with plain green head cabbage. I have tested the filling with a combination of beef and pork, and with pork only, and I find the latter richer and better. I also have had trouble finding smoked ricotta, a favorite cheese of Friuli, but I have used *ricotta salata* and even fine gratings of smoked mozzarella in its place. Neither is regionally correct, but they both have tasted good. If desired, serve the cabbage packets with toasted bread for sopping up the rich juices.

FOR THE FILLING

1 1/2 pounds ground pork, or half each ground pork and ground beef

3 cloves garlic, minced

1 small yellow onion, minced

1 cup fresh bread crumbs

1 egg

3 tablespoons chopped fresh flat-leaf parsley

1 teaspoon sweet paprika

Salt and freshly ground black pepper

To make the filling, in a bowl, combine the meat, garlic, onion, bread crumbs, egg, parsley, paprika, and 1 teaspoon each salt and pepper. Mix well and set aside.

Bring a large pot two-thirds full of water to a boil. Meanwhile, using a sharp knife, cut out the tough core of the cabbage(s). Salt the water lightly and slip the cabbage into the pot. When the water returns to a simmer, adjust the heat to maintain a gentle simmer and cook gently until the cabbage leaves soften, about 10 minutes. Lift the cabbage out of the water and drain it in a colander. If using 2 cabbages, repeat with the second cabbage. Remove only the outer large leaves from the head(s). You need 15 to 18 leaves in all. Reserve the remaining cabbage for another use.

Spread out the cabbage leaves, inside facing upward, on a work surface. Place a few tablespoons of the filling on the center of a leaf, fold the top of the leaf over to cover it, fold in the sides, and then fold up the bottom, making a neat package. Secure closed with toothpicks. Repeat until all of the filling is used.

1 large or 2 medium Savoy cabbages, 1¹/₂ to 2 pounds

Salt

2 tablespoons unsalted butter

2 tablespoons olive oil

1 large yellow onion, chopped

1 teaspoon sweet paprika

About 3 cups meat stock

¹/₂ cup grated smoked ricotta, ricotta salata, or smoked mozzarella cheese

¹/₂ cup toasted bread crumbs (page 276)

In a large Dutch oven or other heavy pot, melt the butter with the olive oil over medium heat. Add the onion and sauté until softened and almost golden, about 10 minutes. Add the paprika and cook for 5 minutes longer. Place the cabbage packages in the pot, toothpick side up, add the stock to cover, and bring to a gentle boil. Reduce the heat to low, cover, and simmer gently until aromatic, the pan juices are somewhat reduced, and the cabbage leaves are very tender, 1 to 1¹/₂ hours.

If you want to reduce the pan juices further, use a slotted spoon to transfer the cabbage packages to a plate and cover them with aluminum foil to keep warm. Reduce the juices over high heat until they are the desired consistency.

Transfer the cabbage packages to warmed individual bowls and ladle on the pan juices. Garnish with the cheese and toasted bread crumbs. Serve at once.

WINE: *Look for a Pinot Nero, Tocai, or Riesling from Friuli.*

———————————

NOTE: You may also proceed as directed, and once the stock has been added, place the pot in a preheated 350°F oven and cook for 1¹/₂ hours.

Braciolettini di maiale al ragù
Little Stuffed Pork Rolls in a Rich Sauce

SERVES 4

Neapolitans understand and appreciate *braciole,* large or small, not that they have a monopoly on the concept. These little pork bundles are also popular in Calabria, Basilicata, and Sicily. While you can prepare scallops of veal or beef the same way, pork *involtini*—yet another term for these rolls—are especially succulent; they have a bit more fat, which keeps the meat juicier during the braising process. Because the resulting sauce is worthy of adorning *ziti* or rigatoni or a mound of mashed potatoes, I have made sure that you will have leftover sauce.

FOR THE ROLLS

1/4 cup chopped lardo *(page 211) or pancetta*

4 cloves garlic, minced

4 tablespoons chopped fresh flat-leaf parsley

Freshly ground black pepper

8 slices pork loin, each about 1/4 inch thick, about 2 pounds total weight

4 long slices prosciutto, about 2 ounces total weight, cut in half to fit pork slices

1/2 cup pine nuts

1/2 cup raisins

1/4 pound provolone cheese, cut into 8 equal strips

To make the rolls, combine the *lardo* or pancetta, garlic, and parsley on a cutting board and chop together to form a rustic paste. Season the mixture with pepper.

Lay the pork slices on a work surface. Top each pork slice with a half slice of prosciutto, one-eighth of the paste, and 1 tablespoon each of the pine nuts and raisins. Place a strip of cheese in the center. Roll up each pork slice, and tie each end and the center with kitchen string.

In a large sauté pan, heat the pancetta fat or *lardo* and olive oil over medium-high heat. Add the pork rolls and brown on all sides, 8 to 10 minutes. Add the onion and let it color a bit. Reduce the heat to low, add the tomato purée and 1 1/2 cups of the wine, cover, and simmer until the meat is tender, 1 to 1 1/2 hours. Check from time to time and add wine or water if the liquid has reduced too much.

3 tablespoons chopped pancetta fat or lardo
(page 211)

1 tablespoon olive oil

1 yellow onion, chopped

2 cups tomato purée

1¹/₂ to 2 cups dry red wine

Salt and freshly ground black pepper

Using a slotted spoon, transfer the pork rolls to a plate. Snip and discard the strings. Taste the sauce and season with salt and pepper and keep over medium-low heat. Return the meat rolls to the hot sauce and turn them in the sauce to coat them well for about 5 minutes. Serve the rolls with some of the sauce spooned over the top. Reserve the remaining sauce for another use (see recipe introduction).

WINE: *To drink locally, pour Aglianico from Mastroberardino or a Taurasi from Caggiano or Villa Matilde. Your usual house red would be perfect here as well.*

———————————

VARIATION: You can use boneless pork chops in place of the pork loin slices, but you must butterfly them first. Using a sharp knife, cut each pork chop nearly in half horizontally, stopping within about ¹/₂ inch of the opposite side. Open it up to lie relatively flat, like a book. Place between 2 sheets of plastic wrap and, using a meat pounder, pound to flatten to an even ¹/₄ inch thick.

Salsiccia, patate e lampascioni in tortiera
Sausage, Potato, and Wild Onion Casserole

SERVES 4

Lampascioni are the slightly bitter hyacinth bulbs so popular in Apulia. They are a type of onion, once only wild and now cultivated as well, but are perhaps an acquired taste, and must be soaked to remove some of their bitterness before using. It is unlikely that you will find them easily outside of southern Italy, so I have used the sweeter flat-topped cipollini onions here in their place. The choice of sausage is up to you. I prefer a spicy fennel sausage, although milder ones would work well, too. The Apulians cook this dish in a *tortiera,* a typical terra-cotta casserole of the region, but a gratin dish or other baking dish can be used.

1 1/2 pounds hot or mild fresh pork sausage, casings removed and meat broken up into small pieces

1 pound russet potatoes, peeled and cut into thick slices

3/4 pound cipollini onions, parboiled for 8 minutes, drained, and peeled

5 or 6 tomatoes, peeled, seeded, and cut into strips (fresh or canned)

2 cloves garlic, minced

1/4 cup chopped fresh flat-leaf parsley

1/2 cup grated pecorino cheese

1/4 cup water

Salt and freshly ground black pepper

Preheat the oven to 350°F. Oil a 2-quart gratin dish or other baking dish.

Combine the sausage pieces, potatoes, onions, tomatoes, garlic, parsley, and 1/4 cup of the cheese in the prepared dish and mix well. Drizzle in the water, season with salt and pepper, and cover with aluminum foil.

Bake for about 30 minutes. Uncover, sprinkle the remaining 1/4 cup cheese over the top, and continue to bake until the potatoes are tender, the sausage is cooked through, and the cheese is golden, about 30 minutes longer. Serve directly from the dish.

WINE: *Drink a Primitivo from Apulia or a Zinfandel from California.*

VEGETABLES

As a form of protest to decades of overcooked, mushy vegetables, many of us now eat only barely cooked vegetables, their bright colors and crispness a welcome antidote to the gray and soggy vegetables of the past. But sometimes I think that the pendulum has swung too far, and I become tired of eating grassy-tasting, almost raw "cooked" vegetables. Pure cellulose holds little appeal for me.

There is a big difference between over-cooking and slow cooking. In Italy, an established slow cooking tradition exists that renders vegetables truly tender and full of flavor. Vegetable braises, sometimes called "suffocated" because they cook in so little liquid, coax layers of flavors from vegetables that would be monodimensional if quickly steamed or sautéed. Gratins, *tortini* (vegetable tarts without a crust), and *sformati* (unmolded vegetable flans) combine diverse textures and subtle flavors and make vegetables intriguing and delicious.

Simply put, there is a time for crisp and crunchy vegetables and a time for vegetables that reveal their inherent flavors through slow, gentle cooking. The recipes in this chapter will show you the beauty and the appeal of the latter. Remember, too, in Italy vegetables are served on their own plates, as a separate course. They are culinary stars treated with respect, and not to be regarded as either an afterthought or only a touch of color.

Most of the recipes in this chapter are *contorni,* that is, side dishes, so I have not included wine recommendations with them. There are also some savory pies, however, that may be served as *primi* or even *secondi,* and for those recipes I have made wine suggestions.

Baked Pumpkin with Mint and Almonds

Mediterranean pumpkin-like squashes have a bumpy, dark green peel and bright red-orange flesh. Some of them are so large that markets sell them by the slice. In flavor, they are reminiscent of butternut and kabocha squashes, and they are especially prized in the Veneto, Lombardy, and Sicily. This savory gratin is Sicilian in inspiration and makes a wonderful accompaniment to roast chicken, duck, or pork, especially if it has a slightly sweet sauce.

SERVES 6 TO 8

1 butternut squash, about 2 pounds

1/4 cup olive oil, or as needed to coat all of the squash

1 tablespoon finely minced garlic

2 tablespoons sugar

2 tablespoons balsamic vinegar

Salt and freshly ground black pepper

2 to 3 tablespoons chopped fresh mint

1/2 cup slivered blanched almonds or chopped pistachios, toasted

Preheat the oven to 400°F. Oil a 1¹/₂-quart gratin or other baking dish.

Using a vegetable peeler, peel the squash. Cut the squash in half lengthwise and scoop out the seeds. Cut each half crosswise into ¹/₂-inch-thick slices. You should have 4 to 4¹/₂ cups half-moon pieces. Alternatively, cut the squash into 1-inch pieces.

In a bowl, toss the squash with the ¹/₄ cup olive oil, garlic, sugar, vinegar, and a little salt and pepper until evenly coated. If there seems insufficient oil to coat the squash, add a little more oil. Transfer the squash to the prepared gratin dish. Pour water into the dish to a depth of ¹/₂ inch, then cover with aluminum foil.

Bake the squash for 30 minutes. Uncover the dish and continue to bake until the squash is meltingly tender, about 10 minutes longer.

Transfer the squash to a serving dish and sprinkle with the mint and nuts. Serve hot or warm.

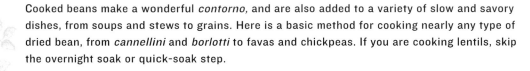

Cooked Dried Beans

Cooked beans make a wonderful *contorno,* and are also added to a variety of slow and savory dishes, from soups and stews to grains. Here is a basic method for cooking nearly any type of dried bean, from *cannellini* and *borlotti* to favas and chickpeas. If you are cooking lentils, skip the overnight soak or quick-soak step.

SERVES 6 TO 8

1 pound (2 rounded cups) dried beans, picked over and rinsed

2 quarts water

3 cloves garlic

1 yellow onion, chopped (optional)

A few fresh sage leaves, or 1 bay leaf

Extra virgin olive oil for serving

Salt and freshly ground black pepper

If you have time, soak the beans in water to cover overnight, then drain. If you need the beans in a hurry, you can use the quick-soak method: Place the beans in a saucepan with water to cover and place over high heat. Bring to a boil, boil for 2 minutes, then remove from the heat. Cover and let stand for 1 hour, then drain. (Although you can use the quick-soak method for chickpeas and favas, it will not measurably shorten cooking time.)

In a saucepan, combine the beans with the water. Bring to a gentle boil over medium-high heat and add the garlic, onion (if using), and sage or bay leaf. Reduce the heat to low, skim off any foam from the surface, cover, and simmer gently until the beans are tender, 40 to 60 minutes; the timing will depend on the age and variety of the beans. (Chickpeas and favas will take up to 1 1/2 hours if the quick-soak method has been used.) Add 2 teaspoons salt after the first 15 minutes of cooking.

When the beans are done, discard the garlic and sage or bay leaf. Drain the beans if you plan to eat them as is, and dress them while still warm with a few tablespoons of olive oil and some salt and pepper. If you will be using them in another dish, leave them in their cooking liquid until needed.

VARIATION: To prepare Tuscan *fagioli all'uccelletto,* or beans cooked in the manner of small birds, cook the beans as directed, then drain and reserve the liquid. In a sauté pan, heat 2 tablespoons olive oil over medium heat. Add 3 cloves garlic, chopped, and sauté until softened, about 3 minutes. Add the cooked beans; $^1/_2$ cup peeled, chopped tomatoes; 6 fresh sage leaves, chopped; 1 cup reserved bean cooking liquid; and salt and pepper to taste. Simmer for 15 minutes to blend the flavors. Drizzle with extra virgin olive oil just before serving.

To Salt or Not to Salt

According to assorted grandmothers and old wives, you must not salt beans until they are cooked or they will never become tender. The salt supposedly toughens the skins and makes the beans split. This notion has been disproved quite nicely by *Los Angeles Times* food editor Russ Parsons, who writes on the subject of beans and salt in his book, *How to Read a French Fry.* I usually salt beans after they have been simmering for 10 to 15 minutes. There is no point in salting the cooking water after the beans are cooked because the beans will never absorb it—and they need salt. Cooking beans too rapidly is what causes splitting. The water must bubble quietly. Some cooks add a pinch of baking soda to the soaking water to soften the skins. I have done this with chickpeas, but I do not think it is necessary with other beans, except perhaps dried favas that have not been peeled.

Fava Purée with Wild Greens

SERVES 6

When once asked what she would eat at her proverbial last meal, cookbook author and teacher Marcella Hazan said she would want *macco e verdure*. This robust fava purée topped with greens appears throughout the Italian south and goes under a variety of names: *macco e verdure*, or *maccù* in dialect, in Sicily; *'ncapriata* in Apulia; and *fave e bietole* or *fave e cicoria* in Calabria. The bean purée is similar to the Greek spread called *fava* (made with yellow split peas), which is served drizzled with olive oil and topped with shaved red onion. In Sicily, the purée is topped with wilted greens—wild fennel fronds, curly endive (chicory), Swiss chard, beet greens, wild mustard greens, even broccoli rabe—sometimes with the addition of chopped tomatoes. Dried favas usually can be purchased already peeled. They are beige-yellow. If you can only find them with the skins intact, you will need to start out with more beans and then peel them after you soak them.

1 pound dried fava beans if peeled or 1¹/₄ pounds if unpeeled, picked over, rinsed, and soaked overnight

2 quarts water

2 or 3 cloves garlic, peeled but left whole, plus 2 cloves garlic, minced

Salt

6 tablespoons extra virgin olive oil, plus more for serving

1 cup chopped yellow onion

2 cups peeled, seeded, and chopped tomatoes (optional)

8 cups coarsely chopped assorted greens (see recipe introduction)

Freshly ground black pepper

Grated pecorino cheese for serving (optional)

Drain the beans, then peel them if necessary. In a heavy soup pot, combine the beans with the water, place over medium-high heat, and bring to a boil. Add the whole garlic cloves, reduce the heat to low, and simmer uncovered, stirring occasionally to prevent sticking, until the beans are very soft and can be easily mashed, 1 to 2 hours; the timing will depend on the age of the beans. Add 2 teaspoons salt after the first 15 minutes of cooking. Check from time to time and add water if the liquid reduces too much.

Remove from the heat and mash the beans with a large spoon or a potato masher. Stir in 4 tablespoons of the olive oil and season with salt.

Meanwhile, in a wide sauté pan, heat the remaining 2 tablespoons olive oil over medium heat. Add the onion and minced garlic and sauté for a few minutes until starting to soften, 5 to 8 minutes. Add the tomatoes (if using) and then the greens, which should begin to wilt just from the rinsing water still clinging to them. If there is too little moisture, add about 1 cup water to create sufficient steam to wilt them. Reduce the heat to low and simmer uncovered, stirring occasionally, until the greens are tender, about 20 minutes. Remove from the heat, season with salt and a generous amount of pepper, and drain off any excess liquid.

Spoon the fava purée into warmed bowls and arrange the greens on top. Generously drizzle with olive oil and then sprinkle with pecorino, if desired. Serve at once.

VARIATION: You can also make the purée with fresh fava beans. Shell 4 to 5 pounds fava beans, blanch the beans in boiling water for 1 to 2 minutes, drain, and peel the beans. Cook with the salt and garlic as directed, reducing the cooking time to about 20 minutes, then proceed as directed.

A Pair of Mixed Fava Purées

Sometimes fava beans are combined with other vegetables for a purée. For example, at the Ristorante Bufi in Molfetta, in Apulia, the chef makes a delicious *crema di favette e cavolfiore* (fava and cauliflower purée). It is simple to prepare: Shell 3 pounds fresh fava beans, blanch for 1 to 2 minutes in boiling water, drain, and peel. In a saucepan, combine the fava beans, 1 pound cauliflower florets, and water to cover. Bring to a boil over high heat, add about 2 teaspoons salt, reduce the heat to low, and simmer, uncovered, until both vegetables are soft, about 20 minutes. Drain the vegetables, mash with a fork or potato masher, season with salt, and drizzle liberally with extra virgin olive oil. Serve on grilled or toasted bread.

Fave 'ngreccia, an ancient recipe from the town of Picerno, near the city of Potenza in Basilicata, calls for mashing equal parts cooked favas and potatoes with lots of chopped mint, some parsley, garlic, olive oil, salt, and a bit of vinegar to taste. Again, serve on grilled or toasted bread.

Pumpkin Squash with Mozzarella and Tomato

SERVES 8

In Sicily and Apulia, there are many dishes described either as *alla parmigiana*, usually translated elsewhere as "in the style of Parma," or *parmigiano di*, and although they nearly always include Parmesan cheese, it is typically their only connection to Parma. This Sicilian gratin calls for the local pumpkin-like squash (page 239), tomato sauce, *caciocavallo* cheese, and only a topping of Parmesan. The interplay of the saltiness of the cheese and the sweetness of the squash is especially appealing. When shopping for butternut squash, select the one with the longest neck. It will yield the largest number of round slices and produce the least waste.

1 butternut squash, about 2 pounds

2 eggs

About ³/4 cup all-purpose flour

Salt and freshly ground black pepper

Freshly grated nutmeg

Extra virgin olive oil for frying

1¹/2 cups Rich Tomato Sauce (page 69), Tomato Sauce (page 69), or canned tomato sauce

¹/2 cup dried bread crumbs

1 pound caciocavallo, fresh mozzarella, or scamorza cheese, thinly sliced

¹/2 cup grated Parmesan cheese

Preheat the oven to 350°F. Butter or oil a 2-quart baking dish or a 10-inch round gratin dish.

Using a vegetable peeler, peel the squash. Cut the squash in half lengthwise and scoop out the seeds. Cut each half crosswise into ¹/2-inch-thick slices. You should have 4 to 4¹/2 cups half-moon pieces.

In a shallow bowl, lightly beat the eggs. Spread the flour on a plate and season with salt, pepper, and nutmeg.

Place a large, deep skillet or sauté pan over medium heat and film the bottom with olive oil. One at a time, dip the squash slices in the beaten eggs and then in the flour, coating evenly. Working in batches, and adding more olive oil as needed, fry the squash slices, turning once, until golden on both sides, 3 to 4 minutes on each side. Using a slotted spoon, transfer to paper towels to drain.

Layer half of the squash in the bottom of the prepared dish. Top with half of the tomato sauce, then half of the bread crumbs, and finally half of the sliced cheese. Repeat the layers with the remaining squash, tomato sauce, bread crumbs, and sliced cheese. Top with the Parmesan cheese.

Bake the squash until it is tender when pierced with a fork and the cheese is golden, 40 to 50 minutes. Serve immediately directly from the baking dish.

SERVES 6

These eggplants are easy to prepare and are a flavorful accompaniment to poultry, fish, or lamb. Look for firm, unblemished eggplants that feel heavy in your hand. Store them in the refrigerator in a paper bag, not plastic, and they will remain fresh until you are ready to cook them.

3 small to medium globe eggplants, about 2 pounds total weight

Salt

4 cloves garlic, chopped

1/4 cup chopped fresh flat-leaf parsley

3 tablespoons chopped fresh basil

1/4 cup salt-packed capers, rinsed and chopped

1/2 cup peeled, seeded, and chopped tomatoes

Freshly ground black pepper

1/4 cup toasted bread crumbs (page 276)

Extra virgin olive oil for drizzling

Preheat the oven to 350°F. Oil a baking pan that will accommodate the eggplant slices in a single layer.

Cut the eggplants in half lengthwise. Using a small, sharp knife, deeply score the flesh in a diamond pattern on one side of each eggplant slice, then sprinkle with salt. Place the slices in a colander and leave to drain for about 30 minutes. Rinse the slices and dry well with paper towels.

Meanwhile, in a small bowl, mix together the garlic, parsley, basil, capers, and tomatoes to form a coarse paste. Season with salt and pepper.

Press the paste into the scored side of each eggplant half. Place the halves, scored side up, in the prepared pan. Sprinkle with the bread crumbs. Drizzle generously with olive oil.

Bake the eggplants until they are soft when pierced with a fork, about 1 hour. Serve hot or at room temperature.

VARIATION: In the winter, substitute 1/4 cup olive oil–packed sun-dried tomatoes, chopped, or 1/2 cup seeded and chopped, canned tomatoes for the fresh tomatoes.

Five Less-Familiar Italian Vegetables:
Broccoli Rabe, Cardoons, Fennel, Kale, and Radicchio

Broccoli rabe: Also known in English as rape and in Italian as *broccoletti di rapa, cime di rapa,* and *rapini,* this deep green leafy vegetable is related to the turnip. It has small flowering buds and ruffly green leaves atop long stalks. It is considered a bitter green, and is often, although not always, braised or parboiled for use in other recipes.

Cardoons: This dramatic vegetable resembles giant, prehistoric, jagged stalks of celery, but it tastes like artichokes. In Italian, cardoons are known as *cardi* and also sometimes as *gobbi,* a rather unfortunate name that means "hunchback," a reference to the curved nature of the stalks. When shopping for cardoons, buy the largest, tightest, crispiest bunch. You will probably have to discard some of the outer ribs. If the bunch weighs about 3 pounds, your yield, after trimming, will be about 1 1/2 pounds of edible stalks. Remove the prickly leaves, then peel each stalk with a vegetable peeler or a knife, removing the fibrous, stringy outer layer. Cut the peeled stalks into 2- or 3-inch pieces and immediately put the pieces into a bowl of water to which lemon juice has been added. Have a cut lemon on hand, too, because when you handle the cardoons, just as when you work with lots of artichokes, your fingers can become stained black. Cook the cardoon pieces in water that has been liberally seasoned with salt, lemon juice, and a few tablespoons of flour. I like to add at least 1/2 cup olive oil to the water as well, which is something the Italians do when they cook artichokes to ensure that the vegetable develops a creamy texture. Simmer the cardoons until they are tender, 45 to 60 minutes. (If the stalks were very large, the pieces may take longer to cook.) Drain the cardoons and use them in gratins and vegetable stews.

Fennel: Called *finocchio* in Italian, fennel grows wild all over Italy and is celebrated for its long, arching stems, feathery leaves, and pungent seeds. In contrast, cultivated fennel has stouter stems and a swollen base that is appreciated in the kitchen. To prepare, trim away any discolored or bruised outer sheaths and tough core portions; if the fronds are still attached, reserve them for cooking or to use as a garnish. Eaten raw, fennel tastes strongly of anise; when cooked, the anise flavor mellows. Raw fennel provides a sweet and crunchy accent in a salad of bitter greens and pairs well with cheese and nuts. It can also be parboiled in salted water for use in other recipes, it can be braised in oil or butter with some stock or water, and it can used in gratins.

Kale: A member of the big cabbage family, kale is a mildly bitter, leafy green. Two main types are used. The most common variety comes in the form of loose, medium-green bunches of ruffled leaves. *Lacinato* kale, also known as dinosaur kale and *cavolo nero* (black cabbage), has smaller, narrower, crinkly dark blue-green leaves. Before cooking either type, discard the thick stems and the central ribs, as they are both tough. Cut the leaves into strips and sauté in olive oil and then steam in liquid until tender, or simply parboil for use in soups and braises.

Radicchio: This colorful chicory is the prize of the Veneto. Two major varieties are cultivated, *radicchio di Verona,* fluffy, round, burgundy red heads, and *radicchio di Treviso,* with long pointy leaves, large white veins, and a paler shade of red. Castelfranco and Chioggia are two additional varieties. Sometimes the leaves are almost white with pale pink, red, or green streaks. Radicchio is mildly bitter and may be braised, grilled, or sautéed. It is also used in salads.

This simple gratin is typical of Tuscany, and is an excellent accompaniment to roasted or grilled meats. In Umbria, cooks make a similar dish *gobbi alla parmigiana*. They parboil the cardoons, dip them in flour and egg, and then fry them until golden before covering them with the *besciamella* and baking them.

SERVES 8

1 lemon, halved, plus 3 to 4 tablespoons fresh lemon juice

2 pounds cardoons

1/2 cup olive oil

6 tablespoons all-purpose flour

6 tablespoons unsalted butter

1 cup milk, heated

1 cup heavy cream, heated

2 egg yolks

1/2 cup grated Parmesan cheese, plus 3 to 4 tablespoons (optional)

Salt and freshly ground black pepper

Freshly grated nutmeg (optional)

1/4 cup toasted bread crumbs (optional; page 276)

Squeeze the juice from the lemon halves into a large bowl of cold water. Trim the prickly leaves from the cardoon stalks, then, using a vegetable peeler or knife, peel off the fibrous, stringy outer layer from each stalk. As each stalk is trimmed, cut it into 3-inch pieces and drop them into the lemon water.

When all of the stalks are trimmed, drain them and place in a large saucepan with water to cover generously. Add the olive oil, the 3 to 4 tablespoons lemon juice, and 2 tablespoons of the flour. Bring to a boil over medium heat and cook until tender, 40 to 60 minutes. (If the cardoon stalks are very large, they may take as long as 1 1/2 hours to become tender.) Drain well and set aside.

Meanwhile, prepare a *besciamella,* or cream sauce: In a small saucepan, melt 4 tablespoons of the butter over low heat. Add the remaining 4 tablespoons flour and cook, stirring, until the flour is well incorporated with the butter, about 3 minutes; do not let the mixture color. Slowly whisk in the hot milk and cream and bring almost to a boil. Reduce the heat to low and cook, stirring often, until the mixture is quite thick and the flour has lost all of its raw taste, about 8 minutes. Remove from the heat, whisk in the egg yolks and the 1/2 cup Parmesan cheese, and season with salt and pepper and a little nutmeg, if desired.

Preheat the oven to 350°F. Butter a 2-quart gratin or other baking dish.

Place the drained cardoon pieces in the prepared baking dish. Spoon the *besciamella* evenly over the top. If you like, sprinkle the top with the toasted bread crumbs and the 3 to 4 tablespoons grated Parmesan cheese. Cut the remaining 2 tablespoons butter into small pieces and use to dot the top.

Bake until the top is golden and the sauce is bubbling, about 30 minutes. Serve immediately directly from the dish.

VARIATION: To prepare fennel the same way, trim off the stems and fronds if intact, then cut the bulbs lengthwise into quarters or eighths, remove some of the tough core, and boil until tender, about 15 minutes. Place in the baking dish, cover with the *besciamella* seasoned with nutmeg, and top with the crumbs and cheese. Bake as directed.

Braised Radicchio with Balsamic Vinegar

SERVES 4

You cannot visit the Veneto without dining on radicchio prepared in myriad ways. This colorful bitter green, a type of chicory, is cultivated primarily in the areas around Treviso, Castelfranco, Chioggia, and Verona (page 247). It is often used in salads, but it is also wonderful braised or grilled. Here, sweet balsamic vinegar tames its natural bitterness. Two methods are given: you can blanch the radicchio, halve it, and then braise the halves, or you can cut it into strips, sauté them, and then braise the strips.

Salt

4 small round heads radicchio

4 tablespoons extra virgin olive oil

2 tablespoons aged balsamic vinegar

Freshly ground black pepper

Preheat the oven to 350°F.

Bring a large saucepan three-fourths full of water to a boil. Salt lightly, drop in the radicchio, and cook for 2 minutes. Push them under the water, as they have a tendency to float. Drain well and, when cool enough to handle, carefully squeeze out excess moisture. If they are large, cut them in half through the stem end. If the cores are large and tough, trim them, but do not cut them away completely or the radicchio halves will fall apart.

Alternatively, omit the blanching step. Instead, cut the radicchio heads into narrow strips. In a sauté pan, heat 2 tablespoons of the olive oil over medium heat, add the radicchio, and sauté briefly to soften slightly, 5 to 7 minutes.

In a small cup, whisk together the balsamic vinegar and the 4 tablespoons olive oil if you have not sautéed the radicchio, or the remaining 2 tablespoons olive oil if you have sautéed it. Place the radicchio in a gratin dish, sprinkle with salt and pepper, and drizzle the oil-vinegar mixture evenly over the top. Cover the dish with aluminum foil.

Bake the radicchio until meltingly tender, about 30 minutes. Serve at once.

VARIATION: Wrap each radicchio half in a slice of prosciutto before putting it in the baking dish. Bake as directed, basting with pan juices from time to time. The prosciutto will take on color in the oven.

"Suffocated" Cabbage

Italians use the term *suffocated* (*sofegae* is Venetian dialect, from the verb *soffocare*, "to suffocate") to describe the technique of cooking vegetables in olive oil over low heat with little additional liquid. Many other vegetables can be cooked in this same way, including carrots, cauliflower, broccoli, squashes, beans, and other greens.

SERVES 8

2 Savoy cabbages

¼ cup olive oil

1 yellow onion, chopped

2 cloves garlic, minced

2 ounces lardo *(page 211), chopped (optional)*

Dash of red or white wine vinegar or fresh lemon juice

Salt and freshly ground black pepper

Cut each cabbage through the stem end into quarters. Cut away the tough central core, then cut the quarters crosswise into narrow strips.

In a large sauté pan, warm the olive oil over low heat. Add the onion, garlic, and the *lardo* (if using) and sauté until the onion is softened, about 8 minutes. Add the cabbage, vinegar or lemon juice, and a sprinkle of salt and pepper and mix well. Reduce the heat to the lowest setting, cover, and cook until the cabbage is tender, about 1 hour.

Taste and adjust the seasoning, then serve.

VARIATION: In the Abruzzo, *cappuccio strascinato* calls for preparing cabbage in much the same way, but adds about 1 pound waxy potatoes such as Yukon Gold, peeled and cut into 1-inch cubes with the cabbage and adds 1 cup dry white wine during the last 20 minutes of cooking.

NOTE: Some cooks prefer to add the vinegar at the end of cooking because it bleaches the green from the cabbage.

"Drowned" Broccoli Rabe with Tomatoes and Pancetta

SERVES 8

Broccoli rabe (page 247) is a favored green in Apulia. In this recipe, it is cooked in two stages, with liquid added as needed. Do not be alarmed to see that you will need 3 pounds of greens. The tough stems are discarded, and the leaves shrink substantially, so you will end up with a reasonable amount. *Affogare* means "to drown" or "to smother"; this technique is a variation on the "smothered" method used for cooking cabbage on page 251.

1/3 cup extra virgin olive oil

6 cloves garlic, minced

1/3 pound pancetta, cut into small dice

3 pounds broccoli rabe, tough stems discarded and cut into 2-inch pieces

1 cup water, or as needed

10 Slow-Roasted Tomatoes (page 262), or 1 cup olive oil–packed sun-dried tomatoes

Pinch of chile pepper flakes, or to taste

Salt and freshly ground black pepper

In a large saucepan with a tight-fitting lid, warm the olive oil over medium heat. Add the garlic and pancetta and sauté until they take on a bit of color, about 5 minutes. Add the broccoli rabe and 1/2 cup of the water, reduce the heat to low, cover, and cook for 15 minutes. Add the tomatoes, the remaining 1/2 cup water, the chile pepper flakes, and a little salt and black pepper and mix well. Re-cover and continue to cook over low heat until the greens are tender, 15 to 20 minutes longer. Check from time to time and add a little water if the greens threaten to scorch.

Taste and adjust the seasoning. Transfer to a serving dish and serve warm or at room temperature.

VARIATIONS: Add 6 to 8 olive oil–packed anchovy fillets, chopped, or 3 or 4 salt-packed anchovies, rinsed, filleted, and chopped, with the garlic. Or, add 1 cup diced *caciocavallo* cheese with the chile pepper flakes.

NOTE: Some recipes for this dish recommend using red or white wine instead of water, but I find that the wine makes the broccoli rabe taste excessively bitter.

Artichokes Braised in Citrus Juices

SERVES 6

Artichokes and citrus are a natural combination, and I have braised artichokes in orange juice in recipes from Morocco and Turkey. But this Sicilian classic combines three citrus juices and vinegar, adds salt in the form of anchovies, and uses sugar for sweetness and flavor balance. These spectacular artichokes, which are best served at room temperature, are stellar in an antipasto assortment.

1 lemon, halved

6 artichokes

1/2 cup olive oil, plus 1 tablespoon

3 yellow onions, cut in half and thinly sliced

1/2 cup fresh orange juice

1/2 cup fresh tangerine juice

1/2 cup fresh lemon juice

1/4 cup white wine vinegar

2 cups water

Salt

2 tablespoons salt-packed capers, rinsed

4 olive oil–packed anchovy fillets, finely minced, or 2 salt-packed anchovies, rinsed, filleted, and finely minced

2 tablespoons sugar, or to taste

Chopped fresh mint for garnish (optional)

Squeeze the juice from the lemon halves into a large bowl of cold water. Working with 1 artichoke at a time, remove all of the leaves, then trim away any dark green parts from the base and the stem, trimming the stem to a length of 2 inches. If the stem seems tough, cut it off flush with the base. Cut the artichoke in half lengthwise. Scoop out the prickly choke from each half with a spoon, or cut it out with a paring knife. As each artichoke is trimmed, drop the halves into the lemon water and leave them in the water until ready to cook.

In a Dutch oven, heat the 1/2 cup olive oil over low heat. Drain the artichokes and add them to the oil along with the onions, citrus juices, vinegar, water, and 1 teaspoon salt. Mix well, cover, and cook very slowly until the artichokes are tender when pierced with a knife, 35 to 40 minutes.

Using a slotted spoon, transfer the artichokes to a serving bowl. Return the pan to high heat and add the capers. Cook over high heat until the sauce is reduced and thickened, 10 to 15 minutes.

In a small sauté pan or saucepan, warm the anchovies in the remaining 1 tablespoon olive oil over low heat. When they have dissolved, add them to the sauce along with the 2 tablespoons sugar. Cook for 5 minutes longer, then taste and adjust the sweetness of the sauce with more sugar if necessary.

Spoon the sauce over the artichokes. Serve at room temperature, garnished with mint, if desired.

Stuffed Artichokes in Tomato Sauce

SERVES 4 TO 8

San Fernandino, in the Apulian province of Foggia, is considered the artichoke capital of the Salento peninsula. The locals have long prepared slow-cooked vegetables, and this braise fits perfectly into that culinary tradition. In keeping with the everyday thriftiness of the Italian kitchen, the recipe was designed to use leftover bread. Please keep in mind that, unlike many artichokes cultivated elsewhere, most Italian artichokes do not have a hard, hairy choke that must be removed before the artichoke can be stuffed. This dish can be a wonderful *contorno* or *primo* (serve one artichoke per person) or a satisfying *secondo* (serve two artichokes per person).

1 lemon, halved

8 artichokes

FOR THE FILLING

2 or 3 slices coarse country bread, crusts removed, soaked in water, and squeezed almost dry

2 eggs, lightly beaten

3 tablespoons dried bread crumbs

3 tablespoons grated Parmesan cheese

3 cloves garlic, minced

2 tablespoons chopped fresh flat-leaf parsley

2 tablespoons chopped fresh mint

Salt and freshly ground black pepper

Squeeze the juice from the lemon halves into a large bowl of cold water. Working with 1 artichoke at a time, trim off the stem flush with the bottom. Pull off all of the tough outer leaves until you reach a pale green, pointy core that measures $1^1/_4$ to $1^1/_2$ inches in diameter at its base. Trim away any dark green parts from the base. Using your fingers, open the leaves, being careful not to crack them at their base. Using a melon-ball scoop or small pointed spoon, scoop out the prickly choke, then immediately drop the trimmed artichoke into the lemon water.

To make the filling, in a bowl, combine the bread, eggs, bread crumbs, cheese, garlic, parsley, and mint. Mix well, then season with a little salt and pepper.

To make the sauce, in a pan just large enough to hold all of the artichokes in a single layer, warm the olive oil over medium heat. Add the onion and sauté until softened, about 8 minutes. Add the tomatoes, bring to a gentle boil, reduce the heat to low, and simmer, uncovered, until the tomatoes break down to form a sauce, about 15 minutes. Season with salt and pepper.

Meanwhile, stuff the artichokes: Remove the artichokes from the water and drain well. Gently open the leaves and spoon the filling into the center, dividing it evenly among the artichokes and closing the leaves over the stuffing.

FOR THE SAUCE

1/2 cup extra virgin olive oil

1 large yellow onion, finely chopped

2 pounds fresh plum tomatoes, peeled, seeded, and chopped, or 4 cups seeded and chopped, canned plum tomatoes

Salt and freshly ground black pepper

When the sauce is ready, stand the artichokes upright in the sauce, placing them close together. Raise the heat to medium and bring the sauce to a gentle boil. Reduce the heat to very low, cover, and cook until the artichokes are very tender when pierced with a knife, about 1 hour. Check from time to time and add hot water in small amounts if needed to keep the sauce from scorching.

Transfer the artichokes to a platter and spoon the sauce around them. Serve warm.

Roman Artichokes

The Romans also appreciate the thistly artichoke. Two of their most famous dishes are *carciofi alla romana* and *carciofi alla giudia.* The first is similar to Apulian-stuffed artichokes, with mint and garlic slipped between the leaves, but rather than cooking them in tomato sauce, they are braised (or occasionally baked) in olive oil and wine. Sometimes bread crumbs, prosciutto, or anchovies are added to the filling as well. Alas, *carciofi alla guidia,* or "artichokes Jewish style," are not slow and savory, but they are delicious. The first tender, young artichokes of the season are flattened and then deep-fried in olive oil until they are tender and have taken on the appearance of flowers in bloom.

Pomodori ripieni di riso
Rice-Stuffed Tomatoes

SERVES 6 TO 12

Rice-stuffed tomatoes, fragrant with herbs and glistening with oil, say summer in Italy to me. Other fillings are based on bread crumbs or ground meat (you could use the mixture for Meatballs from Sardinia on page 225, doubling the bread crumbs), but the fillings based on rice are my favorites. You can serve the tomatoes as a side dish to roast chicken or baked fish, as a light supper, or as an antipasto.

12 large, ripe but firm tomatoes

Salt

2 tablespoons sugar

1/2 cup extra virgin olive oil, plus more for drizzling

1 yellow onion, chopped

1 cup Arborio rice

1 1/2 cups water

3 cloves garlic, finely chopped

1/4 cup chopped fresh flat-leaf parsley

1/4 cup fresh basil leaves, finely shredded

Freshly ground black pepper

Cut a 1/2-inch slice off the top of each tomato and reserve the caps. Using a small spoon, scoop out the pulp and juice from each tomato, leaving a shell about 1/2 inch thick. Chop the pulp and set aside with the juices. Sprinkle the cavity of each tomato with a little salt and with the sugar. Set aside.

Preheat the oven to 375°F. Oil a baking dish just large enough to hold all of the tomatoes in a single layer.

In a large sauté pan, heat 1/4 cup of the olive oil over medium heat. Add the onion and sauté until softened, about 8 minutes. Add the rice and sauté for 2 minutes longer. Add 1 cup of the water and simmer, uncovered, until the water is absorbed, about 10 minutes. Remove from the heat and fold in the reserved tomato pulp and juices, the garlic, parsley, basil, and the remaining 1/4 cup olive oil. Season with salt and pepper.

Spoon the rice mixture into the tomatoes, dividing it evenly and filling each tomato about three-fourths full (the rice will expand). Place the tomatoes in the prepared dish. Cover with the reserved tomato tops. Pour the remaining 1/2 cup water into the dish, and drizzle the tomatoes with olive oil. Cover the dish with aluminum foil.

Bake the tomatoes for about 30 minutes. Uncover the dish and continue to bake until the rice kernels are puffed and fully tender, about 30 minutes longer.

Remove from the oven and, if desired, drizzle with more olive oil, then let cool. Serve the tomatoes at room temperature.

cont'd

VARIATIONS: Other vegetables can be stuffed with the same filling. To make stuffed bell peppers, cut the tops off 6 bell peppers and set the tops aside. Remove and discard the seeds and veins. Make the filling as directed, diluting 1 tablespoon tomato paste in the water. Parboil the peppers in boiling water for 4 to 5 minutes, then drain. Stuff the peppers, replace the caps, and bake as directed.

To make stuffed eggplants, cut 6 small globe eggplants (each 6 to 7 ounces) in half through the stem end. Scoop out some of the pulp, leaving a shell about 1/2 inch thick. Chop the pulp, discarding as many seeds as possible. Make the filling as directed, but sauté the eggplant pulp with the onion until tender before adding the rice. Sauté the eggplant cases in olive oil for about 5 minutes to soften them. Stuff the eggplant cases and bake as directed.

To make stuffed zucchini, cut 8 medium-sized zucchini in half lengthwise. Scoop out and discard the seeds from each half, then scoop out some of the pulp, leaving a shell 1/4 to 1/3 inch thick. Chop the pulp and sauté with the onion until tender before adding the rice. Parboil the zucchini cases in boiling water for 3 minutes, then drain. Stuff the zucchini cases and bake as directed.

Primizie

Years ago, when I first moved to Italy, the vegetable markets, with their overflowing stalls of vibrant-colored foods, quickly seduced me. Having grown up in Brooklyn during the era of frozen vegetables, I found Italian produce a revelation. The Roman countryside produced the sweetest, most flavorful vegetables I had ever eaten, and thus began an informal vegetable tutorial. Every day I talked with the vendors at the competing stands, comparing prices and culinary opinions. I would ask how they prepared the artichokes, the favas, the wild greens. Then I would rush home to cook my purchases before I forgot all the detailed instructions.

The vendors' greatest enthusiasm was, and still is, for the *primizie,* the early crops of fruits or vegetables that appear at the market just before the main season begins. For example, in Venice, excellent artichokes are grown on some of the islands in the lagoon. When the *castraure* appear at the Rialto market, however, they are the talk of the town. These are the first cuts from the artichoke plants; they are prized because each plant has only a single first bloom, and they are particularly flavorful. So, too, are the first pencil-thin asparagus, the tiny new peas, the pale green fava beans. They seem even sweeter and more precious because they have been out of season and off the menu for a year, and their reappearance at the market is cause for celebration.

Roman Spring Vegetable Stew

SERVES 6

Said to be what the wife of the wine maker *(la vignarola)* serves for supper, this classic Roman spring vegetable dish has many different names and interpretations all over Italy. Some cooks start with minced *guanciale* (page 211) or pancetta, and others keep the dish strictly vegetarian. A number of recipes suggest braising the artichokes or peas in a mixture of water and white wine to preserve their color. I find this to be a futile step, however, as they still turn a grayish green. You can peel the potatoes or not, and in addition to halving or quartering them, you can slice them, or, if they are tiny, you can even leave them whole. The herbs of choice are mint and parsley. I have fond memories of eating this stew at Al Moro, a venerable Roman restaurant just off the via del Corso.

1 lemon, halved

6 artichokes

4 pounds fava beans in the pod, shelled (about 2 1/2 cups)

1/2 cup olive oil

1/4 pound pancetta, diced

3 spring onions or 6 to 8 green onions, including tender green tops, chopped

2 cloves garlic, minced

1 pound small new potatoes, halved or quartered

1 cup water

2 1/2 pounds English peas in the pod, shelled (about 2 1/2 cups)

1 pound asparagus, tough ends discarded, cut into 2-inch lengths, blanched for 3 minutes, and drained (optional)

2 to 3 tablespoons chopped fresh flat-leaf parsley

2 tablespoons chopped fresh mint

Salt and freshly ground black pepper

Squeeze the juice from the lemon halves into a large bowl of cold water. Working with 1 artichoke at a time, remove all of the leaves, then trim away any dark green parts from the base and the stem, trimming the stem to a length of 2 inches. If the stem seems tough, cut it off flush with the base. Cut the artichoke into quarters lengthwise. Scoop out the prickly choke from each quarter with a spoon, or cut it out with a paring knife. As each artichoke is trimmed, drop the quarters into the lemon water and leave them in the water until ready to cook.

Bring a small saucepan three-fourths full of water to a boil. Add the favas, blanch for 1 to 2 minutes, and drain. When cool enough to handle, slip off the thin skin covering each bean. (It is a meditative activity, so keep smiling.) Set aside.

In a Dutch oven, heat the olive oil over medium heat. Add the pancetta and onions and sauté until the onions are softened and the pancetta has given off some fat, about 8 minutes. Drain the artichokes and add to the pan along with the garlic, potatoes, and water. Bring to a boil, then reduce the heat to low, cover, and simmer until the artichokes and potatoes are tender, about 25 minutes. Add the favas, peas, and the asparagus (if using) and cook for 10 minutes longer.

Stir in the parsley and mint and season to taste with salt and pepper. Transfer to a serving dish and serve hot or warm.

Summer Vegetable Stew

SERVES 8 TO 10

This rustic vegetable dish is variously called *ciambotta* in Calabria, *ciammotta* in Basilicata, and *cianfotta* in Campania and Lazio. The last spelling is used by famed author Luigi Carnacina and is gleefully translated by the irrepressible Faith Willinger as "John Fuck." One story suggests that the dish was first made by a famous madam in a Naples brothel, and that the name is derived from *cian* (slut) and *fotta* (made). Regardless of how the name evolved, the dish is delicious. In summer and early fall, eggplants have few or no seeds and are creamy white throughout. If you should make this dish when eggplants are more mature, be sure to salt the cut-up eggpplant, leave it to drain in a colander for an hour, and then rinse and pat dry before sautéing. Try to find the medium-sized black, salt-cured Gaeta olives from Lazio. Some families serve this dish at room temperature. Others serve it as a hot *contorno*.

1/4 cup extra virgin olive oil

2 yellow onions, chopped

4 cloves garlic, minced

1 eggplant, peeled and cut into 1-inch pieces

2 red or green bell peppers, seeded and cut into large dice

1 pound new potatoes, unpeeled, cut into large dice

2 tomatoes, peeled, seeded, and chopped

Salt and freshly ground black pepper

1/4 cup chopped fresh flat-leaf parsley

1/4 cup finely shredded fresh basil

1/2 cup Gaeta olives (optional)

Ricotta salata or fresh ricotta cheese for garnish (optional)

In a large, deep sauté pan, heat the olive oil over medium heat. Add the onions and sauté until softened, about 8 minutes. Add the garlic, eggplant, bell peppers, potatoes, and tomatoes and bring to a lively simmer. Reduce the heat to low, cover, and cook gently, stirring from time to time, until the vegetables are meltingly tender, about 45 minutes. If the mixture is too wet, uncover, and cook over high heat to evaporate the excess juices.

Season to taste with salt and pepper. Transfer to a serving bowl and serve hot or at room temperature. Just before serving, add the parsley and basil and the olives, if using. Top with crumbled *ricotta salata* or dollops of fresh ricotta, if desired.

VARIATIONS: You can cook this dish in the oven rather than on the stove top. Sauté the onions as directed, then toss the onions with the other ingredients except the herbs and the olives, if using. Place in a baking dish and bake in a 350°F oven for 1 hour. Add the herbs and olives just before serving. To prepare the dish as they do on Pantelleria, a small island off the coast of Sicily, swirl in 6 eggs, lightly beaten, at the end of cooking. They will thicken the juices and give them a creamy consistency.

NOTE: The easiest way to prepare this dish is to cook all the vegetables together over low heat. However, some purists prefer to sauté each vegetable separately until softened and golden, and then to combine them with the tomatoes and garlic for a final 30 minutes.

Cavolfiore seduto

"Sitting Down" Broccoflower

SERVES 4

Broccoflower is a cross between cauliflower and broccoli, but looks like the former. It is a striking chartreuse and here, in a dish from Basilicata, it is cooked whole: the leaves are removed and a cross is cut in the bottom so that heat can penetrate and cook the central core. The pot is tightly covered and the broccoflower, along with a handful of pitted olives and a sliced onion, is left to braise over very low heat with little moisture. As it cooks, it softens and "sits down."

1 head broccoflower, 1 1/2 to 2 pounds

1/4 cup extra virgin olive oil

1 yellow onion, thinly sliced

1/2 cup pitted oil- or brine-cured black olives

Remove the outer leaves from the broccoflower. Turn it stem end up and, using a small, sharp knife, cut a deep cross in the bottom of the central stem.

In a heavy saucepan or Dutch oven, warm the olive oil over medium heat. Add the onion and sauté until softened, about 8 minutes. Add the broccoflower, stem side down, and the olives, and then pour in water to a depth of 1/4 inch. Bring to a simmer, reduce the heat to low, cover, and cook until the broccoflower is tender when pierced with a knife, 30 to 40 minutes.

Serve the broccoflower directly from the pan, using a large spoon and being sure to include some olives and onion in each portion. Alternatively, carefully transfer the broccoflower to a serving bowl and spoon the olives and onion on top.

Slow-Roasted Tomatoes

Plum tomatoes, sometimes called Roma tomatoes, are pretty but rarely highly flavorful. This simple recipe, however, concentrates the tomato flavor and brings out the best in them. You can serve the tomatoes as a side dish on their own, or add them to other dishes when full-flavored tomatoes are needed.

SERVES 6 TO 8

16 to 18 plum tomatoes, halved lengthwise and seeded

4 or 5 cloves garlic, minced

1/4 cup chopped fresh flat-leaf parsley

4 to 6 tablespoons extra virgin olive oil

Salt and freshly ground black pepper

Preheat the oven to 350°F. Oil a rimmed baking sheet.

Arrange the tomatoes, cut side up and side by side, on the prepared baking sheet. In a small bowl, stir together the garlic, parsley, and enough olive oil to create a spreadable consistency. Season with salt and pepper. Rub the garlic mixture evenly over the tomato halves.

Roast the tomatoes until they are very soft and fragrant, 40 to 60 minutes. Remove from the oven and let cool completely. Serve at room temperature, or store in an airtight container in the refrigerator for up to 5 days and use in other dishes.

Slow-Roasted Onions with Aged Balsamic Vinegar

SERVES 6 OR 12

In Emilia-Romagna, many markets sell onions already roasted. But it is worth it to roast them at home, where they will fill your kitchen with a wonderful aroma as they cook and are best served warm from your oven. Here, the onions are treated to a simple glaze made from the pan juices and balsamic vinegar, a legendary product of the region. Be sure to use a good-quality balsamic vinegar, one that has been aged for at least a decade. If you are not using the best quality (and you'll know by what you paid for it!), simmer the vinegar over medium heat until it is thickened and rich in flavor, reducing it by at least half, before using. Serve these sweet, meltingly tender onions with roast meats.

6 large red onions

Olive oil

Salt and freshly ground black pepper

1/3 cup aged balsamic vinegar

1/2 cup slivered blanched almonds, toasted (optional)

Preheat the oven to 350°F.

Rub the onions liberally with olive oil and sprinkle with salt and pepper. Place in a deep roasting pan just large enough to hold them.

Roast the onions until they are tender when pierced with a knife, 1 to 1 1/2 hours. The timing will vary depending on the size of the onions. Remove from the oven, transfer the onions to a cutting board, and cut them in half through the stem end. Arrange the onions cut side up on a platter.

Place the roasting pan on the stove top over medium heat, add the vinegar, and deglaze the pan, scraping up all of the brown bits. Add the almonds (if using) and heat briefly, then drizzle the pan juices over the onions. Serve hot or warm.

VARIATIONS: Stud each onion with 2 whole cloves and baste the onions occasionally with dry or sweet Marsala as they roast. You can also do as cooks in the Abruzzo do and roast new potatoes, halved and rubbed with olive oil, along with the onions. Or, you can cut the roasted onions in half crosswise, scoop out the center from each half, leaving a 1/2-inch shell, fill the halves with herbed *robiola* cheese or a similar herbed cheese, and return the onions to the oven to melt the cheese. No vinegar, no almonds.

Cipolline in agrodolce
Sweet-and-Sour Pearl Onions

These onions from the Veneto are a wonderful side dish for roast pork, pork chops, or duck. The classic Levantine addition of pine nuts and raisins plays up the sweetness side of the culinary equation. Slivered blanched almonds may also be used in place of the pine nuts.

SERVES 6

2 1/2 pounds small white, yellow, or red onions, each 1 to 1 1/2 inches in diameter, or the slightly larger cipollini onions (about 18 total)

6 tablespoons unsalted butter or olive oil

2 tablespoons sugar

6 tablespoons red wine vinegar

1 tablespoon tomato paste (optional)

1/4 cup dark or golden raisins

1/4 cup pine nuts, toasted

Salt

Trim the root ends of the onions carefully, leaving the bottom of each bulb intact. Cut a shallow cross in each root end to prevent the onion from telescoping during cooking. Bring a large saucepan three-fourths full of water to a boil. Add the onions and boil until barely cooked and still firm, about 5 minutes. Drain, let cool until they can be handled, and slip off the skins.

In a large sauté pan, heat the butter or olive oil over medium heat. Add the onions and sauté, stirring occasionally, until golden brown, about 8 minutes. Reduce the heat to low and add the sugar, vinegar, tomato paste (if using), raisins, and pine nuts. Cover tightly and simmer until the onions are completely tender, 25 to 30 minutes.

Season the onions with salt and transfer to a serving dish. Serve warm or at room temperature.

Sformato, Torta Salata, and Tortino

The Italian kitchen has a sizable repertory of savory puddings and pies that may be served as *primi* or *contorni,* or as main courses for a lighter meal. *Sformati,* which are found all over the country, are essentially custard puddings, or flans, and are among the easiest of this big family to make. Your only anxiety may come when you need to unmold them (*sformare* means "to unmold"). You can try using a nonstick ring mold, tube pan, or baking pan as insurance, or you can line the bottom of the baking dish with buttered baker's parchment, which guarantees a better "release." You can also use custard cups, which are much easier to unmold because of their size; just remember to reduce the cooking time. Test the pudding with the point of a knife. When it emerges clean, the pudding is ready. Let it sit for 10 minutes, then run a knife blade around the inside edge of the dish, invert a serving plate on top, and invert the mold and the plate together. Finally, lift off the mold. If this is too much pressure, tradition can be disregarded. You can bake the mixture, cut it into squares or wedges, and serve it directly from the mold.

Sformati can be baked dry or in a water bath *(bagnomaria).* Many cooks cover the pan to prevent a crust from forming on the surface and to keep the texture of the pudding somewhat moister or creamier. I have included two *sformati* in this chapter, each made with a slightly different technique and producing a different texture. One relies on a classic cream sauce to bind the vegetables, and the second one uses eggs and milk and adds the flour at the end.

Torta is the Italian word for "cake," but it also can refer to a savory pie, or *torta salata. Torte salate* are specialties in particular of Liguria and the Piedmont, but they are also found as far south as Sardinia and Sicily. Some have a single crust, others are enclosed completely in flaky pastry, and still others call for thin pastry layered almost like filo or for a heartier yeast-dough crust. Although traditionally round and typically baked in springform pans, *torte* are sometimes baked in large rectangular pans and cut into squares for ease of serving when volume is a consideration. They are best served at room temperature.

A *torta* filling can also be baked in a buttered baking dish without a crust. It is then called a *tortino.* In other words, a *tortino* is essentially a *sformato,* but it does not have to be unmolded. It is freed from a springform pan, or it is cut and served directly from the baking dish.

Steamed Carrot Pudding

On a trip to Venice, I was served this lovely carrot pudding as a first course. It was very pretty and delicate, steamed in individual molds and then served with a light cream sauce. It would be a fine accompaniment for a roast chicken, duck, or turkey. Serve it with just a garnish of fresh parsley, or perhaps mint, or dress it up with a sauce of *fonduta* (page 102).

SERVES 8 TO 10

Salt

2 pounds carrots, peeled and thinly sliced (about 6 cups)

1 tablespoon chopped fresh sage

5 tablespoons unsalted butter

3 tablespoons all-purpose flour

1 1/4 cups milk, heated

4 eggs, lightly beaten

1/2 cup grated Parmesan cheese

Freshly ground black pepper

Freshly grated nutmeg (optional)

Chopped fresh flat-leaf parsley for garnish

Bring a saucepan three-fourths full of water to a boil. Salt lightly, add the carrots, and cook until very soft, about 15 minutes. Drain, transfer to a food processor, and purée until smooth. You should have about 3 cups purée. Fold in the sage.

Preheat the oven to 350°F. Butter a 1 1/2-quart ring mold or tube pan, soufflé dish, or baking dish with 3-inch sides, or ten 1/2-cup ramekins. Alternatively, butter the bottom and sides of the soufflé dish or baking dish as directed, then line the bottom with buttered baker's parchment.

In a small saucepan, melt the butter over medium heat. Add the flour and cook, stirring, until the flour is well incorporated with the butter, 3 to 5 minutes; do not let the mixture color. Slowly whisk in the hot milk and bring almost to a boil. Reduce the heat to low and cook, stirring often, until the sauce is quite thick and the flour has lost all of its raw taste, about 8 minutes.

Fold the sauce into the puréed carrots, then let cool for a bit. Add the eggs and cheese and mix well. Season the mixture with 1 teaspoon salt, a little pepper, and some nutmeg, if desired. Spoon into the prepared mold(s). Place the mold(s) in a baking pan and pour hot water into the pan to reach halfway up the sides of the mold(s).

Bake the *sformato(i)* until golden and set, about 1 hour for the large pudding and 25 minutes for the small puddings. Remove from the oven and let rest for 10 minutes. Run a knife blade around the inside edge of the large or a small mold, invert a warmed serving plate on top, shake the mold once, and invert the mold and the plate together. Lift off the mold. Sprinkle with parsley and serve hot.

VARIATIONS: Bake the *sformato* in an 8-inch springform pan. Butter the pan as directed, then dust the bottom and sides with 3 tablespoons fine dried bread crumbs. Omit the water bath and bake as directed. Let rest for 10 minutes, then release the pan sides, transfer to a warmed serving plate, and cut into wedges.

Substitute 3 cups cauliflower purée for the carrot purée, bake as directed, and serve with *fonduta*. You can also substitute 3 cups butternut squash purée for the carrot purée, bake as directed, and serve with a sprinkle of chopped toasted hazelnuts and chopped fresh sage.

Spring Greens and Rice Pudding

Surrounded by rice fields, Piedmont is known for its varied rice dishes. So it is no surprise to find a vegetable rice pudding as a *stellun primo*, traditionally served the day after Easter. While this pudding is good warm, it is equally tasty served at room temperature, and would be fine fare for a picnic. The recipe is from the town of Monferrato in the Piedmont.

SERVES 6 TO 8

Salt

1 1/2 pounds assorted tender spring greens such as spinach, dandelion greens, and Swiss chard, tough stems discarded

1/2 pound assorted wild or bitter greens and herbs such as sage, borage, arugula, and cress

3 tablespoons olive oil or lard

2 small leeks, including tender green portions, halved lengthwise and sliced crosswise

1 small yellow onion, chopped

3/4 cup Italian short-grain rice

1/2 cup dry white wine

1 1/4 cups poultry or vegetable stock

4 eggs

3/4 cup grated Parmesan cheese, plus more for sprinkling

Freshly ground black pepper

Freshly grated nutmeg

4 tablespoons fine dried bread crumbs

1 small fresh rosemary sprig

1 1/2 cups Tomato Sauce with or without cream (page 69), heated (optional)

Bring a large saucepan three-fourths full of water to a boil. Salt lightly, add all the greens, and boil until tender, about 5 minutes. Drain well, chop, and drain again.

In a large saucepan, heat the olive oil or lard over medium heat. Add the leeks and onion and sauté until softened, about 10 minutes. Add the rice and sauté until coated with the oil or lard, 3 to 5 minutes. Add the white wine and simmer for a few minutes until it is absorbed by the rice. Gradually add the stock 1/2 cup at a time, allowing each addition to be absorbed before adding more. When all of the stock has been added, remove from the heat. The rice should be quite firm.

Add the greens to the rice and let the mixture cool for a bit. Lightly beat 3 of the eggs, then stir them into the rice mixture along with the 3/4 cup cheese. Season the mixture with salt, pepper, and nutmeg.

Preheat the oven to 400°F. Butter an 8-inch springform pan or a round or square baking dish with 3-inch sides and sprinkle with 2 tablespoons of the bread crumbs. If using a springform pan, wrap the outside of the pan in heavy-duty aluminum foil to prevent leaking. Spoon in the filling and smooth the top. Lightly beat the last egg and pour it evenly over the top. Sprinkle the top evenly with a little cheese and the remaining 2 tablespoons bread crumbs. Top with the rosemary sprig.

Bake the *tortino* until golden and set, 45 to 50 minutes. Remove from the oven and remove and discard the rosemary sprig. If using a springform pan, let rest for 10 minutes, then release the pan sides, transfer to a serving plate, and cut into servings. If using a baking dish, let rest for 5 minutes, then cut into servings. Serve immediately with the sauce, or let cool to room temperature and serve without the sauce.

WINE: *Drink a Barbera d'Asti or a full-flavored white such as Chardonnay.*

———————————

VARIATION: To transform this *tortino* into a *torta,* that is, a pudding baked in a crust, you can make a typical Ligurian pastry dough. In a bowl, stir together 4 cups all-purpose flour and 2 teaspoons salt. Mix in 1/2 cup olive oil, then gradually add 3/4 to 1 cup water, or equal parts water and dry white wine, and stir and toss with a fork until the dough is evenly moistened and comes together in a mass. (You can also mix this dough in a food processor, using the pulse function to mix in the oil and water or water and wine.) Gather the dough into a ball and divide into 2 portions, one slightly larger than the other. Flatten each portion into a disk, wrap separately in plastic wrap, and let the dough rest at room temperature for at least 30 minutes. On a lightly floured work surface, roll out the larger pastry disk into a 14- to 16-inch round about 1/4 inch thick. Carefully transfer the dough round to a well-oiled 10-inch springform pan and ease it into the bottom and sides. Spoon the cooled rice mixture into the prepared pastry. Roll out the remaining dough disk into a 10-inch round about 1/4 inch thick. Moisten the edges of the bottom crust with water. Carefully transfer the second dough round to the pan, placing it over the filling. Trim away any excessive overhang, then turn the edges of the top and bottom crusts under and pinch together to seal. Cut a few steam vents in the top crust, then brush the surface with 1 tablespoon olive oil. Bake until the filling is set (test with a knife blade inserted through a steam vent) and the crust is golden, about 40 minutes. Transfer to a rack and let cool for at least 10 minutes. Release the pan sides and transfer to a serving plate. Cut into wedges and serve warm with the tomato sauce, or let cool completely and serve at room temperature without the sauce.

SERVES 8

The famed Easter pie of Liguria has many variations. For the filling, some cooks use only greens, some use only artichokes, and some add peas to the greens or artichokes. Traditionally, this pie is multilayered—thirty-three layers to be exact, one for every year of Christ's life, and it is prepared with a very thin and elastic strudel-type dough. You also can prepare it with *pasta frolla salata,* a short pastry crust that gives it a wonderful richness. If you are not locked into the multilayer concept, you can use the rich and buttery pastry recipe here, the leaner Ligurian pastry for the Spring Greens and Rice Cake variation on page 269, or buttered filo (see variation). Some cooks also make indentations in the filling and break a whole egg into each one before adding the top crust.

FOR THE PASTRY

2 1/2 cups all-purpose flour

1/2 teaspoon salt

1/2 cup plus 1 tablespoon chilled unsalted butter, cut into 1-inch pieces

1 egg, lightly beaten

2 to 4 tablespoons ice water, or as needed

To make the pastry, in a bowl, stir together the flour and salt. Scatter the butter pieces over the flour mixture and, using a pastry blender, cut in the butter until the mixture resembles coarse meal. Add the egg and 2 tablespoons ice water and stir and toss with a fork until the dough is evenly moistened and comes together in a mass. If the dough is too dry, add more water 1 tablespoon at a time. (You can also mix this dough in a food processor, using the pulse function to mix in the butter, egg, and water.) Gather the dough together into a ball, and divide it into 2 portions, one slightly larger than the other. Flatten each portion into a disk, wrap the disks separately in plastic wrap, and refrigerate for 1 hour.

To make the filling, squeeze the juice from the lemon halves into a large bowl of cold water. Working with 1 artichoke at a time, remove all of the leaves, then trim away any dark green parts from the base, and trim the stem flush with the base. Scoop out the prickly choke with a spoon, or cut it out with a paring knife. Cut the base vertically into 1/4-inch-thick slices. As each artichoke is trimmed, drop the slices into the lemon water and leave them in the water until ready to cook.

In a large sauté pan, heat the 1/4 cup olive oil over medium heat. Add the onion, parsley, and marjoram and sauté until softened, about 5 minutes. Drain the artichokes and add to the pan along with the greens and peas. Reduce the heat to low, cover, and cook until the mixture is almost dry, 10 to 15 minutes. Remove from the heat,

FOR THE FILLING

1 lemon, halved

4 large or 5 medium artichokes

1/4 cup olive oil

1 large yellow onion, chopped

1 large bunch fresh flat-leaf parsley, chopped
(about 1/3 cup)

3 tablespoons chopped fresh marjoram

1 pound beet greens or spinach, tough stems
discarded and coarsely chopped

2 pounds English peas in the pod, shelled
(about 2 cups)

Salt and freshly ground black pepper

1/2 teaspoon freshly grated nutmeg, or to taste

3 eggs, lightly beaten, plus 5 whole eggs
(optional)

1 cup ricotta cheese

1/2 cup grated Parmesan cheese, plus more if
using the whole eggs

1 tablespoon unsalted butter, cut into 5 equal
pieces, if using the whole eggs

1 tablespoon olive oil, or 1 egg, lightly beaten,
for brushing on the top crust

let cool completely, and season with 2 teaspoons salt, 1/2 teaspoon pepper, and the nutmeg. Mix in the 3 beaten eggs, the ricotta cheese, and the 1/2 cup Parmesan cheese.

Preheat the oven to 375°F.

On a lightly floured work surface, roll out the larger pastry disk into a 14-inch round about 1/8 inch thick. Carefully transfer to a 9-inch springform pan and ease it into the bottom and sides. Spoon in the filling. If you like, make 5 deep, evenly spaced indentations in the filling and break an egg into each well. Top each egg with a piece of butter and a sprinkle of Parmesan cheese. Roll out the remaining dough disk into a 10-inch round about 1/4 inch thick. Carefully transfer the second dough round to the pan, placing it over the filling. If you have used the whole eggs, lay it gently on top so as not to break them. Trim away any excessive overhang, then turn the edges of the top and bottom crusts under and pinch together to seal. Cut a few steam vents in the top crust, then brush the surface with the olive oil or beaten egg.

Bake the pie until the crust is golden, about 40 minutes. Remove from the oven and transfer to a rack to cool for 10 to 15 minutes, then release the pan sides. Transfer to a serving plate and serve warm. Alternatively, let cool completely before removing the pan sides, then release them, transfer to a serving plate, and serve at room temperature.

WINE: *Sip a Sauvignon Blanc from Friuli.*

VARIATION: To use filo in place of the pastry crust, have ready 10 filo sheets and 1/2 cup melted unsalted butter. Brush a filo sheet with the butter. Stack 4 additional sheets on top, brushing each one with butter. Fit the stack of filo sheets into a 9-inch springform pan, allowing the edges to overhang the pan rim. Spoon in the filling, and fold the overhang over the top of the filling. Make a stack of 5 additional filo sheets, again buttering each one. Lay the stack over the filling and tuck the overhang into the sides of the pan. Bake as directed.

Spread a 2-foot square of cheesecloth or a dish towel of the same size on the work surface and dust it with flour. Place the dough on top and roll it out into a rectangle 14 to 15 inches long, 12 inches wide, and ¼ inch thick, with a long side facing you.

Sprinkle the dough with the ½ cup Parmesan cheese. Leaving a 1-inch border uncovered on all sides, spread the toasted bread crumbs evenly over the dough. Then, beginning at the long side closest to you, roll up the rectangle into a cylinder, using the cheesecloth (or towel) to lift it and enclosing the roll in the cheesecloth. Using kitchen string, tie both ends of the cheesecloth securely.

Pour enough water into a fish poacher or large roasting pan to cover the potato roll once it is added and place the pan over 2 burners on the stove top. Salt the water lightly and bring to a boil. Carefully lower the potato roll into the pan and simmer gently until the potato dough feels firm, 40 to 60 minutes, like gnocchi it floats to the top of the water when it is done. Using the tails of the cheesecloth or the insert of the fish poacher, carefully lift the roll out of the water, set it aside on a platter, and let cool to room temperature. Do not unwrap the roll until it has completely cooled. (The cooled roll can be covered and refrigerated for up to 1 day before continuing.)

Preheat the oven to 400°F. Butter 1 large baking dish or 2 smaller ones.

In a small saucepan, melt the 1 cup butter with the sage leaves over medium-low heat and then remove from the heat. Unwrap the potato roll and cut crosswise into slices about 1 inch thick. Lay the slices flat in a single layer in the prepared dish(es). Drizzle evenly with the melted sage butter and sprinkle with the ¾ cup Parmesean cheese.

Bake the slices until golden, about 20 minutes. Remove from the oven and divide among individual warmed plates. You can serve it as is, or spoon the meat or tomato sauce over the top and serve at once.

WINE: *If you have used the bread-crumb filling and the meat* ragù, *select a robust red such as Barbera d'Alba, a moderately aged Barbaresco, or a Refosco from Friuli. If you have used the greens and cheese filling, pick a red wine that is neither too big nor too oaky, such as Ghemme or Spanna from the Piedmont. Or, choose a big, full-flavored white from Friuli.*

———————————————

VARIATION: To fill the potato roll with a mixture of greens and ricotta cheese, bring a large saucepan three-fourths full of water to a boil. Salt lightly and add 2 pounds assorted greens such as Swiss chard, curly endive (chicory), beet greens, and dandelion greens, tough stems discarded. Boil until tender, 8 to 10 minutes, drain well, chop finely, and squeeze dry. (You may also use Swiss chard alone, preparing it in the same way, or spinach, which can be placed in a saucepan with only the rinsing water clinging to the leaves and cooked until wilted, 3 to 5 minutes. Again drain well, chop finely, and squeeze dry.) In a large sauté pan, melt 4 tablespoons unsalted butter over medium heat. Add 1 small yellow onion, chopped, and sauté until softened and just beginning to color, about 10 minutes. Add the greens and toss them in the butter for a few minutes. Transfer the mixture to a bowl and add 2 cups (1 pound) ricotta cheese, drained in a cheesecloth-lined sieve in the refrigerator for 3 hours; 2 eggs, lightly beaten; 1/4 cup grated Parmesan cheese; and 1/4 cup dried bread crumbs. Mix well and add 1/2 teaspoon each salt and freshly ground black pepper and 1/4 teaspoon freshly grated nutmeg. Mix well again and let cool to room temperature before filling the potato roll. If the mixture seems too moist just before using, add more bread crumbs. Spread on the potato dough. Roll and poach as directed. Cool completely, then slice. Top the slices with the melted sage butter and the Parmesan and bake as directed. Omit the meat or tomato sauce for serving. Alternatively, dress with sage butter and cheese before baking and serve topped with cream-enriched Tomato Sauce (page 69).

SERVES 6

In the eighteenth century, noble families in Naples and Sicily hired French chefs to cook for their families and impress their friends. These chefs were called *monzù,* a corruption of the French word *monsieur.* One of their creations was the *gatto di patate,* which is essentially a *tortino. Gatto* in this instance does not mean "cat," however, but is instead yet another corruption, this time for the French word *gâteau,* or "cake."

FOR THE TOASTED BREAD CRUMBS

2 thick slices coarse country bread, crusts removed

4 tablespoons unsalted butter, melted, or olive oil

Salt and freshly ground black pepper

3 pounds russet potatoes (if baking) or Yukon Gold (if boiling)

Salt

³/4 cup grated pecorino cheese

2 eggs, lightly beaten

6 tablespoons unsalted butter

¹/2 cup milk, or as needed

Freshly ground black pepper

To make the toasted bread crumbs, preheat the oven to 350°F. Cut the bread slices into 1-inch cubes. You should have 1 to 1¹/2 cups. Place in a food processor and pulse until fine crumbs form. Transfer to a bowl and drizzle with the butter or olive oil, then sprinkle with ¹/2 teaspoon salt and ¹/4 teaspoon pepper. Toss well to coat. Spread the bread crumbs on a baking sheet. Bake, stirring occasionally, until the crumbs are golden, about 20 minutes. Remove from the oven and let cool. You should have about 1 cup. (The toasted crumbs will keep in a covered container at room temperature for 4 to 5 days.)

If you are using russet potatoes, raise the oven temperature to 425°F. Prick the potato skins in a few places with a fork and place the potatoes on a rimmed baking sheet. Bake until tender, about 1 hour. Remove from the oven and, when cool enough to handle, cut in half lengthwise and scoop the pulp out into a bowl. Discard the skins. If using Yukon Gold potatoes, peel them, cut into chunks, and place in a saucepan with water to cover. Salt lightly, bring to a boil over high heat, reduce the heat to medium, and cook until tender, 20 to 30 minutes. Drain well.

While the potatoes are still hot, put them through a ricer placed over a bowl. (In the absence of a ricer, mash them in a bowl with a potato masher as smoothly as possible.) Add the pecorino cheese, eggs, butter, and milk and knead together a spoon or your hands to make a soft purée. Season with salt and pepper. Set aside.

FOR THE FILLING

¹/₄ pound salami, diced, or ¹/₂ pound sweet sausages with or without fennel, cooked and crumbled

1 cup shelled English peas, parboiled

¹/₂ pound fresh mozzarella cheese, diced

About 1 cup Tomato Sauce (page 69) or canned tomato sauce

Extra virgin olive oil for drizzling

To make the filling, in a bowl, combine the salami or sausage, peas, and mozzarella and mix well. Add just enough of the tomato sauce to bind the mixture together.

Preheat the oven to 350°F. Oil a 9-by-12-by-2-inch baking dish or a 10-inch round baking dish or pie dish.

Sprinkle the bottom of the prepared baking dish evenly with ¹/₂ cup of the bread crumbs. Place half of the mashed potatoes in the pan, patting them down to form an even layer. Spread the filling evenly over the potato layer. Top with the remaining potatoes, again patting them down to form an even layer. Drizzle with olive oil and top with the remaining ¹/₂ cup bread crumbs.

Bake the potato cake until golden, about 40 minutes. Remove from the oven and let rest for at least 8 to 10 minutes. Cut into servings and serve warm or at room temperature.

Torta alla tarantina
Layered Potato and Tomato Gratin from Taranto

SERVES 6

Simple yet satisfying, this easy-to-assemble dish comes from Taranto, a lively seaside town in Apulia originally settled by the Greeks when the heel of the Italian boot was called Magna Graecia. Unlike a *gatto* (page 276), which layers mashed potatoes, this *torta* calls for sliced potatoes, like a gratin. It tastes like a pizza but without a crust.

2 pounds new potatoes, peeled and thinly sliced

Salt and freshly ground black pepper

8 small tomatoes, peeled and diced or sliced (fresh or canned)

4 cloves garlic, thinly sliced

1 tablespoon dried oregano

²/₃ pound fresh mozzarella cheese, thinly sliced or diced

Extra virgin olive oil for drizzling

Preheat the oven to 400°F. Liberally oil an 8-by-12-by-2-inch baking dish or a 10-inch pie dish.

Using one-third of the potato slices, arrange them in a layer, overlapping them slightly, on the bottom of the prepared dish. Sprinkle with salt and pepper. Top with a layer of half of the tomatoes. Sprinkle with half of the garlic and half the oregano and then top with half of the cheese. Repeat the layers, using half of the remaining potato and garlic slices, and then end with a layer of potato slices. Sprinkle with salt and pepper and drizzle generously with olive oil. Cover the dish with aluminum foil.

Bake the gratin for 30 minutes. Uncover and continue to bake until the top is golden and the potatoes are tender, 30 to 45 minutes longer. Remove from the oven and let rest for 8 to 10 minutes, then serve hot.

VARIATION: Using essentially the same ingredients, you can also make a gratin that is not layered. In a bowl, toss together 2 pounds new potatoes, peeled and cut into 1-inch dice; 2 red onions, chopped; 2 cups peeled, seeded, and chopped tomatoes (fresh or canned); 2 tablespoons dried oregano, and ¹/₂ cup extra virgin olive oil. Sprinkle generously with salt and pepper and toss again. Transfer to an oiled 8-by-11-by-2-inch gratin dish and drizzle with more olive oil. Cover with aluminum foil and bake in a 350°F oven for 30 minutes. Uncover and continue to bake until the potatoes are tender, 30 to 45 minutes longer. Serve warm.

Bibliography

To ensure as much authenticity as possible, the majority of my research was done with Italian source material, rather than contemporary English language cookbooks. At the end of the bibliography, I have included eleven titles that I explored from the excellent Slow Food series on recipes from regional *osterie*.

Adami, Pietro. *La cucina carnica*. Padua: Franco Muzzio, 1985.

Agostini, Pino, and Alvise Zorzi. *A tavola con i dogi*. Venice: Arsenale, 1992.

Alberini, Massimo. *Antica cucina veneziana*. Casale Monferrato: Edizioni Piemme, 1990.

Allegranzi, Antonio. *La cucina del pesce del Po a Trieste*. Padua: Franco Muzzio, 1980.

Bastianich, Joseph, and David Lynch. *Vino Italiano: The Regional Wines of Italy*. New York: Clarkson Potter, 2002.

Bellei, Sandro. *La cucina modenese*. Padua: Franco Muzzio, 1995.

Boni, Ada. *La cucina romana*. Rome: Newton Compton, 1983.

Butazzi, Grazietta. *Toscana in bocca*. Palermo: Edikronos, 1981.

Capnist, Giovanni. *La cucina polesana*. Padua: Franco Muzzio, 1985.

———. *La cucina veronese*. Padua: Franco Muzzio, 1987.

Cardella, Antonio. *Sicilia e le isole*. Palermo: Edikronos, 1981.

Carnacina, Luigi, and Vicenzo Buonassisi. *Il libro della polenta*. Florence: Martello-Giunti, 1984.

Capacchi, Guglielmo. *La cucina popolare parmigiana*. Parma: Artegrafica Silva, 1985.

Cavalcanti, Ottavio. *Il libro d'oro della cucina e dei vini di Calabria e Basilicata*. Milan: Mursia, 1979.

Celant, Ennio. *Valle d'Aosta in bocca*. Palermo: Il Vespro. 1979.

Cernilli, Daniele, and Carlo Petrini. *Italian Wines*. Bra: Gambero Rosso Editore, Slow Food Editore, 1999, 2001.

Cernilli, Daniele, and Gigi Piumatti. *Italian Wines 2003*. Rome: Gambero Rosso and Slow Food Editore, 2003.

Cernilli, Daniele, and Marco Sabellico. *The New Italy: A Complete Guide to Italian Contemporary Wine*. London: Mitchell Beasley, 2000.

Colacchi, Marina, and Pino Simone. *Le tre Venezie*. La cucina regionale italiana. Rome: Panda Libri, 1990.

Coltro, Dino. *La cucina tradizionali veneta*. Rome: Newton Compton, 1983.

Contini, Mila. *Friuli e Trieste in bocca*. Palermo: Il Vespro, 1978.

———. *Veneto in bocca*. Palermo: Il Vespro, 1977.

Coria, Giuseppe. *La cucina della Sicilia orientale*. Padua: Franco Muzzio, 1996.

Correnti, Pino. *Il libro d'oro della cucina e dei vini di Sicilia*. Milan: Mursia, 1976.

———. *Milano in bocca*. Milan and Palermo: Il Vespro, 1976.

Cunsolo, Felice. *Guida gastronomica d'Italia*. Novara: Istituto Geografico de Agostini, 1975.

Da Mosto, Ranieri. *Il Veneto in cucina*. Florence: Giunti-Martello, 1985.

Davidson, Alan. *Mediterranean Seafood*. London: Allen Lane, 1981.

Del Conte, Anna. *Gastronomy of Italy*. New York: Prentice Hall Press, 1987.

Deplano, Francesco. *Sardegna in bocca*. Palermo: Il Vespro, 1978.

Di Francesco, Nelda. *Antica cucina abruzzese*. Guardiagrele: Carsa Edizioni, 2000.

Dossolo, Francesco. *Regioni a tavola*. Milan: Libreria Meravigli, 1984.

Eramo, Cia. *La cucina mantovana*. Padua: Franco Muzzio, 1980.

Fast, Mady. *Mangiare triestino, storie e ricette*. Padua: Franco Muzzio, 1993.

———. *La cucina istriana*. Padua: Franco Muzzio, 1990.

Ferrari, Ambra. *Emilia in bocca*. Palermo: Edikronos, 1981.

Field, Carol. *Celebrating Italy*. New York: William Morrow, 1990.

Francesconi, Jeanne Carola. *La cucina napoletana*. Rome: Newton Compton, 1992.

Franconeri, Silvana. *La cucina montanara*. Bussolengo: Demetra, 1994.

Fosca, Martini. *Romagna in bocca*. Palermo: Il Vespro, 1978.

Goria, Giovanni. *La cucina del Piemonte*. Padua: Franco Muzzio, 1990.

Gossetti della Salda, Anna. *Le ricette regionale italiane*. Milan: Casa Editrice Solares, 1967.

Gossetti, Fernanda. *Primi piatti della cucina regionale italiane*. Milan: Fabbri, 1994.

Grimaldi, Gianni. *Liguria in bocca*. Palermo: Il Vespro, 1979.

Iori Galuzzi, Maria Allesandra, and Narsete Iori. *La cucina reggiana*. Padua: Franco Muzzio, 1987.

Iori Galuzzi, Maria Allesandra, Narsete Iori, and Marco Ionotta. *La cucina ferrarese*. Padua: Franco Muzzio, 1987.

Kasper, Lynne Rossetto. *The Splendid Table: Recipes from Emilia-Romagna, the Heartland of Northern Italian Food*. New York, William Morrow, 1992.

Kramer, Matt. *A Passion for Piedmont: Italy's Most Glorious Regional Table*. New York: William Morrow and Company, 1997.

Kurt, Eva. *Bolzano in bocca*. Palermo: Il Vespro 1978.

Lantermo, Alberta. *Piemonte in bocca*. Palermo: Edikronnos, 1981.

Lingua, Paolo. *La cucina dei genovese*. Padua: Franco Muzzio, 1989.

Liri, Clotilde. *La polenta, ricette e tradizioni*. Bussolengo: Demetra, 1995.

Lucchesi, Emiliana. *La cucina della lucchesia*. Padua: Franco Muzzio, 1989.

Maffioli, Giuseppe. *La cucina padovana*. Padua: Franco Muzzio, 1980.

———. *La cucina trevigiana*. Padua: Franco Muzzio, 1983.

———. *La cucina veneziana*. Padua: Franco Muzzio, 1987.

Mantovano, Giuseppe. *La cucina italiana, origini, storie e segreti*. Rome: Newton Compton , 1985.

Marchese, Salvatore. *La cucina di Lunigiana*. Padua: Franco Muzzio, 1989.

———. *La cucina ligure di levante*. Padua: Franco Muzzio, 1990.

Marini, Marino. *La cucina bresciana*. Padua: Franco Muzzio, 1993.

Massara, Elena Prevede. *Polenta*. Milan: La Spiga, 1998.

Montani, Sandra, and Anita Veroni. *La cucina della bassa padana*. Padua: Franco Muzzio, 1986.

Muzi, Beatrice, and Allan Evans. *La cucina picena*. Padua: Franco Muzzio, 1991.

Nollo, Beppe. *Calabria in bocca*. Palermo: Il Vespro, 1978.

Natali, Carlo. *Abruzzo e Molise in bocca*. Palermo: Il Vespro, 1979.

Padovan, Rachele. *La cucina ampezzana*. Padua: Franco Muzzio 1985.

Perisi, Giuseppina. *Cucine di Sardegna*. Padua: Franco Muzzio, 1989.

Perna Bozzi, Ottarina. *Vecchia Brianza in cucina*. Florence: Giunti-Martello, 1979.

———. *Vecchia Milano in cucina*. Florence: Giunti-Martello, 1985.

Petrini, Carlo. *Slow Food: The Case for Taste*. New York: Columbia University Press, 2001.

Petroni, Paolo. *Il libro della vera cucina emiliana*. Florence: Casa Editrice Bonechi, 1978.

———. *Il libro della vera cucina fiorentina*. Florence: Casa Editrice Bonechi, 1974.

Piccinardi, Antonio. *Il libro della vera cucina milanese*. Florence: Casa Editrice Bonechi, 1989.

Pignatelli Ferrante, Maria. *La cucina delle Murge, curiosità e tradizioni*. Padua: Franco Muzzio, 1991.

Plotkin, Fred. *La Terra Fortunata*. New York: Broadway Books, 2001.

———. *Recipes from Paradise: Life and Food on the Italian Riviera*. Boston: Little, Brown and Company, 1997.

Pomar, Anna. *La cucina tradizionale siciliana*. Rome: Giuseppe Bancato, 1988.

Pozzetto, Graziano. *La cucina romagnola*. Padua: Franco Muzzio, 1995.

Pradelli, Alessandro Molinari. *La cucina abruzzese*. Rome: Newton Compton, 2000.

———. *La cucina ligure*. Rome: Newton Compton, 1996.

———. *La cucina milanese*. Rome: Newton Compton, 2002.

———. *La cucina sarda*. Rome: Newton Compton, 1997.

Righi, Igino. *Marche in bocca*. Palermo: Il Vespro, 1979.

Riveccio, Maria Zaniboni. *Polenta, piatto del re*. Milan: Idealibri, 1986

Root, Waverley. *The Food of Italy*. New York: Atheneum, 1971.

Sada, Luigi. *La cucina della terra di Bari*. Padua: Franco Muzzio, 1991.

———. *La cucina pugliese*. Rome: Newton Compton, 1994.

———. *Puglia in bocca*. Palermo: Il Vespro, 1979.

Sandri, Amedeo. *La polenta nella cucina veneta*. Padua: Franco Muzzio, 1980.

Sandri, Amedeo, and Maurizio Falloppi. *La cucina vicentina*. Padua: Franco Muzzio, 1980.

Santini, Aldo. *La cucina fiorentina*. Padua: Franco Muzzio, 1992.

———. *La cucina livornese*. Padua: Franco Muzzio, 1988.

———. *La cucina maremmana*. Padua: Franco Muzzio, 1991.

Santolini, Antonella. *Napoli in bocca*. Palermo: Edikronos, 1981.

———. *Roma in bocca*. Palermo: Il Vespro, 1979.

———. *Umbria in bocca*. Palermo: Il Vespro, 1979.

Sassi, Maria. *Trento in bocca*. Palermo: Il Vespro. 1978.

Sassu, Antonio. *La vera cucina in Sardegna*. Rome: Casa Editrice Anthropos, 1983.

Schwartz, Arthur. *Naples at Table*. New York: Harper Collins, 1998.

Scudelotti, Chiara. *Ricettario italiano, La cucina dei poveri e dei re*. Bussolengo: Demetra, 1994.

Serra, Anne, and Piero Serra. *La cucina della Campania*. Naples: Franco di Mauro, 1991.

Simeti, Mary Taylor. *Pomp and Sustenance*. New York: Alfred A. Knopf, 1989.

Sola, Pino. *Ricette e vini di Liguria*. Genoa: Sagep Editrice, 1993.

Stelva, Maria. *La cucina triestina*. Trieste: Edizioni Italo Svevo, 1987.

Tedeschi, Edda. *Le regioni italiane in tavola*. Milan: Sperling & Kupfer, 1994.

Truini Palombo, Maria Giuseppina. *La cucina sabina*. Padua: Franco Muzzio, 1991.

Willinger, Faith. *Red, White & Greens: The Italian Way with Vegetables*. New York: Harper Collins, 1996.

Valli, Emilia. *La cucina friulana*. Padua: Franco Muzzio, 1992.

Vigano, Fiorenzo, and Fiorenzo Baroni. *Polenta: Storia e civiltà del mais*. Rimini: Idealibri, n.d.

Wright, Clifford. *Cucina Paradiso: The Heavenly Food of Sicily*. New York: Simon and Schuster, 1992.

Zanini deVita, Oretta. *Il Lazio a tavola: Guida gastronomica tra storia e tradizioni*. Rome: Alfabyte Books, 1994.

Ricette di osterie Series, Slow Food Editore

Ricette delle osterie di Langa, 1992.

Ricette di osterie dell'Abruzzo, 1997.

Ricette di osterie della Lombardia, Cremona e il suo territorio, 1998.

Ricette di osterie dell'Emilia dall'uovo al maiale, 1997.

Ricette di osterie del Veneto, quaresime e oriente, 1996.

Ricette di osterie di Firenze e Chianti: desinari di casa tra città e contado, 1997.

Ricette di osterie di Puglia: mare, erbe fornelli, 2000.

Ricette di osterie e di porti marchigiani, 1994.

Ricette di osterie e famiglie dell'Umbria, 1999.

Ricette di osterie e genti di Liguria, 1995.

Ricette di osterie e ristoranti del Monferrato, 1997.

Index

Table of Equivalents

The exact equivalents in the following tables have been rounded for convenience.

LIQUID/DRY MEASURES

U.S.	METRIC
1/4 teaspoon	1.25 milliliters
1/2 teaspoon	2.5 milliliters
1 teaspoon	5 milliliters
1 tablespoon (3 teaspoons)	15 milliliters
1 fluid ounce (2 tablespoons)	30 milliliters
1/4 cup	60 milliliters
1/3 cup	80 milliliters
1/2 cup	120 milliliters
1 cup	240 milliliters
1 pint (2 cups)	480 milliliters
1 quart (4 cups, 32 ounces)	960 milliliters
1 gallon (4 quarts)	3.84 liters
1 ounce (by weight)	28 grams
1 pound	454 grams
2.2 pounds	1 kilogram

LENGTH

U.S.	METRIC
1/8 inch	3 millimeters
1/4 inch	6 millimeters
1/2 inch	12 millimeters
1 inch	2.5 centimeters

OVEN TEMPERATURE

FAHRENHEIT	CELSIUS	GAS
250	120	1/2
275	140	1
300	150	2
325	160	3
350	180	4
375	190	5
400	200	6
425	220	7
450	230	8
475	240	9
500	260	10